ULTIMATE

Skiing & Snowboarding

FLIP BYRNES

Hardie Grant

EXPLORE

Above Swiss precision in Mürren, Switzerland

The tree-lined runs of Mount Buller, Australia

INTRODUCTION

There is a lot of snow in the world. 'Not nearly enough!' I hear the powder hounds cry. But when writing a book vowing to leave no powder drift un-poked, no run unconsidered, no après bar un-danced on, trust me, it's a big world. With So. Much. Skiing. And boarding – we are all snowbirds of a feather and this book is deliberately inclusive; if you ride one plank or two, go uphill or downhill, this is a safe space no matter which way you bend your knees. We all have the same chills, thrills and spills.

The problem when wading through the blizzard debris of notes and experiences from a billion ski areas, each as unique as a snowflake (true), is narrowing it down to the Ultimate. It would be far easier to write a never-ending book, that would never be read or finished, simply to keep mentally (and as often as possible physically) immersed in anything and everything snow.

But all good things must come to an end, and so what has made a McTwist (front flip with a 540-degree rotation) into these pages is the best in its class. It's the big kahunas of snow (hello Aspen, Chamonix and Whistler). But along with the can-can kicking showgirls are the quiet achievers, the sometimes less good-looking but more interesting siblings. Here, you'll find underrated gems like the USA's Big Sky with its big stats

or Austria's Fieberbrunn (the newcomer to the Saalbach-Hinterglemm-Leogang-Fieberbrunn party) with its freeriding caché. And should you really go to France's Avoriaz, even just for a raclette panini? Oui.

If you're wondering whether this book is full of opinion, it is, based on a 30-year snow-industry career spanning three continents and riding experience on all seven. But above all, fairness has been the objective. Not every day is a powder day. Not every day is mid-week when crowds are spare and runs aplenty. But we've aimed to rise above that and see the *potential*.

You won't have the exact same experience that's on these pages, but what you *will* have is a face shot full of inspiration, a mountain of motivation and an exhaustively curated worldwide book of where to go to find your next, ultimate, white line.

I hope this guide inspires you to seek your own ultimate – whatever it may be. You'll know it when you find it, because it will make your soul sing.

Happy hunting.

Flip Byrnes

Frozen tree 'snow monsters' at Canada's Big White stud the landscape

HOW TO READ THE MOUNTAIN STATS

Each destination entry includes mountain stats, indicating the size, number of lifts, lift capacity (skiers per hour it can move), vertical and elevation and percentage of terrain according to beginner, intermediate and advanced.

Sizes matter

Actually, let's clarify that: crowds matter more than size. What use are a billion acres of terrain if every powder line is hoovered by 10am? Reading the resort stats can determine your riding choice. The question is, which statistic to read when surfing sites? For example, at Big White (*see* p. 65), technically, the 'skiable terrain' is the patrolled area, which is 11sqkm (2765 acres). Other resorts may only disclose the 'resort area', which is the controlled recreational boundary. For Big White, that framed number almost triples to 29.8sqkm (7355 acres). So be statistic savvy to ensure you're comparing like with like.

Also, Europe rates its areas by the kilometres of runs if stitched end-to-end. The USA uses acres, Australia and New Zealand hectares. In Japan, it's a course, not a run, while in Europe it's a piste. And the linked resorts with village-to-village riding can be called a circuit, circus, itinerary or carousel.

Likewise, there's summit elevation and lifted elevation, which can differ remarkably. A peak within a ski area is often not the highest lifted elevation – but may fall within the ski area and can be accessed by boot packing (hiking). See if an area has used 'summit' or 'lift' elevation for their statistics. Some ski areas will list both: for example in Telluride (*see* p. 23) the lifted elevation is 3831m (12,570 ft) and the summit elevation is 4008m (13,150 ft).

Run

In general, runs are graded as colours, as follows:

- **Green** Beginner: the slightest of inclinations.

- **Blue** Intermediate: inclination less than 25 per cent.

- **Red** Advanced: won't exceed a 40 per cent gradient, can be ungroomed, narrow.

- **Black** Expert only: for the most experienced and professional skiers and boarders.

Decoding the run colour grading system can throw some curve balls. For example, Austria doesn't have any green (beginner) runs, easiest runs are marked blue, followed by red and black. At France's Courchevel (*see* p. 95) a blue (intermediate) may not be the same as, say, a blue in the Pyrénées Grandvalira (*see* p. 167). Mammoth Mountain in California (*see* p. 33) invented a few extra, like a green circle in a black square to denote a more difficult green. Southern Hemisphere resorts don't have red runs (but have green, blue and black). The only consistent colour across continents is black for expert.

DON'T BREAK THE BANK

You can understand why Butch Cassidy robbed a bank in Telluride (*see* p. 23). And he wasn't even a skier. Skiing and boarding are not cheap sports, but there are ways to keep gold bullion robberies at bay. Because going downhill (or uphill) is only one element of a ski trip – half the fun is in the gourmet meals to be had and experiences like dog-sledding, paragliding and meeting reindeers. Although experiences can be pricey as it's a captive audience on a mountain (and operators need to offset their own mountain price costs from fuel to feed), there are some you simply won't want to miss.

Here are a few ways to get extra fancy flakes for your ski buck.

Go shoulder season

If you're trapped by school holiday windows, I feel you. And while we all yearn for a white Christmas, it's when ski resort prices go sky high in every category (with no guarantee of snow). December in general has become a dice roll; snow seems to fall later and it can be a literal wash out.

But there's a solution – if you can, go high (easiest if you're in the Northern Hemisphere). Anywhere over 1800m (5905ft) is the general rule of thumb for a snow-sure early season trip.

Likewise for late season. Aspen Snowmass in Colorado (*see* p. 13) receives the majority of its snowfall in March and regularly extends its season through early April, and closes on a 4m (13ft) base. California's Mammoth Mountain (*see* p. 33) parks keep hucking through to June. In Europe, high-altitude French resorts like Tignes (*see* p. 83) hit a sweet-spot in spring with long days, warm temperatures and solid snow. There are even slopes that never close, like Austria's Hintertux and some glaciers in Switzerland, such as Zermatt's Theodul Glacier, where over one hundred ski teams from 22 countries train in summer.

Another benefit of late season skiing and boarding is there's added value with festivals, deals, extra-long happy hours, ski gear sales and a kind of dizzy lunacy in relaxed staff that only the end of a full-skiing, full-party season can bring.

Be flexible

Check around your dates as even changing by a week or so on either side (you may inadvertently avoid local or major school holidays) can mean you hit a jackpot.

Book ahead

Everything – airfares, hotels – is cheaper the earlier you book (most flights come online a year in advance). Also sign up to the socials of resorts for any flash sales or earlybird alerts.

Package it

Skiers and boarders like to do things independently. But even with great deals booking tickets, hotels, and rentals separately, it simply can't compare with the buying power of a ski travel operator who purchases in bulk and passes those discounts onto the customer. Find an operator who suits your style of holidaying and see what they can bundle. If there's a Ski Expo near you, go along as there are often deals associated (and loads of prizes to be won).

Beg and borrow

Many resort rentals will have annual model updates which means you can hire nearly the latest gear – arguably better than buying, and you can swap them out if the fit's not perfect.

Although tempting, don't borrow boots and skis/boards. Nothing will kill your trip buzz quicker than a set-up better suited to your six-foot neighbour.

However, go bananas on borrowing all else. Especially if courting the sport, borrow jackets, pants, gloves, thermals, and ski bags before committing, or keep the planet happy and buy second hand. Borrowing high ticket, fragile items like goggles (which can be easily scratched) is stretching a friendship.

Self-cater

The oldest trick in the book. Prices ascend in synchronicity with the terrain. The closer to the mountains, the more expensive the item, including food. Do your research beforehand to find out where the nearest towns or grocery stores are en route to the ski resorts.

Get the beginner specials

Beginners don't need 50 lifts. Aware of this, at some resorts like Mammoth Mountain (*see* p. 33), novices can skip the full-price ticket and buy a pass valid only on beginner chairs.

Must-have insurance

You shouldn't be skiing or boarding without insurance. All it takes is one intoxicated skier descending from a mid-slope après drink to take you out and, hello Stateside $20k USD medical bill.

Not without reason, since 2022 Italy now has a zero-tolerance on riding under the influence of drink or drugs and riders are required by law to have third-party liability insurance when buying a lift pass.

Skiing and boarding are often an 'Extra' sport coverage on standard insurance – and may not be available on credit cards with inbuilt travel insurance – but it is not a prohibitive amount. Don't wait 'til you get there to buy, and make sure you read the fine print. If purchasing insurance at the destination, having left your home country, there can be a 48- to 72-hour lag before it comes into effect to deter people buying insurance on the day on or after an accident.

Some insurance is only valid if you're wearing a helmet (some ski areas require them, such as Italy until age 18 and Mammoth Mountain in the USA for all riders). Some ski resorts offer a version of insurance in-house. In Austria's St. Anton am Arlberg (*see* p. 107), the Arlberg Safety Card (ASC) covers all rescue costs within their bounds.

Pause before hopping on that snow mobile! 'Extreme' activities include paragliding, out of bounds riding, plus anything mountain-related once crampons or ropes are introduced. Specialised insurance is available but you need to research it carefully.

If you want to do expeditions involving remote locations, glaciers or Arctic regions, your nationality may play a role – some insurers classify certain country's citizens as higher risk than others!

THE GEAR

Fellow #geargeeks will understand the euphoria of finding the perfect piece of kit. For me that's been a pair of knitted wool knickerbockers (#passionkillers) that kept static kiteskiing thighs warm in Arctic temperatures; a -40° down sleeping bag I'd happily live in; a pair of expedition quality down mitts which are like permanent hand jacuzzis; and a mesh inside, wool-backed top that both allows sweat to escape AND wicks the moisture away, keeping me warm and dry when sledge hauling or back country hiking. Genius.

Choose your activity

The first consideration is – what are you doing? Sweat is the enemy in cold environments, so if moving uphill or intensely, you need clothes that will breathe and vent – pants and jackets with full zips.

Wear layers

Layers are key. The most important layer is thermal underwear wicking sweat away from the body. The next layer should be a fleece (or something equivalent) for core warmth. Then the final element-resisting outerlayer. If it becomes ridiculously cold, add in goggles, a buff or balaclava and mitts to expose less skin.

Style isn't everything

I am outing myself as a baggy one-piece wearer (think boilersuit). It isn't fashionable, but I'll take function over being steezy every day. You'll get the last laugh when your friends need warm-up breaks on powder days and you can keep on riding in your personal, Jamaica-like biosphere.

Powder ace shots are great, not so much tummy or face shots. If you're not into onesies (I get it) a bib'n'brace or overall set up

Saint-Gervais Mont-Blanc is a favourite among the French

will avoid any mid-body snow drifts (and adds an extra layer of core warmth), and make sure that your jacket hood can cover your helmet (helmets have a double function of keeping you safe and warm – needing vents for spring). If you're a snowboarder, a longer line jacket keeps your tush warmer on the snow.

Consider your feet

Invest in heated ski boots, combined with thin (not chunky) socks made from high-quality wool, which will promote blood flow keeping your feet warmer and more comfortable. While heated boots may seem like a luxury, these can be a game changer and you won't regret the expense.

Wear bright colours

Lastly, choose bright colours even if you're a neutrals lover. Family and friends can spot you, as can a rescuer off-piste – your bold, bright colours could save your life.

Select your materials

If you're sipping suds at a brewery or lounging like a lizard, cotton's comfortable. But on the mountain, cotton kills. Its natural characteristic is to absorb and hold onto moisture, so it doesn't wick and lowers your core temperature when wet (and loses all insulation value). Go with these materials instead, some of which are even recycled if you're hunting for sustainably-produced garments.

- Merino wool is a natural fibre that wicks/pulls moisture away from your body, so you don't overheat or get the chills. It's one of the few materials that deflects moisture from the skin even when sweat is in a vapor state, as the wool fibre shape allows air to pass through. Not only is there more chance of staying dry if breaking a sweat, but odour-causing bacteria is less likely to linger, meaning you won't scare away the snow bunnies (or leopards) at après.

- Polypro is a solid synthetic fibre, made from plastic, designed to move liquid moisture through the holes in the weave. This fibre cannot breathe, but it's light and dries quickly. However, bury your nose in a polypro armpit after a big day touring and you may just pass out.

- A third, recent option is a bamboo layer, a good choice for skin irritated by wool fibres. Bamboo is natural, sustainable, odour-resistant (not quite as good as merino, but still pretty good) and is more durable than wool with a softer (almost silky) feel than both wool and synthetics. The natural scales of bamboo fibre retain the thermal energy but won't be as warm as merino when wet.

A view of Dent du Villard and chalets in Courchevel 1850, France

Mitts vs gloves

Mittens win for warmth every time. Yet gloves are more dexterous. If cold hands make or break your ski day, down gloves will take you to a happy place. Yes, down gloves are expensive and can rip easily, but they're for cold sensitive risk takers. There are now down/ hybrid gloves with down sections on top and sturdier material palms.

If you'll be ripping a slalom, gloves are the go. For an average piste day, you know best if you suffer cold hands or not and which way to go (some ski gloves have inbuilt pockets to add hand warmer pouches).

Choose clothing for the location

It pays to research the climate and weather factors. If you're in Banff in Canada (*see* p. 59), for example, purchase a full-face balaclava for those frostnip days. In Australian resorts and during spring in Canada's Whistler (*see* p. 43), I've seen people wear rubber gloves (no ski gloves are 100 per cent waterproof). If you're on a European spring or summer glacier, add in the darkest lense goggles available or glacier glasses protecting the side eye area. And Japan? Even a powder skirt may not do the job, so go with the overalls AND powder skirt. Cold countries like Scandinavia have specialised products not available (or needed) elsewhere. Peruse the local stores when there for an exciting find – and ask the locals what they wear too. You might end up with a pair of lovingly hand-knitted knickerbockers by an Arctic dwelling Norwegian.

Pee before you ski!

This may seem like a no-brainer, but your body utilises an incredible, unnecessary amount of energy to keep urine warm. Direct that energy instead to warming up fingers, toes and nose.

THE SPORTS

Snowboarding

When snowboarding became mainstream in the late '80s, ski areas had no idea what to do with it. Was it a fad like mono skiing or (gulp) ski ballet? Should they develop instruction techniques and snowboard schools? Invest in snow hungry halfpipes? Market it?

Fast forward 30-plus years and it's come a long way from the 1964 Snurfer (with reins attached to the nose), the 1970s Swallowtail Winterstick, and the era of Tom Sims and Jake Burton Carpenter pitting their metal-edged, turned-up-nose mass-produced boards into a boarding battle. The game changer was when Burton added more responsive highback bindings. And once binders locked the feet to the board, increasing rider-to-board connection, the sport never looked back.

So, here's where we're at: the modern snowboard has (mainly) a fat nose and tail, skinny waist, parabolically curved edges, camber (midsections that arch off the snow slightly when unweighted), rocker (midsections that rest on the snow and tips and tails that curve up, also called reverse camber). Choose a preference (or blend) so it hits in all the right spots to either float or carve turns. Skiing, you're welcome.

New style skiers

Just as skiing was fading in popularity, usurped by this unruly snowboarding upstart, it was reinvented. Snowboarding changed skiing. Skiing has its own storied and impressive history, long-bound by tradition and conservatism. The longer the skis, the better the skier (210cm/82in anyone?). But the snowboard innovations spurred the ski industry into action; to mimic snowboards, skis became twin tip, with side cut and upturned tails with development extending to fat powder skis. Suddenly skiers were sliding rails and landing switch in between off-axis spins, wearing spiked belts and session-ing halfpipes.

If there's anyone to thank for turning skiing new-school, it's a group of Québécoises – JF Cusson (now a Canadian Olympic coach), Vincent Dorion, and the late JP Auclair. Free skiing was truly ushered in at the Winter X Games in 1999 in Crested Butte, Colorado, where big-air skiing debuted. Cusson, skiing on Salomon Teneighty's, won the event with a 720 – two full rotations of 360 degrees, taking off and landing switch (backwards).

While snowboarding has plateaued, skiing has had a huge resurgence, with twin tips the halfpipe, slopestyle courses and big airs are equally their domains. Some snowboarders both ski and board, simply because skis can now do everything snowboards can, and often more.

Halfpipe

In a pipe, shaped like a U, riders compete in the following:

- Amplitude: the height the riders reach during the runs.
- Difficulty: The technicality of the tricks that are used in the runs.
- Variety: A diverse mix of tricks.
- Using the full pipe throughout the run.
- Performing a combination of tricks and moves back-to-back.

Slopestyle

Slopestyle skiing is where riders string a run together through a park section with features and multiple jumps. If in a competition form, judges look for amplitude – clean take-off, controlled flight path, landing on a sweet spot; originality – such as a new trick or taking a different route through the course; and quality of tricks – if the rider performs a clean grab and lands steadily.

Big air

Riders throw their biggest tricks off a single, large jump. In an Olympics finals (as an example) riders are scored on their best two jumps out of three, but they must be different in rotation or direction. This typically leads to higher scoring corked tricks or off-axis flips with high degrees of rotation. While a snowboarder might do a triple cork 1440 in slopestyle, they could try a triple cork 1800 in big air, for instance.

Park

Snowparks are the winter-friendly version of a skate park and are huge drawcards for areas like Switzerland's Mayrhofen (*see* p. 147), Stubai, LAAX and Crans-Montana (*see* p. 145), or California's Mammoth Mountain (*see* p. 33) and Colorado's Aspen Buttermilk, home of the X Games. Features can vary from ride-on butter boxes to triple-kinked handrails and include rounded top tubes, benches and jumps built as hips, spines and table tops, or a jump line (a stacked set of jumps).

Switzerland's Zermatt is a prime access point for backcountry ski touring, like the multi-day hut trip on the Spaghetti Route

Boardercross and ski cross

The term boardercross comes from Motocross, as the course is similar. Boardercross (SBX) and Ski Cross involves a group of four or six riders who simultaneously start atop a winding and inclined course, and race to reach the finish line.

Courses include turns, various jumps, berms, rollers, drops, steep and flat sections, and are designed to challenge the rider's ability to stay in control and hold speed simultaneously. The tracks are deliberately narrow and racing is aggressive with competitors often colliding.

Alpine skiing

Commentator Ellen Jobling says: 'Alpine skiing can be summarised with three words: "fastest down wins". Although there are four main events within alpine skiing, they are just slight variations on the same concept: skiers are timed, one by one, coming down the race slope, and the one with the quickest time wins. There is something beautiful about the simplicity of alpine skiing and you do not have to learn a whole bunch of complicated rules to be able to sit down and follow a race.

It is technically an individual sport, in that each skier comes down the slope by themselves, and their result is based purely on their own performance during that run. However, each of the big skiing nations operates a strong team, with their skiers training together and supporting each other. In fact, even skiers across many different countries are often quite close and supportive of each other.

It is also one of the precious few sports than can boast of gender equality, with men's and women's events given equal attention and equal respect. Apart from some steeper downhill slopes for the men, there are not many differences between the layout of the men's and women's races. They are all given equal weight in television coverage (at least in Switzerland and Austria), receive plenty of funding and sponsorship, and are both followed passionately by fans.'

Alpine skiing comprises four core events that range from very technical (lots of narrow turns) to very fast (flying down the slope with minimal turns). In order from technicality to speed, the events are:

- Slalom

- Giant Slalom

- Super G

- Downhill

Cross-country and telemark skiing

Cross-country skiing is easily one of the best cardio exercises among winter sports, doesn't involve buying a lift pass, and can be done gently or at competition level. It requires power, endurance, and speed. In cross-country skiing only the toe of the boot is attached to the ski, and will involve classic skiing (with skis parallel, kicking and gliding) or dynamic skate skiing, which requires shorter skis, and an ice-skating movement. If you see tracks of twin grooves when out hiking or snow shoeing, these are likely prepared cross-country trails maintained by ski areas so keep them undisturbed.

If you want a similar workout while still going downhill, free the heel! Telemark skiing leaves the heel free at all times, and downhill turns are made by lunging. It's beautiful to watch, challenging to master and incredibly fun.

Ski touring and split boarding

At some point, you will wonder what lies beyond the pistes, and once you score a taste of the rare air 'out there', it's hard to go back. The first step in taking the leap from pistes to untamed, avalanche-prone wilderness is to sign up for a course (of which there are many) and head out with a guide.

So what are ski touring and split boarding? According to International Federation of Mountain Guides (IFMGA) guide Till Karmann, 'You have special gear that allows you to walk uphill with skis on, including skins on the bottom which grip the snow. And then you peel the skins off, lock your bindings down and ski down, off-piste.' It's the same for split boards, which have come a long way in the past 10 years. There are now cleaner ways to reattach the board (which splits in two) to smoother bindings that rotate from sideways to facing forward for walking uphill. And crucially, Mr Chomp crampons – that inside edge is not bite-y and needs some teeth.

You'll need to do your research about the terrain and be properly geared up with the likes of adhesive skins for going uphill, a hydration system, a backpack, glacier goggles, full-length zip waterproof pants, a down jacket for the stops, impenetrable sunscreen, a GPS, and a compass/altimeter.

You'll also need avalanche gear, including an air bag, an avalanche transceiver, a metal blade shovel, and a rescue beacon, as well as the knowledge to use it correctly and quickly. Be warned: backcountry ski touring is physically demanding and peak fitness and experience are the keys to maximum thrills (have a taste before biting off a big adventure).

You also want a full-cert mountain guide. Not all guides are created equal. An International Federation of Mountain Guides Association (IFMGA) guide, also known as Union Internationale des Associations de Guides de Montagne (UIAGM), spends years passing rigorous ski-touring, ice-climbing, rock-climbing, mountaineering, glacier-travel and safety exams for this overall certificate. In North America, guides are permitted to have one certification for an individual speciality, such as Canadian heli-ski guiding, where they have sole access to their company's tenure and know the area best.

SLOPE SAFETY

Slope safety isn't just about you, but *everyone*. Speed, metal equipment and static objects like trees or people are not a good mix. If you were to hit or injure another slope user, legal consequences can include manslaughter. Likewise, not remaining at the scene of an accident you are involved with becomes a police matter and is treated as a road hit and run. Every country's laws vary but The National Ski Areas Association (NASAA) in the USA developed a '7 Rules of Slope Safety', often printed on the back of a lift pass:

1. Always stay in control and be able to stop or avoid other people or objects.

2. People ahead of you (including downhill) have the right of way. It's your responsibility to avoid them.

3. Don't stop where you obstruct a trail or aren't visible from above.

4. Whenever starting downhill or merging into a trail, look uphill and yield to others.

5. Always use devices to help prevent runaway equipment.

6. Observe all posted signs and warnings. Keep off closed trails and out of closed areas.

7. Prior to using any lift, you must have the knowledge and ability to load, ride, and unload safely.

The International Ski Federation's (FIS) skiers' code of conduct can be added to this, which are legally binding and include overtaking only if leaving enough space for any voluntary/ involuntary movements by the skier in front, keeping to the side of the run if on foot, and every skier and snowboarder is duty bound to assist in the case of an accident on the slope. Lastly, wear a helmet – according to a John Hopkins Medicine-led study, severe head trauma accounts for around 20 per cent of all ski- and snowboard-related injuries.

FITNESS

Heading to altitude and downhill piste skiing can require more fitness than anticipated, especially if you're desk jockeying for much of the year. Try these before you hit the slopes:

- Mountain Biking - great for keeping legs strong and working on agility.

- Trail running - an excellent way to stay fit through the warmer months while also enjoying nature.

- Gym - hit the gym and work on your cardio, balance, endurance, flexibility (for injury prevention) and muscle power. In particular, strengthen the areas that do the heavy lifting: quads, glutes, hamstrings, hips and supporting muscles, especially around injury prone areas like knees. Some gyms host ski fitness classes pre-season or do them online.

- Boost your confidence - this may seem odd to add into fitness but confidence in your preparation and abilities elevates mountain fun, so when you're there also choose a slope suited to your ability.

Five basic rules of off-piste

1. Never go alone and know your partner's skill level.

2. Know how to use the avalanche and rescue beacon equipment you're carrying.

3. Carry enough food/water/layers for sudden weather events.

4. Notify a third party of your route and time to alert authorities if contact has not been made.

5. Always have one person in a position to commence a rescue (i.e, not riding a slope simultaneously).

Opposite Picturesque Wānaka, Aotearoa New Zealand, is where to find Northern Hemisphere racing teams and pro riders off season

TICKET TO RIDE

To explore many different ski resorts around the world and broaden your horizons too, look into a ski pass which can offer incredible value by bundling access to different resorts and ski spots in one price. Choosing the right pass is like scoring a golden ticket to Willy Wonka's chocolate factory. So much skiing candy, so little time.

Epic Pass

Vail Resorts in Colorado changed the ski travel game in 2008 when it introduced the Epic Pass: the first season pass offering access to multiple world-class (and relatively expensive) ski areas for the price of a single resort pass. Since then, the father company of Vail has acquired or partnered with ski areas around the world, bringing more than 80 US and international resorts under its Epic umbrella. The most tantalising Vail with its 21sqkm (5289 acres) of skiable terrain and glitzy village atmosphere, Utah's Park City (the largest resort in the USA, *see* p. 29), and Canada's Whistler (the largest in North America, *see* p. 43). But possibly the most exciting thing about holding an Epic Pass is being able to ski year-round in both Northern and Southern Hemisphere resorts. Epic covers a handful of areas in Australia including Perisher (the largest resort in the Southern Hemisphere, *see* p. 183), plus Japan, and a handful of European hotspots including Les 3 Vallées in the French Alps (*see* p. 95), Ski Arlberg in Austria (*see* p. 107), and 4 Vallées in Switzerland (*see* p. 139).

Ikon Pass

The strongest competitor to Epic Pass covers almost every US resort that Epic does not. Ikon Pass began with fabled mountains such as the historic mining town and four resort areas of Aspen Snowmass (*see* p. 13), the Hollywood ski scene of Deer Valley in Utah (*see* p. 31), and bucking cowboy steeps of Jackson Hole (*see* p. 9). It now boasts access to more than 50 destinations across the US, Canada, Europe, South America, Australia, New Zealand and Japan. Ikon partners with many resorts, rather than acquiring them, so often the pass access extends for a seven-day period rather than a whole season. However, this distinction also has advantages. Many people rave about Ikon resorts for their distinctive villages and cultures, which have remained refreshingly unique and 'Ikonic', despite the corporate conglomerate they have joined.

Mountain Collective

Mountain Collective is perfect for the road-tripping powder hound who gets bored quickly and wants to hit multiple resorts in a single trip or try different runs each weekend. It allows two days at each location for a combined total of 46 days skiing in a season. However, it has always been substantially cheaper than Ikon and Epic and does offer 50 per cent off the purchase price of additional days at collective destinations. Many of the resorts included in the Ikon Pass also fall under Mountain Collective, including Aspen Snowmass (*see* p. 13), Big Sky (*see* p. 5) and Mammoth Mountain (*see* p. 33), as well as a handful of Aotearoa New Zealand resorts, Thredbo in Australia (*see* p. 177) and Chamonix in France (*see* p. 99).

SNOWPASS

SNOWPASS was the very first pan-European season pass, touted as the 'biggest ski pass in the world' going by the number of ski resorts it offers access to. More than 100 resorts across 12 European countries are on offer – but only for a maximum of 10 days at each resort. This is a great option for explorers who want to make memories in quieter, lesser-known European resorts that are off the beaten track.

Paradiski

The pass that combines the French word for 'paradise' with 'skiing' is hard to oversell, as your wildest dreams for both is what you'll get with the Paradiski pass: 425km (264mi) of skiable terrain and 264 pistes across three famous resorts in the Tarentaise Valley in the French Alps. They're popular playgrounds closest to the beguiling alpine villages of Tignes (*see* p. 83) and Val d'Isère (*see* p. 87).

Dolimiti Superski

Ski 1200km (745mi) of pistes over 15 ski areas and experience breathtaking scenery in the Dolomite Alps, a UNESCO World Heritage Site. This is the pass for lovers of dramatic scenery, bluebird days, wide, sweeping runs and quaint resorts with a unique Austrian-Italian blend of culture. Some of the most iconic skiing here links multiple resorts and runs for full days of leg-burning exploration. The 40km Sella Ronda route, for example, links Alta Badia (*see* p. 127) to Val Gardena, Val di Fassa and Arabba Marmolada, and the 80-plus kilometre 'Great War Tour' showcases historic World War I sites.

Mont Blanc Unlimited

This pass covers Europe's most iconic mountains: Chamonix, Les Houches Saint-Gervais, Megève Evasion Mont-Blanc, Courmayeur and Verbier 4 Vallées. The namesake mountain, Mont Blanc, is the highest peak in the Alp, and a must-ski for thrill seekers, and is part of Chamonix (*see* p. 99) – one of the oldest and most famous ski areas in France.

THE WORLD IS YOUR SNOW OYSTER

So you have done your research, you have the gear; now where are you going? Are you looking to carve your name on Northern Hemisphere slopes, or is the Southern Hemisphere calling? Do you need an easy-access airport, have a road trip in mind or do you want to embrace the adventure of long-distance public transport? Are you thinking of an iconic big-name destination or a low-key lesser-known place? Do you want a luxe resort, no-frills budget accommodation or something that suits the whole family? The choices are endless!

Canada has small ski towns bursting with personality like Revelstoke (*see* p. 55) and easily accessible day terrain or fly-in infrastructure – get dropped at a backcountry lodge for a week by heli. If you like spring corn snow, the Pyrénées (such as Grandvalira, *see* p. 167) has different snow than the wind-affected Alps' powder (it's wetter), and has a more stable bond during gloriously long sunny days. In Austria's St. Anton am Arlberg (*see* p. 107) and Switzerland's Mürren (*see* p. 149), you'll be surrounded by dazzling mountain peaks that serrate the sky. France's cliff-perched, sustainably designed Avoriaz (*see* p. 77) is a Modernist masterpiece – and if you need snow surety, see you in Tignes (*see* p. 83), not too far away.

And that's not even digging into slopes further south, where you'll discover Japan's 'Japowder' is the stuff of legend and Australia is producing an exponential number of snowboarding world champions – there must be something in the slopes.

Then theres off OFF track, where your skis or board become the only passport you need to explore the wilds. Dream big and creatively – to the world's highest gondola in the Indian Himalayas (*see* p. 261), or the monstrous mountains of Alaska (*see* p. 267).

The final step – polar travel. This includes touring South Georgia, Antarctica or sled hauling or kite skiing across an ice cap like Greenland. This latter has been my own Ultimate – for the challenge, the beauty, the portal to another universe (but on this planet) and camaraderie born through adversity. Being on the ice is transformative on a cellular level, the pinnacle for anyone with a passion for both adventure and snow.

Snow hangs in the trees like Christmas baubles at Furano, Japan

BEST OF THE BEST

Most charming ski areas

Most iconic runs

Best resorts for non-skiers

Best value

Best for families

Best extreme

Top Snowman building is always a winner - this one at Falls Creek, Australia *Bottom* Nestled in Italy's Dolomites, Alta Badia is both a feast for skiers and for gourmands *Opposite left* The dazzling lakeside location of Chile's Portillo *Opposite right* The character-rich streets of Colorado's Telluride, USA

MAP OF THE WORLD

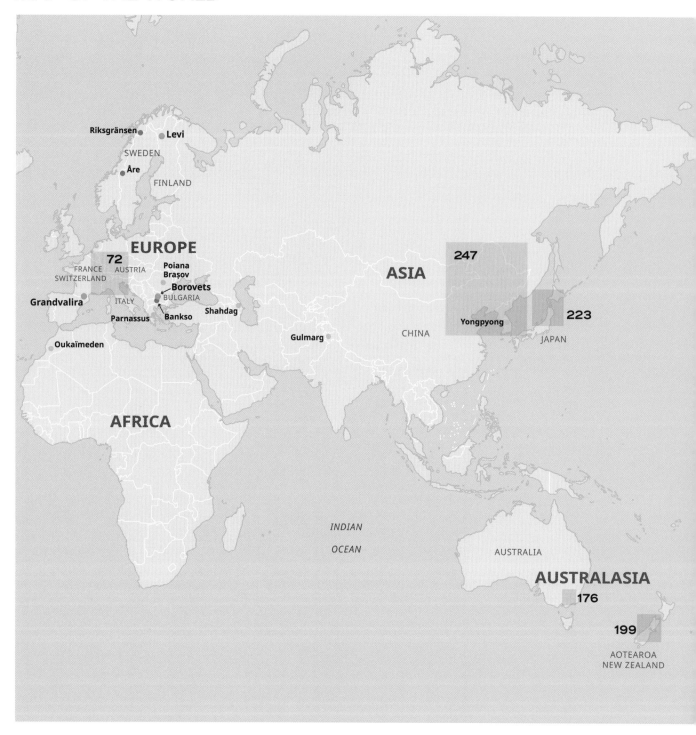

Riksgränsen • • Levi
SWEDEN
• Åre
FINLAND

EUROPE
72
FRANCE   Poiana
SWITZERLAND   AUSTRIA Braşov
                        Borovets
                        BULGARIA
Grandvalira
                ITALY
Parnassus   **Bankso**   **Shahdag**

Oukaïmeden

ASIA
247

Yongpyong   223
CHINA   JAPAN

Gulmarg

AFRICA

INDIAN

OCEAN

AUSTRALIA

AUSTRALASIA
176

199
AOTEAROA
NEW ZEALAND

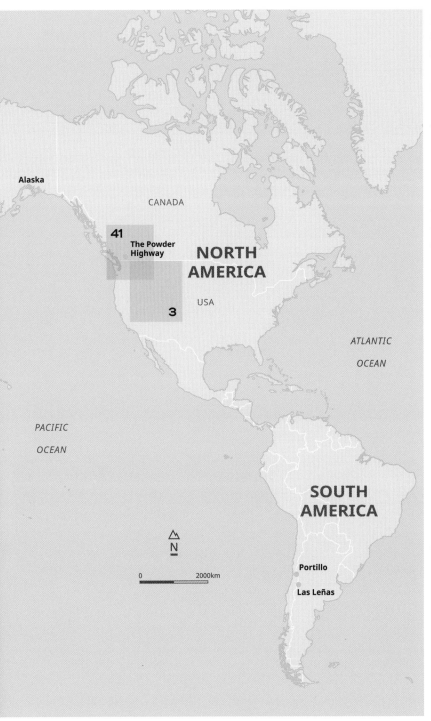

Legend

- Featured ski destination
- Alternative destination
- Ski the World destinations

North America

From Canada's superstars and quirky mountain towns to the USA's unbeatable hospitality and feast of resorts, North America is a super-sized adventure on every front.

USA

The United States of America: land of the free and home of the brave. Home of mega mountains and more ski resorts than you could poke a pole at. Home of free hot-chocolate refills, organised ski slopes and the friendliest people on the planet. The USA is top of the menu for a plate heaping with options and a side serve of hospitality. No one will ankle-tap you here while trying to get ahead in a ski queue (looking at you, France).

And this is the thing – skiing in the USA is civilised. This will be hugely exciting to beginner and intermediate skiers, and potentially massively disappointing for those used to backcountry skiing out of bounds. Due to liability issues, the USA has heavily regulated ski areas and skiing is absolutely inbounds. Having said that, it has some of the best inbound (patrolled) out-of-bounds-style riding in the world. Look at the adrenalin-inducing Highlands Bowl in Aspen (*see* p. 13), or nooks like Corbett's Couloir in Jackson Hole (*see* p. 9). You won't lose thrills, but the way they operate means slopes may just be a little safer. And backcountry wilderness can still be yours – just grab a guide and venture forth.

Some people complain about the generic homogeneity and regulated ski areas. Sure, you can't cross countries, you won't end up in an onsen and there are no Northern Lights. But there's cowboy culture (giddy up Steamboat Springs, *see* p. 19), endless space (feel it at Big Sky, *see* p. 5), and did I mention the red-carpet welcome? Resorts are genuinely happy to see you and the next-level service (slopeside ski concierge anyone?) creates hassle-free holidays. Once you've said 'yay' to the US of A, it's hard to settle for anything else.

Coolest winter selfie
Seated on the chairlift seat adorned with prayer flags atop Highlands Bowl in Aspen Snowmass (*see* p. 13) at 3777m (12392ft), wallowing in Steamboat's thermal springs (*see* p. 19), catching an Olympian in the terrain parks at Mammoth Mountain (*see* p. 33) or riding like a pro in the tram at Jackson Hole (*see* p. 9).

Get appy
If you're in Colorado, the CAIC (Colorado Avalanche Info Centre) app, including user-uploaded photos for current on-site reports, is literally a lifesaver (also follow @friendsofCAIC).

Skilynx has one-touch messaging and interactive real-time maps, which can show you where your gang is on the mountain.

Don't break the bank
Statistically, many resorts in Colorado get their biggest snowfalls in March. Take advantage of shoulder and low-season prices through to April with great spring snow.

If you're a foreigner, jump on a package from a ski operator - they can bundle passes, accommodation and rentals for better prices than what is available independently.

When it snows
The USA is a big animal, so it stands to reason that weather patterns differ from tip to tail. Cold-smoke snow is the prized trophy: it's the type of snow that isn't just dry, but retains a low percentage of moisture for flotation, like in Utah and Big Sky (*see* p. 5), where moisture is sucked out along the flats. The coastal proximity of Mammoth Mountain (*see* p. 33) results in heavier snow, and the good news for Colorado is that when there's an Arctic blast coming from the North Pole and a Pacific low-pressure system from the north-west, the clashing systems produce ample snowfall and extremely light powder.

Previous In the white room on a bluebird day, a snowboarder scores a light and dry spray in Aspen, Colorado

Unplug and lose the crowds, this Montana mountain stars 'America's Matterhorn'.

Big Sky, Montana

THE LOWDOWN

I have no idea why Big Sky near Yellowstone National Park gets overlooked. None. It's not even hard to access – an hour's scenic drive (complete with elk and bighorn sheep spotting) through the Gallatin National Forest south of Bozeman, with over 30 non-stop flights. That makes Big Sky the best-served mountain destination in the country.

Here, you'll find uncrowded bliss with over an acre per skier, the most consistent snowfall in the Northern Rockies in the form of cold-smoke powder and, like the name says, it's capital-B Big. Big Sky is the second largest resort in the US, and third largest in North America.

The multi-page piste map can double as a tablecloth, and just when you think you've seen everything, there's another ridge, another lift, and another run to ride. The map expanded when Boyne Resorts purchased Moonlight Basin, but the highlight addition is the Lone Peak 75-person tram, which replaced the 15-person tin can after more than 25 years of service to the gnarliest cliffs and chutes in the USA.

Big Sky's claim to fame is Lone Peak, offering 300 degrees of skiing and inbounds black runs that can only be described as aggressive. Yet 40 per cent of the terrain is for beginners and intermediates.

Unlike many other purpose-built resorts, Big Sky doesn't have a pre-existing town nearby and the many condos are spread out. While this dampens the après and village vibe, it keeps the focus on the mountain, which isn't a bad thing at all.

Big Sky Resort is on the land of Confederated Salish-Kootenai Tribes, Northern Cheyenne Nation, Niitsitapi (Blackfoot Confederacy), Shoshone-Bannock Tribes, Cayuse, Umatilla and Walla Walla, and many other tribes, nations, bands, and confederacies.

 Mountain stats
- Elevation top: 3400m (11,166ft)
- Elevation bottom: 2289m (7510ft)
- Vertical drop: 1326m (4350ft)
- Skiable terrain: 23.6sqkm (5850 acres)
- Longest run: 9.6km (6mi)
- Beginner terrain: 23 per cent
- Intermediate terrain: 25 per cent
- Advanced terrain: 52 per cent
- Lifts: 39

 Run
Big Sky's most iconic run is the 1200ft (366m) Big Couloir with a 39-degree sustained pitch in a narrow couloir.

 Experience
The ambitious Big Sky 2025 is a ten-year project that's transformed the resort. A stylish glass viewing platform has been built atop Lone Peak to appreciate the fanginess of those steep lines without having to ride them.

 Local's tip
It usually takes Ski Patrol a bit longer to complete avalanche mitigation on a powder day. Ski powder lines in the trees off Ramcharger 8 or Swift Current 6 while waiting for the tram to open.

Opposite Dropping into the Big Couloir, one of the most intense inbound experiences in America

THE MOUNTAIN DEBRIEF

The area is easily segmented with room for progression in each zone, except for Lone Peak, where you really want to know what you're doing before hitting the triple-black diamond trails. Skiing off the summit is the closest thing to heli-skiing in Montana, with thousands of acres below, views of three states (Montana, Idaho and Wyoming) and two national parks (Yellowstone and Grand Teton).

It's a magical experience unless you forgot that between you and any blue run is a band of mainly triple-black couloirs, cliffs and chutes. You won't breathe normally until you hit Stillwater, Deepwater or Horsehoe Bowls – unless you take single-black-diamond Liberty backside.

This makes it sound like riding Big Sky is Big Business, but that's far from true. Apart from Lone Peak and the black runs scattered throughout the resort, most of the rest of the terrain is the domain of intermediates and beginners, covering fast and steep groomers, wide thigh-burners, gladed runs, seven terrain parks and natural halfpipes around Explorer.

A RIDING ITINERARY

Grab a beverage from **Treeline Coffee** in Big Sky Mountain Village and do 8am Andesite Mountain laps with the Ramcharger Early Access. Just taking **Ramcharger 8** (complete with heated seats and weatherproof bubbles) provides the ideal Big Sky start – the view of Lone Peak from here is breathtaking.

The intimate lunch stop is **Everett's 8800** at the top of Andesite Mountain. Named by *Architectural Digest* as the Most Beautifully Designed Bar in Montana, pit stop here fireside for elk chilli and glühwein.

Make that glühwein a single, because we're heading up the **Lone Peak Tram**. Off the front side is a basketful of double and triple blacks like the **Gullies**. On the south side, head for the double-black **Marx** or **Dictator Chutes**. My favourite is the gloriously open single-diamond **Liberty Bowl**, before a play in the **Bavarian Forest** trees and the wider open **Aspen Meadows**.

ADVENTURE

Nothing black-run related, it's yellow – **Yellowstone National Park**. On a snowcat excursion you can visit the wildlife and thermal features when most don't – in sparkling winter.

OFF-MOUNTAIN MUST-DO

- Go headlamp night skiing on Wednesdays and Saturdays from **Ramcharger 8**, explore the evening **Enchanted Forest** illuminated trail atop Andesite Mountain or try **winter fly fishing** in one of south-west Montana's five blue-ribbon trout streams (wildtroutoutfitters.com and montanaflyfishing.com).

EAT UP & DRINK DOWN

- One of those tough holiday dilemmas is between the almond trout and the bison at **Peaks Chophouse & Wine Lounge** (bigskyresort.com/dining/peaks); in the Summit Hotel.
- **Chet's Bar & Grill** (bigskyresort.com/dining/chets); named after the Big Sky visionary, late NBC anchorman Chet Huntley is where to get family-friendly burgers.
- Take a **Sleigh Ride Dinner** (lonemountainranch.com) to the Lone Mountain Ranch's historic North Fork Cabin for a cowboy-style dinner.

APRÈS SKI

- The **Scissorbills Saloon** (scissorbills.com), with live music and shareable plates (tater tots!) is the obvious stop for après seekers.
- The **Umbrella Bar** in Mountain Village is a glass-walled yurt with front-row seats to Lone Peak views.

STAY

- **Summit Hotel** (bigskyresort.com/the-summit-hotel), where Presidents Obama and Biden have both spent vacations, is the top-tier choice in Mountain Village.
- **Huntley Lodge** (bigskyresort.com/huntley-lodge), recently renovated, is the kind of place you want as a mountain family home, with the Explorer Lift just out the back door.

ALTERNATIVE: TAOS

Taos (skitaos.com) is out on a geographical limb, a long way from Montana, in New Mexico. Like Big Sky, it has no neighbours and some untamed wilds. Unlike Big Sky, it's a mission to access - a 32mi (51km), 3.5hr drive from Albuquerque. However, a similar no-crowds, awesome terrain reward awaits.

Top The summit on Lone Mountain, the highest point at Big Sky Resort *Bottom* The A-Z/Headwaters Ridge, drop in to the left for the A-Z, drop in to the right to ride Headwaters *Opposite* It's easy to see why Lone Peak is called 'America's Matterhorn'

Surrounded by national parks, the steeps are legendary in this grit-hearted, mountain-loving town that comes with all the cosmopolitan trimmings.

Jackson Hole, Wyoming

THE LOWDOWN

Jackson Hole is badass; let's set that expectation from the start. And I don't just mean the terrain, but the riders who come here. The Big Red (tram) line-up is a parade of hardcores who drop into Corbett's Couloir before breakfast and locals like snowboarder Travis Rice or adventurer-filmmaker Jimmy Chin. The HQ of Teton Gravity Research (creators of pro snow films and media) is here, and while you may find a rare Gucci handbag, this is more of a Gore-Tex town. Steamboat (*see* p. 19) feels Wild West until you come to Jackson.

Surrounded by national parks and forests, this ski town is an island in a sea of protected wilderness where elk and bison roam, overlooked by the Teton's cathedral spires. Jackson is seen as the Holy Grail of inbounds, big-mountain steeps and deeps, fuelled by extreme skiing and cold, dry powder. That's true on Rendezvous mountain, but there's another mountain, Après Vous, with less rowdy blue terrain for mere mortals.

Base yourself at purpose-built Teton Village at the slopes or 19km (12mi) away in Jackson, a proud cowboy town lined with galleries, creative cafes, cosmopolitan restaurants, wine hangouts and bars as wild and fun as the mountain.

Jackson Hole is on the Traditional gathering territory of the Arapaho, Cheyenne, Crow, Shoshone and Ute peoples.

 Mountain stats
- Elevation top: 3185m (10,450ft)
- Elevation bottom: 1924m (6311ft)
- Vertical drop: 1262m (4139ft)
- Skiable terrain: 10sqkm (2500 acres)
- Longest run: 7.2km (4.5mi)
- Beginner terrain: 10 per cent
- Intermediate terrain: 40 per cent
- Advanced terrain: 50 per cent
- Lifts: 16

 Run
If you're game and it's open, Corbet's Couloir is a gnarly (and highly visible) inbounds ski run. Meet Your Maker is another steep, narrow chute with little room for error.

 Experience
The National Elk Refuge, just north of Jackson, is the winter destination for North America's largest migrating elk herd (the ski area closes in April to facilitate their exodus). Ride an open-air sleigh (nersleighrides.com) straight into the heart of the thousands-strong action with insider information about all things Wyoming and elk. It's an absolute trip highlight.

 Local's tip
Don't rely on your phone's weather app. Forecasts from Mountain Weather (mountainweather.com), a global meteorological consulting company located in Jackson, paired with the Teton Forecast from Bridger-Teton Avalanche Center (hbridgertetonavalanchecenter.org), give accurate current conditions.

Also, wearing Stio, a local mountain-gear brand sold only online or in Jackson, is as sure a sign you've been to Jackson as a JAC luggage sticker.

Opposite Body and face shots, the calling cards of Jackson Hole, BYO snorkel

THE MOUNTAIN DEBRIEF

Giddyup cowgirls and cowboys, you're in for a wild ride. In this part of the Wild West, there's room to roam and serious stats: 116 trails and an average annual snowfall of over 11m (450in), which is on par with Utah, including a similar low moisture content. Fifty per cent of the terrain is rated expert (only 10 per cent for beginners); if that's not enough, the open backcountry gate system accesses another 12sqkm (3000 acres).

The 100-person Jackson Hole Aerial Tram (aka Big Red) is the beating heart of the mountain, creating the longest continuous vertical rise of any lift in the United States. It accesses prime blue- and black-rated terrain in just 3.5min.

Download the JH Insider app, which includes Replay My Day, a fun animated trail map visual of your epic day.

A RIDING ITINERARY

As the safety message reads on the tram dock, 'Give this mountain the respect it deserves!' That means stashing an extra breakfast croissant bought from boulangerie **Persephone** (persephonebakery.com) in your pocket as a mid-run saviour. It's tempting to jump on the tram and drop into Rendezvous and Cheyenne Bowls, but dip a toe in the water before diving in by riding the mountain from the mellower right to the more extreme left. One thing you'll notice about Jackson is there's a variety of mid-mountain lifts, so there's little reason to ski to base.

Make your way up to the top of **Apres Vous chairlift** and warm up on blues like **Werner** and **Teewinot**. Then shimmy to **Casper Chair** for blues galore, including **Sleeping Indian** and **Campground**. Then head over to **Thunder chair**, which drops into **Amphitheatre** via some steep blues, or start tasting those blacks like **Thunder** or the **Tower Three Chute**.

Up **Sublette**, which tops out above **Laramie Bowl**, and then decisions, decisions – the Cirque blacks or into the Bowl? The call of the **Alta Chutes** is impossible to resist. At some point, a tram run is needed, even if just to look over the lip of Corbet's and grab a waffle at **Corbet's Cabin** (jacksonhole.com/waffles; the bacon and peanut butter is better than it sounds).

ADVENTURE

Hit the **Teton backcountry** (jacksonhole.com/backcountry) – booking a guide grants access to the early tram then, after transceiver tuition, it's straight out the gates from the summit.

OFF-MOUNTAIN MUST-DO

- Nature options abound. This is the place to go dog sledding with **Frank Teasley** (jhsleddog.com) - an eight-time Alaska Iditarod race musher.
- Grab a camera and shoot with a National Geographic contributor at **Teton Photo Adventures** (jaygoodrich.com) or follow moose tracks on a **Teton National Park fat tyre bike ride** (tetonmtbike.com).

EAT UP & DRINK DOWN

- **Teton Thai** (tetonthaivillage.com) is an institution of Teton Village, small-sized but with big flavours, and crammed with tram mechanics, pros and spice lovers.
- In town, **Coelette** (coelette.com) departs from ski-town comfort food with 'snowline cuisine', featuring ingredients found and grown in alpine environments.
- If you're hankering to try elk bolognese, come with a hungry and hard-skiing crew to **Glorietta's Trattoria** (gloriettajackson.com).

APRÈS SKI

- Go old school at the classic **Mangy Moose Saloon** (mangymoose.com), home of Jackson's best après (and spicy margaritas) since 1967.
- Hang at the patio at **RPK3** (jacksonhole.com/rpk3) or find ski instructors (and fondue) at the **Alpenhof** (alpenhoflodge.com) by the tram tower.

STAY

- If you're keen to be first at the tram, the **Four Seasons** (fourseasons.com/jacksonhole) is a rare ski-in, ski-out property in Teton Village.
- In town **Anvil** (anvilhotel.com), appropriately named for its hundred-year-old blacksmith's shop origins, is a stylish take on the rustic rancher's getaway, and just a few steps from Glorietta's (*see* above).

Top Retro vibes are not intentional, they're original *Bottom* Top of the world waffles at Corbet's Cabin are a local institution *Opposite* Cowboy culture is alive and kicking in JH

ALTERNATIVE: GRAND TARGHEE

Another highlight is Grand Targhee in Wyoming - the unsung hero neighbour to Jackson Hole, which attracts snow by the metre load but very few crowds along with it.

ALTERNATIVE: ALTA AND SNOWBIRD

Alta (alta.com) and Snowbird (snowbird.com) in Utah (two separate Cottonwood Canyon ski resorts that share lift tickets) receive Mother Nature's generous gift of 12.7m (500in) of Wasatch annual powder. While newbies are welcome (and snowboarders at Snowbird only), the terrain is best enjoyed by advanced skiers.

Peek below the glitz and glamour and you'll plug into a tribe of forward-thinking snow lovers who emphasise community and inclusivity. Come for its snow, be hooked by its soul.

Aspen Snowmass, Colorado

THE LOWDOWN

Aspen Snowmass is the best ski area in the world. Am I biased? Absolutely. Am I on the payroll? Completely. Disclaimer – I was the Aspen Skiing Company's first Australian snowboard instructor and, 25 years later, I write the communications plans for their top international market. My career began and continues here, and I'd move back in a heartbeat. Out of the scores of ski resorts I've visited, the fact that this is where I will forever choose to hang my helmet, among decades-old friends and colleagues, tells you something. Nowhere compares.

Very rarely do ski areas get political, but Aspen Snowmass is the snow-industry leader in environmental and social activism. It took its #giveaflake climate campaign all the way to Capitol Hill, invested in converting waste methane from a coal plant into usable electricity, has the longest-running Gay Ski Week (45-plus years) and the management team remain, at heart, ski bums who have never lost the stoke of sharing the snow.

You could come here and never ski. Originally a silver mining town, the cosmopolitan centre features Victorian multi-gabled houses, big-name eateries like LA's Nobu Matsuhisa and art exhibitions at the Aspen Art Museum. Family-owned, non-corporate, multi-layered, exceptional – that's Aspen Snowmass.

Aspen is the ancestral home of the Ute Nation.

 Mountain stats
- Elevation top (Snowmass): 3813m (12,510ft)
- Elevation bottom: 2623m (8604ft)
- Vertical drop: 1340m (4406ft)
- Skiable terrain: 13.5sqkm (3342 acres)
- Longest run: 8.5km (5.3mi)
- Beginner terrain: 5 per cent
- Intermediate terrain: 48 per cent
- Advanced terrain: 47 per cent
- Lifts: 21

 Run
All the runs in the Highlands Bowl or Naked Lady on Snowmass are as curvaceous with rollers and pops as their names suggest.

 Experience
Not many people are aware that Aspen is home to the Aspen Centre for Environmental Studies (ACES), a thriving wildlife sanctuary open to the public. It was donated by Elizabeth Paepcke who, with husband Walter, revitalised Aspen from deserted mining town to cultural hub in the 1950s.

 Local's tip
Rent equipment at Four Mountain Sports (aspensnowmass.com/visit/rentals), which includes free inter-mountain transfers (just hand it to a base concierge) so you're never schlepping skis. Join workers to dine on bar menus at restaurants for around 30 per cent less (and the bar is where the action's at).

Opposite Cat skiing on the backside of Aspen Mountain on a Snowcat Powder Tour with The Little Nell

THE MOUNTAIN DEBRIEF

Aspen Snowmass is a family of four mountains linked by a free shuttle in a 32km (20mi) radius.

Aspen Mountain is the signature mountain, rising above the town as a maze of blue and black runs (no greens), with backcountry-style Pandora's added in 2023. John Denver and Jerry Garcia's shrines are two popular, highly decorated nooks hiding in the trees (Jerry Garcia's off Ruthie's is a popular magnet for Grateful Dead 'Deadhead' fans).

Aspen Highlands was the '70s renegade and retains rogue flair, under-the-radar but beloved by locals. Hiking 45min for bucket list–worthy turns up 12,392ft (3777m) Highland Bowl (the first section accessed by free snowcat) is one of the best inbounds, backcountry-style experiences in North America.

Buttermilk is, as the name suggests, gentle and forgiving, with a US$23 million base makeover creating a seamless beginning experience (parents love the award-winning ski/play centre, the Hideout), but it also hosts X Games Aspen with pro-worthy parks.

And then there's Snowmass (the third largest standalone ski area in the USA), where you'll rarely ride the same run twice.

A RIDING ITINERARY

While you could spend multiple days at any of the mountains, the idea is that you can treat them as a movable feast according to your whims, all linked by free and frequent buses.

If you're keen for a half-day ride, head up the **Silver Queen Gondola** on Ajax (Ajax is the former name of Aspen Mountain and often called this among locals) for first tracks top to bottom (pausing at the top to visit the avalanche dogs at ski patrol, they love a pat). Breakfast at **Bonnie's** mid-mountain with fluffy pancakes is a first tracks' tradition. Then spend a morning exploring multiple fall lines and ending on the deck of **Ajax Tavern** (*see* p. 17) at the bottom of the slopes, all in time for lunch.

The new 2022 base area at Buttermilk makes it a beginner's nirvana as a one-stop shop for rentals and lessons. Tip – if it's a powder day, the more advanced **Tiehack** side of the ski area keeps fresh lines late. As the home to the **X Games Aspen** for more than two decades, this is the place to watch the pros, especially during January. Break for lunch at the **Mongolian BBQ at the Cliffhouse** with Pyramid Peak views (some of the best in the valley).

If you're feeling adventurous, head over to Highlands to hike the **Highlands Bowl**. First, warm up on the playful rolling blues where it's not rare to find yourself alone on a run. Then get ready for the best hike inbounds in the USA, 45min up a boot-packed track from a (free) cat drop point – buy ski straps from the Ski Patrol hut at the start of the hike and get some pointers. After an adventure down the face (or more forgiving angled side trees), stop at **Merry Go Round** for a farm-to-plate, cafeteria-style lunch.

A powder day? Hit up **Snowmass**, with 1343 vertical metres (4406ft), 13.5sqkm (3342 acres) of terrain, 98 trails, 21 chairlifts and access to your choice of cruisers, glades, steeps, terrain parks and halfpipes.

ADVENTURE

How often do you get to ride with a big mountain-sponsored skier? Book private guiding with Aspen local **Chris Davenport** ('Dav'; chrisdavenport.com), a two-time World Extreme Skiing Champion and pioneer in ski mountaineering. Non-skiers can ride the **Breathtaker Alpine Coaster** (adjacent Elk Camp Restaurant), whizzing through a mile of forest up to 45km/h (28mph).

Opposite Get a big mountain, inbound feel atop Highlands Bowl

OFF-MOUNTAIN MUST-DO

- If you're not skiing or boarding, the list of activities is long - go ice skating, snow-shoeing, take an insightful tour with the Aspen Historical Society, peruse art galleries, shop the designer district, or go dog sledding or snowmobiling.

EAT UP & DRINK DOWN

- **Element 47** (thelittlenell.com/dine/element-47) at the Little Nell is the pinnacle of Aspen dining, an art-surrounded gourmet experience.
- **Ellina** (ellinaaspen.com) is a cosy hideout with a sun-drenched Italian countryside menu.
- **Woody Creek Tavern** (woodycreektavern.com) is former resident Hunter S Thompson's drinking hole and a cacophony of memorabilia.

APRÈS SKI

- The **AJAX Tavern** (thelittlenell.com/dine/ajax-tavern) deck at Ajax's base has the best truffle fries and people-watching real estate.
- **Mezzaluna's** (mezzalunaaspen.com) U-shaped bar is the place to meet your gang - or find one.

STAY

- The **Little Nell** (thelittlenell.com), a ski-in, ski-out hotel, all the way - the only five-star, five-diamond Aspen hotel; the ski concierge personally removes your ski boots. Even as a non-guest, you can book for an underground cellar flight with their sommelier.
- The **Limelight Aspen** (limelighthotels.com/aspen) in downtown Aspen has a buzzing après with woodfire pizzas, live music and spacious rooms.

Below Award-winning mountain groomers translate into perfect pinstripe corduroy - part of the stellar service *Opposite* Romantic, snowy strolls in the pedestrian heart of Aspen's downtown

Trademarked 'champagne powder', Wild West hospitality and massive new investments keep this ranching heartland alive and bucking.

Steamboat Springs, Colorado

THE LOWDOWN

Giddy up! Steamboat Springs doesn't just embrace its Wild West heritage; it grabs it by the horns and rides its friendly ranching roots hard. There are no fur coats here, instead you'll see people wearing boots and 10-gallon hats. But this is the real deal, with dry snow so light and fluffy Steamboat trademarked it 'champagne powder' (true story). If anyone else tries to claim they also have champagne powder, it's only sparkling.

Steamboat, whose name originated in the 1800s when French trappers thought they heard a chugging steamboat (it was the mineral springs), has always had a defined niche with ride-or-die fans. While the 3hr drive from Denver tends to thin the weekend warrior herds, it's serviced by five airlines and is one of the easiest ski towns to access.

More fun facts; this is Ski Town USA, having produced more Olympians than anywhere in the USA – 100 and counting (even the Director of Skiing is an Olympian, medallist Billy Kidd).

Already an 'Ultimate', Steamboat bull-charged its way from fifth- to second-largest ski resort in Colorado during a multi-year (2021–23) 'full steam ahead' resort transformation (and it is a transformation). Over US$200 million was dropped on new lodging, an ice rink, even an escalator to the slopes. And if you're sniffing change in the air, that may be the new restaurants that are sprouting like wild mushrooms.

Steamboat Springs in on the Traditional grounds of the Ute, the Yampatika Ute and Arapaho tribes.

Mountain stats
- Elevation top: 3221m (10,568ft)
- Elevation bottom: 2103m (6900ft)
- Vertical drop: 1118m (3668ft)
- Skiable terrain: 11.99sqkm (2965 acres)
- Longest run: 3mi (4.8km)
- Beginner terrain: 14 per cent
- Intermediate terrain: 42 per cent
- Advanced terrain: 44 per cent
- Lifts: 17

Run
Amazing corduroy, playful side rollers, and a consistent and accessible bump field make Buddy's Run, off Storm Peak, a crowd pleaser. Ride by the statue of 1950s ski racing legend Buddy Werner (who died aged 28 in a St Moritz avalanche).

Experience
Coming to Steamboat and not enjoying the hot springs is like going to London and avoiding Big Ben. There are over 150 hot springs in the area.

Local's tip
There are not many resorts where Olympians offer free pointers, but Director of Skiing Billy Kidd and fellow former (and sometimes current) US team members offer free clinics (steamboat.com) throughout the season. Bronze medallist Nelson Carmichael also runs a free bump clinic on his namesake, Nelson's Run throughout the winter.

Opposite Time out from mountain exploring for sun-deck soaking

THE MOUNTAIN DEBRIEF

'No more base!' cried the beginners. So now they're being released, via the new Wild Blue Gondola – the longest, fastest 10-person gondola in North America. Learners can ride halfway to mid-mountain's new skier-perfect Greenhorn Ranch and get that alpine feeling like the more advanced. But everyone benefits, with access from base to 2183m (7163ft) in 13min.

Steamboat isn't one hill but an entire mountain range, including Mount Werner, Sunshine Peak, Storm Peak, Thunderhead Peak, Pioneer Ridge and Christie Peak. As you'd expect with 12sqkm (3000 acres) of terrain, there are groomed cruisers, bumps, steeps, meadows and trees, plus five terrain parks for those budding Olympians (the local school offers online schoolwork to its superstars).

There are a whopping 170 trails to explore, but you'll never feel lost as the locals are almost disarmingly friendly, and the trails are arranged with common themes. If riding down Twister or Cyclone, you're on Storm Peak, Sunshine Peak trails are named after time references, and Pioneer Ridge trails feature early settlers. This is where you'll find the extra 2.6sqkm (650 acres) of expert/advanced terrain added in 2023 and serviced by a new chairlift.

A RIDING ITINERARY

Take the **Steamboat Gondola** and beeline to **Storm Peak Express** taking in **Buddy's Run** on Storm Peak South. You might also catch Olympian Nelson Carmichael giving tips for bumps on Nelson's Run. Take a break and recharge at **Four Points Lodge**. The menu champions local ingredient heroes – try the bison chili or turkey pot pie. Or a not-so-healthy (but delicious) bloody mary.

Refuelled, ride over to **Sunshine** for some fun trails, including **Quickdraw** and **Flintlock**, off the **Sunshine Express** lift. Take **Sundown Express** and you'll be in the time-themed area of the mountain. **High Noon**, **One O'clock**, and **Two O'clock** will keep you entertained until the lifts close at four o'clock (the time, not a run).

On a fresh fall day, it's hard to beat **Shadows** and **Closets** side by side with abundant powder stashes; another run not to miss is **Tomahawk** for the views, which starts as a blue along the top face and then mellows out with fun, rolling hills.

ADVENTURE

For something totally different, head to **Bridgestone Winter Driving School** (winterdrive.com), the only one of its kind in North America, where you'll do more 360s than intended tackling an obstacle course of regularly abused traffic cones.

OFF-MOUNTAIN MUST-DO

- A guided winter horseback ride at **Del's Triangle 3 Ranch** is a true western experience, with stunning views through the Routt National Forest.
- Alternatively, go night skiing, snowmobiling or cross-country skiing and winding through aspen groves and along beautiful Fish Creek.

—

EAT UP & DRINK DOWN

- The most genius invention to ever hit the snow is **The Taco Beast**, a food truck on a snowcat, roaming the slopes leaving no hungry rider in its wake. You can track its latest location down on Twitter (@TacoBeastSBT).
- For a true Steamboat steak experience head to **The Ore House**, a former barn, for a 6oz, bacon-wrapped, centre-cut filet with crab meat and bearnaise.

—

APRÈS SKI

- The best après scene is a ski-in, ski-out après hot spot **T-Bar** - an accurately self proclaimed 'five-star dive bar'; blasting '80s hits and chilled reggae. Bang some nails into the Hammerschalgen log or bask in the sunshine with their addictive pulled-pork tacos.
- **Timber and Torch** (steamboat.com) located in the heart of Steamboat Square is the spot for cocktails and an amazing deck to soak up the mountains or catch a concert on the Steamboat Stage.

—

STAY

- There's no shortage of places to stay. The elegant **Steamboat Grand** (steamboatgrand.com) is within a whip flick of the slopes.
- Funky, boutique hotel **Gravity Haus Steamboat** (gravityhaus.com) is one minute from the gondola (timed) and **Moving Mountains** (movingmountains.com) organises luxury vacation homes.

Top Lasso an off-slope activity *Bottom* Wallow in waters after a hard day on the slopes *Opposite* The sleeping giant wakes as the day begins

Famed for Butch Cassidy's first bank robbery, box canyon beauty Telluride has been standing and delivering, handing over skiing gold ever since.

Telluride, Colorado

THE LOWDOWN

Like many who've had a mountain fling, I've retained a wistful crush on Telluride. Is it the utterly unique setting, tucked in a majestic box canyon, the farm-to-table restaurants, the teeny town studded with Victorian-era architecture, or the San Juan Mountain scenery riding? It's the full symphony of elements, singing with an intangible energy. Whatever your expectations of this 140-year-old former mining town tucked deep in a south-west pocket of Colorado, they will be exceeded.

Under the big-name reputation runs the throb of a tight-knit ski-town community with a quiet sophistication, and the brick-and-clapboard facades look much as they did in the 1880s when Cassidy came to town. Sure, landowners may include Oprah Winfrey and Ralph Lauren, but Telluride's vibe is more denim than diamonds.

Telluride is closer to Albuquerque in New Mexico than Denver in Colorado, and getting here is a conscious decision; there isn't a nearby city and most fly into Montrose 90min away. The happy result is there's no blow-ins or any sense of rush; Telluride isn't on the way to anywhere.

There's one decision to make: should you stay at Mountain Village, positioned just shy of 3000m (9545ft) with luxury accommodation in the thick of the ski action, or in Telluride itself, for culture, nightlife and dining? There's no wrong choice as they're connected by a free 13min eco-gondola that runs until midnight.

Telluride is located on ancestral Ute land.

 Mountain stats
- Elevation top: 4008m (13,150ft)
- Elevation bottom: 2659m (8725ft)
- Vertical drop: 1349m (4425ft)
- Skiable terrain: 8.1sqkm (2000 acres)
- Longest run: 7.4km (4.6mi)
- Beginner terrain: 23 per cent
- Intermediate terrain: 36 per cent
- Advanced terrain: 41 per cent
- Lifts: 17

 Run
Feel like you're floating on a cloud on appropriately named See Forever, a blue ridge run, starting from a summit of 3814m (12,515ft). Views extend into Utah, with the La Sal mountains visible near Moab.

 Experience
Telluride went from a stop on the Rio Grande Southern Railway, to an almost ghost town, to a ski town - see the history at Telluride Historical Museum (telluridemuseum.org).

 Local's tip
Telluride is a state-certified Creative Arts District. Download a self-walk Gallery Guide (telluridearts.org/galleries).

Opposite Get amongst the mountains and explore this Colorado corner on snowmobiles

THE MOUNTAIN DEBRIEF

Telluride has it all. Don't let the resort's compact base area fool you – the slopes unfold from mid-mountain and in the Palmyra Peak (4008m/13,150ft) basin with access to multiple bowls and hike-to-steeps.

The mountain is known as a more challenging resort than some of its Colorado counterparts, with 77 per cent of the trails rated intermediate or advanced/expert. Experts love the black fall lines almost free falling into town, then there are more sedate groomers like the 8km (5mi) See Forever blue stunner and green 7km (4.3mi) Galloping Goose.

And the snow isn't shabby, drying out over south-western desert expanses before dropping an annual 7.8m (309in) of light, moistureless powder. If you're a keen spring skier and lover of warmer temperatures, you've found the sweet spot – Telluride's high-elevation slopes and northern exposures maintain snow quality, offering a Rocky Mountain high right through to early April, when the resort closes.

If chutes are your bag, head up the Revelation Lift and hike for as long as you like along the ridge to access one of the ten Gold Hill Chutes. Keep in mind, the further along the ridgeline you go, the steeper and more technical the chutes become. For mogul magic, head down Kant-Mak-M (Frontside, aka Townside); stay on your A Games for the vocal gallery on the Plunge Lift above.

A RIDING ITINERARY

Grab a coffee to start the day at **The Butcher & The Baker** (butcherandbakercafe.com) or the **Coffee Cowboy** (thecoffeecowboy.com) at the base of the free gondola, then head for the Village Express to the **Polar Queen Express** with a mountain face full of blues like **Stormin' Norman** and **Dew Drop**.

Now you're primed to head up **Goldhill Express** and tackle some of the blacks. Telluride's black-diamond slopes comprise 41 per cent of the offerings, and if you're up to it (and acclimated) work for hike-to terrain in the **Black Iron Bowl**, **Revelation Bowl** and **Bald Mountain**. My pick – fit in one of the **Gold Hill Chutes**, accessed via the famed **'Stairway to Heaven'**, a metal staircase along the knife-edge ridge and some of the gnarliest inbounds terrain in the USA. Back up the Gold Hill Express and you have earned your grilled, oozing cheese and antipasti at **Alpino Vino**.

Post lunch enjoy a **See Forever** segment, then kaboom, head down into **Bushwacker** or the **Plunge** and you could play around the **Plunge Lift** all afternoon. Unless you are a snowboarder and bumps aren't your bag days after a fresh fall, in which case the stunning, open expanse of **Revelation Bowl** is a happy place to be.

ADVENTURE

Telluride Helitrax (helitrax.com) has a tenure of over 517sqkm (128,000 acres) of high alpine basins, cirques and summits surrounding Telluride to the north, south and east. It's not just for experts, the terrain graduates from gentle powder fields to peaks.

Opposite top Telluride from above, nestled like a gem in a canyon treasure box *Opposite bottom* The San Juan mountains are spectacular constant companions

OFF-MOUNTAIN MUST-DO

- Have the best of both worlds and signup for a snowmobile tour through the ghost town of Alta and the Alta Lakes area next door to the slopes through **Telluride Outfitters** (tellurideoutfitters.com), or go snowshoeing or cross-country skiing on the Valley Floor.
- For a real adventure, book a beginner ice-climbing excursion with **Mountain Trip** (mountaintrip.com).

———

EAT UP & DRINK DOWN

- The free-range beef will herd you towards the upscale **New Sheridan Chop House** (newsheridan.com); try their Flatliner Martini with cold-brewed espresso.
- For something less spendy, the craft pizzas at **Brown Dog Pizza** (browndogpizza.com) are made by award-winning dough flingers.

———

APRÈS SKI

- Get the party started at rustic **Gorrono Ranch** by skiing the Misty Maiden run off the Village Express to their Snow Beach deck for island vibes and live music.
- In Mountain Village the 4pm après kicks off at the **Madeline** (aubergeresorts.com/madeline) with the sounding of a Swiss alpenhorn (plus there's an ice-skating rink and fire-pits for s'mores) or continue down to **Telluride Distilling** (telluridedistilling.com) to taste its award-winning peppermint schnapps.

———

STAY

- At Mountain Village, it's a drop'n'roll to the slopes from double named **Fairmont Heritage Franz Kalmmer Lodge** (fairmont.com) with luxurious two- and three-bed residences and a pool.
- The **New Sheriden** (newsheridan.com) is a historic gem, with its superb Main Street location giving an immersive Telluride Town experience.

———

ALTERNATIVE: BRECKENRIDGE

Breckenridge (breckenridge.com) has a killer combination of 3962m (13,000ft) snow-sure slopes and a heritage, thriving town. But its base is at 2900m (9514ft), so even going to the supermarket can become an extreme, heart-hammering sport - the base of Val Thorens, Europe's highest ski area, is 600m (1968ft) lower. It's not called the Fridge for nothing.

ALTERNATIVE: COLORADO'S MILLION DOLLAR HIGHWAY

Most people know Colorado for its billionaire playgrounds: Aspen (*see* p. 13), Vail, Beaver Creek. But the most snow, statistically speaking, falls far from these famous areas - down south where little-known clusters of lifts remain the perennial overachievers. How do you find these skiable gems? Follow Colorado's Million Dollar Highway.

This spectacular stretch of road earns its name for two reasons. It reportedly cost a million dollars per mile to drill through the rugged San Juan Mountains, but also because the result was a canyon-clinging drive with million-dollar views at every turn. Slightly terrifying for the vertical drop-offs that lurk inches from your car tyres, the road transports skiers to the south-west corner of Colorado and the doorstep of the 'Four Corners' - where New Mexico, Arizona, Utah and Colorado meet.

The official 'million dollar' section is 40km long but most people drive the full 110km between Ouray in the north and Durango in the south. Ouray is a beautiful hot springs town known as the 'Switzerland of America'. Down south, the historic mining towns of Silverton and Durango are genuine cowboy towns coloured by storied pasts, and now brimming with authentic saloon bars, breweries, restaurants and drawling southern accents.

The outlaw culture lives on in the extensive raw, steep and deep skiing this road trip offers. Alongside Telluride (a short side trip west from Ouray), the other two resorts worth checking out are Silverton Mountain and Purgatory (Durango's main ski resort). Other ski areas include Kendall Mountain, Hesperus and Chapman Hill. For adventure-seekers, there are also myriad backcountry trails (try the Colorado Trail), plus the potential for heli- and cat-skiing in the San Juan Mountains - Purgatory Snowcat Adventures operates the largest cat-skiing operation in Colorado.

Possibly the most unique experience is skiing Silverton Mountain - a one-lift, ungroomed, all-thrills-no-frills ski hill with a whopping 22,000 acres of heli and hike-accessed terrain, and an average 10m (32ft) of average annual snowfall. You're required to ski with a guide most of the season, and carry an avalanche beacon, shovel and probe (guides can provide these). Infrastructure is virtually non-existent, but so are crowd lines. No more than 80 skiers hit the slopes here on any average day.

Opposite Knee-deep fresh powder

This former Olympic Games host, home to the famed Sundance Film Festival, is a certified blockbuster with the most lift-accessible terrain in the USA.

Park City Mountain, Utah

THE LOWDOWN

Once upon a time, pre-2015, Park City Mountain sat on its own, isolated from the neighboring Canyons Resort. Then new owner, Vail Resorts had the brilliant idea of building the connecting Quicksilver Gondola, marrying the two in an everyone-wins union and creating the largest ski area in the USA.

But way before that ski industry checkmate, Park City was a rambunctious 1800s silver-mining town, nearly fading into history in the 1920s, before rising phoenix-like from the campfire ashes into a world-class destination that hosted one-third of the Salt Lake City Winter Olympics in 2002. It's a ski area fairy tale, complete with an annual delivery of Hollywood Prince Charmings when the Sundance Film Festival rolls into town each January.

There's no doubt about it, Park City itself, just 35min from Salt Lake City International Airport's arrival terminal, is exciting. Base yourself in the *joie de vivre* of the historic town, at Mountain Village, at the ski resort base (linked to downtown by electric buses) or at Canyons Village, a quieter ski-in, ski-out outpost with a devoted clientele.

Utah has some fancy flakes, which bring in over five million visitors and almost US$2 billion. A lower water content (8.5 per cent here) means they fall more slowly, allowing the dendrites (arms) to lengthen and create more complex shapes, resulting in a less dense powder. And while Steamboat Springs (*see* p. 19) has trademarked champagne powder, Utah has trademarked its former number-plate slogan 'The Greatest Snow on Earth', all 9m (355in) of it. Only in America.

Park City Mountain operates on the Traditional land of the Ute Tribe.

Mountain stats
- Elevation top: 3056m (10,026ft)
- Elevation bottom: 2072m (6800ft)
- Vertical drop: 953m (3126ft)
- Skiable terrain: 29.5sqkm (7300 acres)
- Longest run: 5.6km (3.5mi)
- Beginner terrain: 8 per cent
- Intermediate terrain: 42 per cent
- Advanced terrain: 50 per cent
- Lifts: 43

Run
Make pro-style jump turns down McConkey's Bowl like the area's namesake, famed skier and later Ski School Director Jim McConkey (father to the late skier and base jumper Shane McConkey).

Experience
After a fresh fall you may need a snorkel for the light powder in the hike-to terrain in Murdock Bowl, Pinecone Ridge, Scott's Bowl and the P-Zone or O-Zone of Jupiter Peak.

Local's tip
Utah is not a dry state as believed, despite over half the population identifying as teetotalling Mormons. But alcohol is state-controlled (like in 16 other US states); liquor stores close at 8pm and all day Sunday. You can also purchase alcohol to go from a licensed restaurant on any day, for elevated prices.

Opposite The colour-popping Orange Bubble Express has become a Canyons Insta fave

THE MOUNTAIN DEBRIEF

Park City Mountain is a mega-resort with the most lift-accessible ski and snowboard terrain in the United States. The highlight is the two-way Quicksilver Gondola linking Park City and Canyons, soaring 2.4km (1.5mi) over Pinecone Ridge (it's worth the ride just for the view). Long a freeski destination, Park City has one of North America's most progressive park and pipe setups with six terrain parks across the mountain.

On the Park City side, the resort is easily divisible in two – the long, wide groomers and trails of the lower mountain, and the multiple powder-filled bowls and gladed tree areas of the upper mountain. Head to the highest point on Park City Mountain to find endless double-black trails to thrill the most avid expert skier.

Intermediates can cruise for days on any run off the King Con Ridge (accessible by the King Con Quad chairlift) around Sunrise. Excellent grooming brings some of the more difficult runs like Jupiter's Access within reach.

At the Canyons, expert runs are sprinkled throughout the terrain, especially off Dreamcatcher and Dreamscape chairlifts, as well as Super Condor Express. Only expert double-black-diamond devotees should head up the Ninety-Nine 90 chairs. Despite the dual ski area connection, this behemoth is best skied one side at a time. It's so big that racing between sections can feel like speed dating and end up being traverse-heavy.

A RIDING ITINERARY

Start with a super healthy Australian-style breakfast (think house-made muesli) at **Harvest Café** (harvestparkcity.com), then take the mellow route up to the mountain via **Town Lift** and carve pristine groomers mid-mountain such as **Silver Queen** or **Assessment**.

After riding Park City's **Orange Bubble Express chair** (with heated seats and shield), make your way down **Chicane** and over to **Dreamcatcher lift** to score hot, fresh doughnuts and soak in some stellar views. Then head towards the Mountain Village side of the resort for laps on iconic runs, including **Tycoon**, **Sundog**, **McConkey's Bowl** and **Georgeanna**.

After lunch, take **Quicksilver Gondola** to northward **Canyons Village** and spend a sunny afternoon arcing turns down the wide, scenic runs of **Pipe Dream**, **Alpenglow** or **Daydream** off Dreamcatcher or Dreamscape. Head down to **Canyons Village** before returning to base.

ADVENTURE

Go dog sledding or snowmobiling with **North Forty Escapes** (northfortyescapes.com), or snow tubing or snow biking at **Round Valley** (visitparkcity.com), and snow tubing at **Woodward Park City** (woodwardparkcity.com).

OFF-MOUNTAIN MUST-DO

- Soak up the history from silver to snow at the **Park City Museum** (parkcityhistory.org) or take a whiskey tour at the **High West Distillery** (highwest.com).
- And shop - **Cake Boutique** (cakeparkcity.com) has a chic curation of brands, housed in a two-storey, grape-hued Victorian building.

EAT UP & DRINK DOWN

- On mountain, the elegant table service at **Lookout Cabin** overlooking the Wasatch Mountains can't be beaten, unless by the beef brisket at **Tombstone BBQ** (parkcitymountain.com).
- **Chimayo** (chimayorestaurant.com) has enchiladas and ceviche with drinks in silver goblets possibly sourced from a *Games of Thrones* set sale.

APRÈS SKI

- It's possible to happily bar-hop all the way down Main Street. Start with the huge patio and fire at **Red Tail Grill** (parkcityrestaurants.com), near Orange Bubble Express.
- **High West Saloon** (highwest.com) is Utah's only ski-in, ski-out distillery with craft cocktails and parmesan fries.

STAY

- The historic, boutique **Washington School House Hotel** (washingtonschoolhouse.com) is in a converted stone schoolhouse, walking distance to Main Street.

ALTERNATIVE: DEER VALLEY

Utah has 15 ski areas, ten within 30min of the airport - you can literally get an Uber from the baggage carousel and step onto a ski run. Deer Valley (deervalley.com) is one of only three skier-only mountains - the other two are Alta (*see* p. 11) and Taos (*see* p. 7). It's super ritzy, you won't just find old wealth here but new wealth and young wealth.

Top Skiers visit the historic Comstock Mine Park City's Silver to Slopes tour *Bottom* The large deck at Mid Mountain Lodge is a favourite spot for friends to rendezvous *Opposite* An adaptive skier schusses towards Canyons Village base area

There's no attitude with the altitude. The highest West Coast area may have bold'n'brash parks but they're stylish with a laid-back California vibe.

Mammoth Mountain, California

THE LOWDOWN

Big. Enormous. Mammoth. The mountain will satisfy every rider level, no matter what you name it. Reclining across the eastern Sierra Nevada Range, Mammoth not only gets a rare 10m (400in) of snow, creating that shimmering coat, but has 300 days of classic California sunshine and an almost immortal season lasting from November to June. Just a 5hr drive away from Mammoth's 3369m (11,053ft) peak, surfers are riding the Malibu waves in one of America's balmiest cities.

The widespread love of Mammoth (apart from the unbeatable parks) lies in the pure air, surrounding ancient pine forests and views of the crown-like Minarets as antidotes for city living. While there's a thriving youth culture and party scene, Mammoth also delivers family-friendly infrastructure and options for those longing to cosy up by a fire in a snow-covered cabin.

Sticking out like a sore thumb, Mammoth gets hit by weather; those 300 days of sunshine means the snow comes in colossal dumps, with long dry spells in between. The resort has several base areas; the main one is pedestrian-friendly Village, or pick Canyon Lodge for ski-in, ski-out, while Mammoth Lakes is just 6.4km (4mi) away.

The mountain comes into its own in spring. For park strutters, there's nowhere else to be; Mammoth has its own brand of cutting-edge parks (Unbound Terrain Parks) and its own athletes in the Mammoth Mountain Ski and Snowboard Team – all six women on the US snowboard team in 2021/22 came from Mammoth. Take a peek in South Park with the early sun or Main Park to see the best in action

Mammoth and June Mountains are located within the ancestral territory of several Indigenous people, including the Nüümü (Bishop Paiute Tribe), the Nim (North Fork Rancheria of Mono Tribe), and the Kutzadika'a (Mono Lake Paiute).

 Mountain stats
- Elevation top: 3369m (11,053ft)
- Elevation bottom: 2424m (7953ft)
- Vertical drop: 945m (3100ft)
- Skiable terrain: 14sqkm (3500 acres)
- Longest run: 4.8km (3mi)
- Beginner terrain: 15 per cent
- Intermediate terrain: 28 per cent
- Advanced terrain: 37 per cent
- Lifts: 25

 Run
Climax always impresses and if the top hasn't popped yet, the trees under Chairs 12 and 14 can still have secret powder stashes when the rest is gone.

Experience
To find stashes leftover on a bluebird day or in the eye of a storm, hook up with an instructor. Knowing those wind drift niches is a highly prized dark art, and you need a local.

 Local's tip
Avoid lines when crossing the mountain by skipping the bases and using mid-mountain lifts. Chair 22 has the more challenging terrain on a powder day if the top is closed.

Opposite Vista of the Ritter sub-range in the eastern Sierra Nevada mountains and its most dramatic formation - the Minarets

THE MOUNTAIN DEBRIEF

This is where you'll find the highest elevation on the West Coast (and slightly colder temps than in Lake Tahoe). All that snowfall is perfect for Mammoth's ten snow-hungry parks, with over 100 jibs, more than 50 jumps, two halfpipes and an aerobag; no wonder it's Team USA's official training venue for snowboarding and freeskiing.

The mountain is easily divided between the top and bottom. Upstairs are bowls, rocky areas and exposed slopes, while lower down are glades, fun natural halfpipes (this was a volcano but hasn't erupted for 700 years) and beginner slopes.

Experts will have a field day on the many chutes and double-black-diamond runs rimming the top of the front side. North-facing Chair 23 is nicknamed the 'Mothership' for its delivery to double blacks and it can get super windy, so that the chairlift has a wind house around it at the top (and it gets a lot of nice snow blowing in that keep tracks up).

Weather patterns are fickle, but the winds dry the snow out, help the mountain re-groom itself and blow crystals off, leaving the famed Mammoth wind buff that's smooth like velvet.

A RIDING ITINERARY

If you're in Mammoth Lakes, don't miss a cold-drip brew from hipster caffeine lab **Black Velvet**. From the Canyon Express take a warm-up groomer on **Downhill** or **Crosswalk**, then head towards the **Rollercoaster Express** where you'll find more playful terrain with scattered trees and glades.

Next, hop on the **Gold Rush Express** over to the glades of **Chair 25** and around **Cloud 9 Express**. When the snow is fresh, it can have some of the best powder stashes. **Ricochet** offers black-level bowl skiing off Cloud 9 Express.

Then it's up **Pandora's Gondola** to the summit, where a heavy set of double blacks is in the line-up (on a powder day, head here immediately when it opens). **Paranoid Flats**, a series of chutes nicknamed 'the Noids' and ranging in pitch from mildly terrifying to white-knuckle, hold some of the best snow.

Then drop backside via **Upper Road Runner** with jaw-dropping views of the Minarets and down for a pit stop at the **Outpost**, with the best vistas (and grilled cheese) on the mountain.

ADVENTURE

Dip your toe into the backcountry with **Sierra Mountain Guides**' (sierramtnguides.com) half-day introductory experience, or explore the nearby **June Mountain** backcountry.

Above Options galore – there's a matrix of lifts and ten parks
Opposite top The eastern Sierra Nevada mountains *Opposite bottom* Mammoth gets the deep, and it certainly has the steep

Mammoth Mountain, California, USA　　35

OFF-MOUNTAIN MUST-DO

- **Wooly's Tube Park** (mammothmountain.com) with high-speed snow tubes is always a winner.
- If the weather cuts in, explore the eastern Sierra Nevada mountains by **dog sled** (mammothdogteams.com), or head to the much-loved bowling alley **Rock'n'Bowl** (mammothrocknbowl.com) or drive 20min east to the mid-fields **Crab Cooker Hot Springs** and **Shepherd Hot Spring** (ask a local for directions).

EAT UP & DRINK DOWN

- Hit **53 Kitchen and Cocktails** for the best Manhattan in town (and occasionally live music).
- **Volcania** (mammothmountain.com) by celebrity chefs Bryan and Michael Voltaggio hits a high-end niche.

APRÈS SKI

- Not much beats springtime at the **Yodler** - walk straight from the lifts at Main Lodge for Bavarian drinks and bratwurst.
- If it's a weekend, find the party at the famed Weekend Après Party at **Canyon Lodge**.
- **Lakanuki** is one of the few places to get your dance on in town.

STAY

- If you like to be mid-action, the **Village Lodge** is your jam with an on-site gondola delivering guests to Canyon Lodge.
- The renovated **Mammoth Mountain Inn** is ski-in, ski-out, opposite to Main Lodge.
- At Eagle Lodge Base, **Juniper Springs Resort**, with a chairlift by the door, is popular with families.

ALTERNATIVE: PALISADES TAHOE

Palisades Tahoe, created when Olympic Valley (formerly Squaw Valley) and Alpine Meadows joined, by exquisite Lake Tahoe is forever Mammoth's frenemy, a northern California stablemate yet competitive in every Best of List.

Below Easy riders making a break for the wilderness
Opposite The Mammoth Mountain Unbound parks are famous for their creative features

Andrew Kurka the downhill adaptive skier

Olympians and Paralympians are made of tough stuff, but if rating toughness on a metallic scale, Andrew Kurka is tungsten. A Paralympic gold medallist and World Champion in downhill sit-ski, he's been clocked at 86m/ph (138km/ph).

His 13 international medal haul includes four World Cup golds and at his maiden Paralympic Winter Games in 2018 in PyeongChang, he added silver in the Super G to his gold. Chasing a second Olympic gold in Beijing in 2022, he was blown into a fence pre-race and broke bones, but still took to the course and claimed fourth place.

Andrew always had this unyielding mentality of an athlete. A six-time Alaskan State wrestling champion he aimed to become an Olympic wrestler before an all-terrain vehicle (ATV) accident at age 13 severely damaged three vertebrae mid spinal cord. Just two years after trying adaptive skiing for the first time, he was on the Paralympic team, riding no-fall chutes in Alaska and has been featured on the cover of *Sports Illustrated*.

Between DJ-ing in his native Alaska, this keen bodybuilder has a reputation for giving back as a coach with Challenge Alaska in his home resort of Alyeska and as an Athlete Mentor for Classroom Champions.

You grew up on a farm in a small Alaskan village (Nikolaevsk) where Russian is the most common language. Did you dream you'd be a world traveller and elite athlete?

I did dream, and that came from starting in sport. I started wrestling when I was eight years old and dedicated everything to it. I had always kind of dreamed of being an Olympic wrestler and being the best in the world. Being in a Russian village, wrestling was taken very seriously, there was a culture of competitiveness, and that has helped me to flourish in my career.

What drew you to skiing?

One of my physical therapists said, 'Hey, you should try it'. And it's something that I had always wanted to do, but never really had the opportunity to try it. And she took me there and paid for it and, lo and behold, I was talented and good at it.

So, what actually is adaptive skiing?

The blanket term is adaptive skiing. And what I specifically do is sit skiing, that's skiing for people who aren't able to ski normally due to a physical disability, or kind of issue. Let's say you have a knee replacement, and you can't ski standing up anymore. So, sit skiing's for you. Or let's say that you lost both your legs in the military. Or let's say you're like me, and you broke your back and so your legs are paralysed.

In both hands, you have outriggers, which work like poles, and also work like skis so that they don't get in your way when you're moving quickly. Shock absorbers are a huge portion of the sit ski, typically larger shock absorbers with more space and a softer compression have a tendency to work a bit better because they are able to absorb more of the bumps and are able to help you manage control on the slopes. Toyota, one of my sponsors, collaborated with me, they created a race sit ski which is definitely very fast. I've only had it for about a year, so I'm still adapting to it.

You are the first person in a monoski to ski the Christmas Chute on the North Face of Mount Alyeska – some of the steepest, most harrowing inbounds terrain in the USA. How did you prepare?

From the start of my ski career, I've always said, 'Well, I'm gonna go for it'. And that's been my entire career. And now it's not really a big deal anymore, I've done it eight to 10 times this year, and I've taken other sit skiers down it. If you can ski steep terrain, and you can ski technical terrain, all you have to do is be able to put those two together.

Of all your medals, what's been a highlight?

My favourite was winning gold at the Olympics in 2018. That was when a dream came true, an accomplishment came to fruition for me. But it was also when kind of everything was made worth it. I've had kind of a tough career with lots of ups and downs. Because I got so good so quickly, I also ended up with a lot of injuries along the way. And those injuries slowed down my career, they were kind of painful and made me question if it was all worth it or not. And that gold medal in PyeongChang made it all worth it for me.

In the 2022 Beijing Winter Olympics, just prior to racing heavy winds blew you into a fence, breaking your humerus and thumb. An hour later you raced and still came fourth in the Downhill. How did you remain composed?

I wouldn't say I was *composed* exactly, but I've lived my entire career for those moments. And the way I see it is the pain I go through throughout the four years preparing was nothing equivalent to the pain I had that one day. If you add all the pain up, to try to get to that point in life, it still doesn't equal the pain of my broken arm and thumb that day. So, for me, it was absolutely worth it. And it's lit a competitive fire inside me for the next Games.

What does being an Athlete Mentor for Classroom Champions involve?

Classroom Champions is a non-profit organisation that partners Olympic and Paralympic athletes with students in under-served communities. It's mentoring underprivileged youth and people who could use inspiration in their lives. And it's a dream of mine, after I've achieved so much to help the next generation achieve those same accomplishments or something greater. I just really want to help make this life and the things that I do as purposeful as possible. And I think mentoring and helping kids to be the best version of themselves, helping the future be the best version of itself, is one of those aims for me.

What's your advice for someone wanting to become an adaptive skier?

Find an adaptive recreational program near you, and speak to someone. Make as many phone calls as it takes, I promise there's opportunities that are near you. These opportunities exist but the programs are not big enough yet where they can seek you out. But hopefully they will be soon enough, the sport is expanding there's something for everyone and it's fun.

CANADA

The 1880s composers of Canada's national anthem 'O Canada' couldn't possibly have anticipated that their phrase would be yelled by skiers and snowboarders out ski-cat windows in RED Mountain (*see* p. 49), through the glades of Big White (*see* p. 65), from the powder-submerged heli runners, down the chutes of Revelstoke (*see* p. 55), across wilderness mountain tops in Lake Louise (*see* p. 59) and pretty much everywhere in Whistler Blackcomb (*see* p. 43), including the dance floors. But now it sounds more like this, 'O Canadaaaaaaaaaaaa....' Before being cut off by a face shot.

And that's the crux of Canada – powder, especially in British Columbia (BC). While Canadian skiing is laid-back, there's nothing nonchalant about the variety of terrain and experiences. Get lost at one of 12 lodges in CMH Heliskiing's three-million-plus acres of private claim (*see* p. 47), splash out on C$10 cat skiing at RED Mountain, burn thighs on new kid Revelstoke's vertical (the longest in North America) or hit the gullies, chutes, alpine bowls and glades where there's no need to fight for powder.

Apart from flakes falling as large as tissues, you'll also find cosy log cabins (basically everywhere), roaring stone fireplaces, craft brews and not just vibrant, friendly locals to share them with, but skiers from all over the world.

Once you've been hit like a deer in the headlights by Whistler Blackcomb's staggering size (the largest ski resort in North America), BC's interior beckons. Jump on the Powder Highway (*see* p. 266), where you'll find authentic towns, audacious ski areas and all the stories that go with them – stories about the original Scandinavian miners whittling their 300cm (118in) skis out of lightning-struck trees 100 years ago, and about the crowd-funding that renewed RED Mountain, and après tales that start with a couple of pitchers, continue with shots, and end with everyone doing the Frankenstein ski boot dance shuffle before embarking on a quest for late-night poutine.

Warm Canadian hospitality, real-deal towns and plentiful pow put Canada in a class of its own.

Coolest winter selfie

In this land of powder aplenty, there are blizzards of snowy opportunities. The fields of 'snow ghosts' - snow-laden trees iced into spooky towering figures - are a Big White signature (accessed off the Snow Ghost Express, *see* p. 66). And any photo perched on the treads of a snowcat, or at the Rock Garden at Lake Louise (*see* p. 60), is one for the 'where's that?' books.

Get appy

Candians often use theweathernetwork.com/ca as their weather source.

FatMap is invaluable for backcountry skiers to plan and navigate a trip, and also features ski resorts, laying runs over its 3D mountain maps. Tap any run for its characteristics and slope profile.

If you're in Whistler Blackcomb, check out Ullr Adventure Maps for on-hill navigation, a trail map on steroids created by Alex Hordal, a Whistler local and ski patroller.

Don't break the bank

Canada has excellent options geared towards the snow-seeking traveller and provides good or comparable value for many currencies. The modern capsule bunks in Whistler's Pangea Pod (*see* p. 47) and high-tech, slopeside hostel Nowhere Special (*see* p. 53) at RED Mountain are two examples; combine with happy-hour meals and you're set. Also explore the smaller resorts with fewer facilities but also lower prices.

When it snows

Revelstoke's bone-dry 10.5m (413in) snowfall results from the perfect location for cold air to sweep down from central and northern BC and collide with moisture from the west. This convergence of hot and cold airflow wrings out the moisture from storm systems and dumps snow on the town and mountains.

Whistler Blackcomb receives heavier snow than Revelstoke with moisture sucked up over the adjacent Pacific Ocean. The Rockies receives a more modest amount and Lake Louise Ski Resort has 3.5m (138in) of snow annually and frigid temperatures - appreciated mainly by ice climbers for top-quality waterfall freezes.

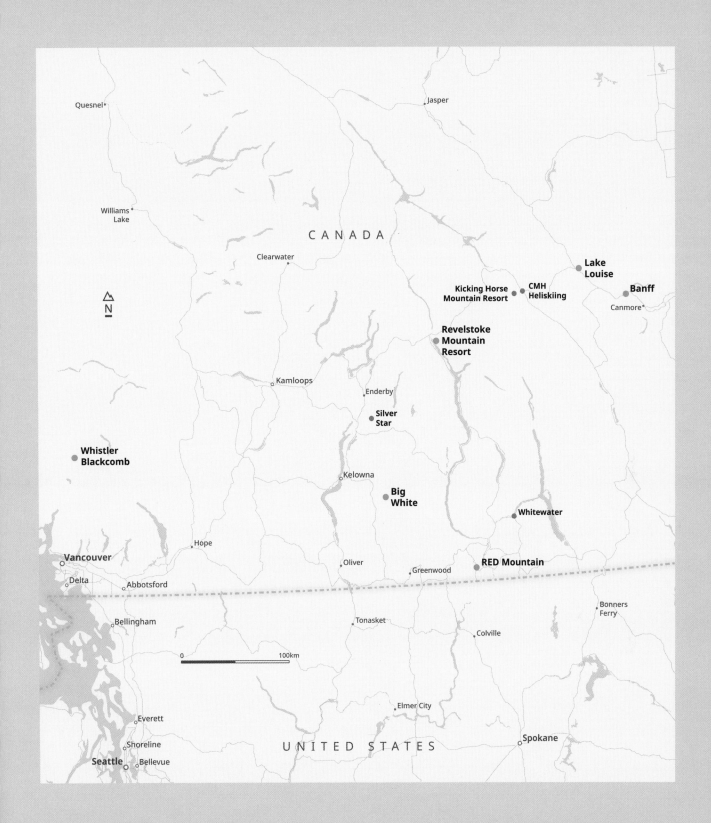

All things to all people, the perennial crowd-pleaser is North America's largest playground.

Whistler Blackcomb

THE LOWDOWN

Let's cut to the chase, what can be said about Whistler Blackcomb that hasn't already been written, filmed and blogged? But there's more to it than riding the two gigantic mountains, soaking in the jaw-dropping scenery or delving into village life. More even than testing the terrain steeps that put a firecracker into even the most extreme skier's back pocket. The fact is that there's always something new to discover here, always a new hidden gem that will keep you coming back for more. There's skiing gold in these hills, so never stop digging.

So how big is big? The advanced skiing area alone – a whopping 9sqkm (2223 acres) – is larger than many world-class resorts. Stitching them into one entity was as seamless as adding the spectacular 3.03km (1.9mi), 436m (1430ft) Peak 2 Peak gondola in 2008.

As the site for the snow events at the Vancouver Olympics in 2010, Whistler Blackcomb scored infrastructure upgrades, including a $1 billion renovation on the Sea to Sky Highway. It's now an easy 2hr trip from Vancouver (a double-edged sword as it brings the crowds on weekends). Once here, there's no need to rent a car; the main Whistler Village, as well as the Upper Village and smaller Creekside, all have gondola access, and Whistler Village is pedestrian-only.

It's a bustling, thriving place with purpose-built faux Euro architecture (love it or loathe it) from French-turreted hotels to Zermatt-style cabins. The pedestrian 'Whistler stroll' is around 1km (0.6 mi) long, lined with shops, bars and restaurants. The second main base, Creekside, is also a happening little village, quieter and with shorter lift lines on powder days and weekends.

Whistler Blackcomb operates on the shared unceded territory of the Squamish Nation and Lil'wat Nation.

Mountain stats
- Elevation top: 2284m (7494ft)
- Elevation bottom: 653m (2140ft)
- Vertical drop: 1609m (5280ft)
- Skiable terrain: 33sqkm (8171 acres)
- Longest run: 11km (7mi)
- Beginner terrain (green): 16 per cent
- Intermediate terrain (blue/red): 55 per cent
- Advanced terrain (black): 29 per cent
- Lifts: 36

Run
You can't visit Whistler without skiing the 11km (6.8mi) Peak to Creek, the longest consistent run in North America. At Blackcomb, Arthur's Choice is a fun and accessible glades run, especially on a powder day.

Experience
Relax with steam baths, saunas and a Nordic waterfall at Scandinave Spa Whistler (scandinave.com), tucked in a fern- and moss-laden rainforest native to British Columbia. For hassle-free holidays, local experts Mabey Ski (mabeyski.com) drill into details so you don't have to, like making dinner reservations and lift-pass delivery.

Local's tip
On a powder day at Peak Chair, the show from the lift line is almost as good as the skiing as riders send it from Air Jordan and Waterfall.

Opposite Mid moment, mid mountain, Whistler Blackcomb

THE MOUNTAIN DEBRIEF

Whistler and Blackcomb are monstrous side-by-side mountains, joined at the foot by the Village and in the middle by the Peak 2 Peak Gondola. Combined, they offer 16 alpine bowls, three glaciers and over 200 marked runs.

Although predominantly suited to intermediate skiers and snowboarders, there are steep bowls, double-black-diamond runs, tricky chutes and additional side-country options with a short hike or two for the more advanced.

Whistler Blackcomb has countless big-mountain features to explore. In particular, there are some epic cliff drops from Café Cliffs (into the Jersey Cream Bowl), the Line Pine drop (the Curl) is via Secret Bowl (marked not-secretly on the trail map) and, of course, the cliffs surrounding Peak Chair Express.

Whistler also has impressive amounts of powder snow. Sure, the lower elevations and coastal proximity mean it's not Utah cold smoke, but at 11.7m (462in) a year, there's still plenty of it. Keep your fingers crossed for temperatures to remain cold to keep the rain off lower elevations. There's amazing tree skiing and a very deep snowpack, so it's important to be aware of tree wells and use the buddy system when skiing in the trees.

A RIDING ITINERARY

Pick your fix at **Lift Coffee** by the Whistler Gondola. Whistler Mountain is sunnier in the morning than Blackcomb, so start with some warm-up laps on blues at **Big Red** in the mid-mountain area or go straight for a black wake-up on **Garbanzo Express** instead.

On a powder day, head to one of Whistler's alpine bowls – **Symphony and Harmony** or **Peak Chair** (hit the West Bowl off Peak Chair for the fluffy stuff) – the excitement in the air is palpable.

If you've got that 'lost in a supermarket' feeling, hook up with a **Mountain Host**, meeting daily at 11.15am at the lightboard at the top of the gondola on each mountain.

Many stop at mega eatery **Roundhouse Lodge**, also home to Whistler's only on-mountain après bar – hidden outside at the back of the restaurant with mulled wine. But switch sides instead and take the 11min **Peak 2 Peak Gondola** to **Blackcomb Mountain** for the afternoon. Here, finally, pause for a Thai curry bowl at the gondola-top **Rendezvous**.

The mid-mountain of Blackcomb offers more steep terrain and is perfect after a Whistler morning. If you're into park skiing or snowboarding, this is the place for big jumps and features; the alpine is also incredible with tree skiing and challenging groomers. Aptly named **7th Heaven** has loads of variety, but you'll also love blue laps around **Crystal Ridge Chair** – **Ridge Run** and **Rock'n'Roll** are two of the most fun runs on the mountain

ADVENTURE

Grab an ACMG guide from **Extremely Canadian** (extremelycanadian.com) and head into Blackcomb's backcountry at the top of the T-bar or around Whistler's newest backcountry hut – Kees & Claire.

The Roundhouse Lodge atop Whistler Mountain
Opposite The top of Whistler Peak looking out to Black Tusk

OFF-MOUNTAIN MUST DO

- Skiers flip through blazing rings at the spectacular **Fire & Ice Show** on Sundays at 6.30pm.
- An absolute must-do is the night walk at **Vallea Lumina** (vallealumina.com), an 80min walk through an old-growth forest with multimedia features, like projections, illuminated trees and strobe lighting. Book ahead online.

———

EAT UP & DRINK DOWN

- **Sushi Village** (sushivillage.com) is a delicious, affordable restaurant (put your name down early).
- You will also want every single soup created by Melissa Craig at **Bearfoot Bistro** (bearfootbistro.com).
- James Walt, former executive chef to the Canadian Embassy in Rome, is at stylish **Il Caminetto** (ilcaminetto.ca); if you can't get a reservation, dine at the bar.

———

APRÈS SKI

- It's a tie between the GLC (Garibaldi Lift Co; whistlerblackcomb.com) above the Whistler gondola building and the **Longhorn** (gibbonswhistler.com) with DJs, smoke machines and champagne guns
- Then segue neatly into 5-7pm happy hour at **Dubh Linn Gate Irish Pub** (whistler.dubhlinngate.com).

- At the base of Blackcomb Mountain, **Merlin's** (whistlerblackcomb.com) old-school rec room spirit can get loose, often.
- **RMU** (mtnculture.com) is where you'll find locals, excellent cocktails and often live music.

———

STAY

- For luxury, park your padded slippers at the impressive, turreted **Fairmont Chateau Whistler** (fairmont.com/whistler), a landmark adjacent to the Blackcomb Gondola.
- Wallet-friendly **Pangea Pod Hotel** (pangeapod.com) has unique, designer 'pod' bed spaces with a chic bar in the heart of the village.

———

ALTERNATIVE: BC'S POWDER TRIANGLE

If variety makes your skis sizzle, **CMH Heliskiing** was the first heli operation in Canada over 50 years ago and as such has retained a huge tenure, over 12,140sqkm (3 million acres) of terrain in BC's Powder Triangle. They have 12 destinations, including backcountry lodges. To figure out which one's your perfect match try this fun quiz: cmhheli.com/quiz.

Bottom left and right Whistler's weekly Fire and Ice show
Opposite Get out early to find your fresh lines

Fiercely independent and resolutely rustic, this former gold mine is a powder pothole where skiers come for the white flaky motherlode.

RED Mountain

THE LOWDOWN

RED (so good it's permanently branded in shouty capitals) is a dynamo of dichotomies. It's the oldest resort in western Canada, yet home to the most significant terrain expansion in the last decade. It's proudly Canadian, yet nudges the US border in the snowy Kootenay mountains. Last millennium it was a rickety lift outpost, now it's catapulted into the Top 10, size-wise, in North America – on par with Breckenridge (*see* p. 27) and Jackson Hole (*see* p. 9).

The numbers are impressive for what was once a community-owned and-run ski hill; over 7.5m (295in) of snowfall, C$10 per run inbounds cat-skiing and five skiable peaks. RED was once under the radar, now it's the Next Big Thing, an unquestioned North American Ultimate.

RED began with a miner from Scandinavia, Olaus Jeldness, who found his real treasure was snow. He introduced skiing here in the 1800s and Canada's first ski competition took place at RED in 1897. Character-filled ski town Rossland, just a 5min drive away, has been voted Canada's number-one ski town multiple times.

It's not just the powder here, it's the passion. To resist being snapped up by a corporate player like Vail Resorts, who purchased Whistler Blackcomb (*see* p. 43) in 2016, RED crowdfunded C$2,556,250 around the globe. Do skiers care who owns the slopes they ride? Turns out they do here. Rebellious RED, owned by many, prisoner to none.

Rossland, RED Mountain and RED Mountain ski resort lie on the traditional, ancestral and unceded territory of the Sinixt People.

Mountain stats
- Elevation top: 2075m (6807 ft)
- Elevation bottom: 1185m (3887ft)
- Vertical drop: 890m (2919ft)
- Skiable terrain: 15.6sqkm (3850 acres)
- Longest run: 7km (4.3mi)
- Beginner terrain: 17 per cent
- Intermediate terrain: 57 per cent
- Advanced terrain: 26 per cent
- Lifts: 8

Run
Booty's Run is initially steep tree skiing that opens into an expansive bowl, then filters into a mellow pitch with a shopfront of pillows and natural features to rip through.

Experience
C$10 cat skiing. Whaaaaat? Unique to RED, usually from 10am to 2pm (check ahead), a 12-person snowcat makes laps between Grey Mountain summit and adjacent Mount Kirkup; simply ski up to the snowcat operator and purchase a cash ticket. No avalanche gear or guide required, just stamina for the 626m (2054ft) vertical drop back to the Grey Chairlift!

Local's tip
Maximise peak moments on your first day with a free Mountain Tour (resresort.com/free-mountain-tours). Departing from the base lodge daily with a Snow Host, it's a fast track to unhooking RED's magic.

Opposite The come-hither twinkling lights of Rossland draw skiers to snow like bees to honey

THE MOUNTAIN DEBRIEF

There are 119 runs over five peaks; RED (the original '40s ski area) Granite (the flagship added in the '70s), Grey (formerly only cat-accessed), Roberts and Kirkup.

The cone of Granite Mountain is the ideal starting peak due to its 360-degree terrain descents and sheer size, with south-facing intermediate and advanced runs at Paradise Basin. The remaining peaks' descents offer up what RED's known for: skiing runs, bowls, natural features and leg-burning pitches.

For the more advanced riders on Granite, Powderfields dishes up tree skiing with an incredible fall line and views. On the other side, both Beer Belly and Oil Can kick off with tree skiing on a steep pitch before becoming a bowl filled with pillows and fun natural features.

If you're an intermediate longing for cruisy groomers, try Rhino's Run (the resort's longest at 7km/4.4mi). It's a journey, wrapping around the mountain down to the base lodge filled with different slope pitches, natural features and tons of scattered mellow-pitch tree-skiing pockets to the sides.

A RIDING ITINERARY

Grab a **Seven Summits** (sevensummitscoffee.com) coffee in Rossland to sip while riding the 5min mountain shuttle. Head to the top of **Granite Mountain** to ski the south-facing **Paradise Basin** for a few laps of mixed tree skiing or groomers. From there, drop in on Granite's north side into the famous **Beer Belly** or other steep, tree-skiing runs which take you over to **Grey Mountain**, 2013's expansion.

Build hunger on **Grey** with some south-facing intermediate tree skiing or steeper north-facing backside options before tearing down 600m (2000ft) vertical to **Topping Creek**, then say *si* to **Taco Rojo** (redresort.com/dining) the Mexican on-snow food truck at the Flyin' Phil's Topping Creek Station.

A day at RED isn't complete without riding the **RED Mountain**. Burrito-fuelled, head to the original **RED**, accessing long groomed fall lines made famous by former World Cup races. Then back to base for après at **Rafters** (*see* p. 53).

ADVENTURE

This is prime-time cat ski nirvana. **Big Red Cats** (bigredcatskiing.com), headquartered right at the base of RED Mountain Resort, is the world's largest cat-skiing operation, covering eight peaks, including numerous ridges and subpeaks, via 220km (137mi) of snowcat tracks.

A bird's-eye view of the layer upon layer of peaks and runs

OFF-MOUNTAIN MUST-DO

• The **Get Lost Adventure Centre** (redresort.com/get-lost) offers tons of information on curated local operators and experiences, from hot spring hunting to fishing, Nordic adventures, and cat and heli-skiing.

EAT UP & DRINK DOWN

• Breakfast needs to be the day's biggest meal (RED's vertical is no joke), so hit up **Alpine Grind** for coffee plus its to-die-for frittata breakfast bagels.
• I love a slashie, and the **Flying Steamshovel** (thefyingsteamshovel.com) restaurant/music venue is a Rossland institution. Live music, pool table and craft beers - get brussels sprouts and the John Candy burger.

APRÈS SKI

• No need for an après crawl: **Rafters** (redresort.com/rafters) at the Red Base Lodge is where you'll find everyone. The list of bonuses includes 18th-century beams (the rafters) from the old mines, local craft beers and post-ski nachos the size of BC.
• If you're hankering for something smarter, **Velvet** lounge (thejosie.com/rossland-velvet-restaurant-lounge) has great cocktails and wine selections (and you'll want to linger for dinner).

STAY

• Once upon a time there was nowhere to stay on-mountain. Now there are pads like misnamed **Nowhere Special** (nowherespecialhostel.com), a tech-forward ski hostel game-changer 2min from the lifts with C$46 beds.
• If 'luxury' is solitude, then chairlift-accessed **Constella** (edresort.com/constella), a collection of six overnight eco-cabins with a central clubhouse, on the backside of Granite Mountain, is five-star.

ALTERNATIVE: WHITEWATER

A 90min drive away, small but mighty Whitewater isn't super-sized but atones for it with a Japanese-style 12m (40ft), feather-light annual fall. The laid-back vibe and over 350 heritage buildings in the legendary satellite ski town of Nelson seal the deal.

Secret stashes pepper the mountains *Opposite* Looking over a cloud sea caused by a temperature inversion

One of the world's newest major ski areas featuring North America's biggest vertical, this former highway pit stop is now a must-see, must-ski, must-live-here destination.

Revelstoke

THE LOWDOWN

New kid on the block Revelstoke Mountain Resort (RMR or Revy for short), is the ultimate ski-resort disruptor. Perhaps that wasn't the aim when it burst on the scene in 2007, but it was certainly a consequence of creating the biggest North American lifted vertical of 1713m (5620ft). This formerly sleepy little town and mountain became a global player almost immediately, heralding a new era of skiing and boarding in the Selkirk Mountains and setting the snow community on fire. Is it worth the hype?

It is, depending on what you're looking for. Going interior British Colombia – and this is remote BC on the north-west section of the famed Powder Highway (*see* p. 266) – you'll always get a more authentic Canadian vibe than playing around the edges. If you want a comparison, Revelstoke is the Canadian answer to Jackson Hole (*see* p. 9); both are unique, with big-mountain skiing and a clutch of cat skiing, a side of heli-skiing, and a bunch of backcountry skiing, all accessed from the one resort.

The locals are welcoming but wary of too much progress. But progress there has been, revitalising Revy from a railway-and-lumber town off the Trans-Canada Highway with no real vibe into a bustling mountain town, drawing adventurers and powder pilgrims from around the world. Now the town features microbreweries and a local-produce culinary scene. Goldilocks would approve – not too gentrified, but with organic porridge that's just right.

Revelstoke is on the Traditional Land of four nations: the Sinixt, the Ktunaxa, the Secwepemc and the Syilx.

 Mountain stats
- Elevation top: 2225m (7300ft)
- Elevation bottom: 512m (1680ft)
- Vertical drop: 1713m (5620ft)
- Skiable terrain: 12.6sqkm (3121 acres)
- Longest run: 15.2km (9.5mi)
- Beginner terrain: 12 per cent
- Intermediate terrain: 43 per cent
- Advanced terrain: 45 per cent
- Lifts: 4

 Run
Do your squats - the Last Spike is a crowd favourite, and 15.2km (9.4mi), from the top of the Stoke Chair down to the village.

 Experience
At Revelstoke Outdoor Art Movement (ROAM), disused alleyways have been turned into art galleries featuring the *Mona Skisa* (by Leonardo da Vinski) made from abandoned ski parts. Pieces like *Le Reve Le Stoke* by Pablo PaCatski are moved unexpectedly around the mountain, turning runs into 'masterpistes'.

 Local's tip
The best lift and lodging rates can be found in April. Head to the mountain and snack in a warming hut with floor-to-ceiling windows at the top of the lifts.

Opposite An adrenaline rush gives that mountain high in Revy

THE MOUNTAIN DEBRIEF

With 88 per cent marked intermediate and above, you know the riding will be spicy – and Revelstoke delivers. There are vertical prairies of powders combined with glade-arama on the front face and bowls on the back. The resort is expanding yearly, so watch for terrain additions until it fulfils its aim of being North America's largest resort.

Currently, when you open the map it looks ... small. But don't be deceived, there are 12sqkm (2965 acres) and 75 runs with four lifts, including the Revelation Gondola, and four bowls with extra hike-to-terrain.

If the backcountry surrounding Revelstoke is your aim, be aware that locals wait weeks (and months) for the conditions to be right before skiing certain lines. Grab a guide in town, like Revelstoke Alpine Adventure (revelstokealpine.ca), if you plan on taking your adventure off-resort. Parks Canada opens areas like Rogers Pass and there's a check-in system at the Rogers Pass Discovery Centre to ski zones above the highway and railway. Play by the rules to keep the areas open.

A RIDING ITINERARY

Start at **Dose Coffee** (dosecoffee.ca), a local hangout created by Australian transplants for all options, including gluten- and dairy-free. Then, if you can ride blacks, get hooked into the mountain with the **First Tracks Breakfast Club**. Loading the lifts an hour early, your guide reveals the goods as the avalanche team opens new terrain throughout the morning, taking you to zones you may never find on your own.

Otherwise, start the day with a few laps on the **Stoke Chair**, enjoy **Critical Path**, **Snow Rodeo** and **South Bowl** while waiting for **Separate Reality Bowl** and **North Bowl** to open (pausing at the top for Columbia River valley and Monashees views). These runs, plus **Pitch Black** or **Mental Health**, will give you a degustation of all that Revelstoke's known for – glades, an alpine bowl and fast groomers.

After a few warm-up runs, earn some turns and hike to the top for the expert-only **North Bowl**. The **Lemming Line** horizontal hike gives exponential rewards for a 5min investment, accessing powder pillows and the face shot nirvana of North Bowl with **Drop In** and steep-pitched **Unlimited Assets**.

Alternatively, hike directly up from the Stoke Chair to **Sub Peak** (2340m/7677ft) for glorious 360-degree and Mount McKenzie views. Drop into **Discipline** or **Powder Assault** and down to **Garcia's Ridge**, where you'll find chutes, drops and cliffs, and all lines funnel into a natural halfpipe and playful glades at the bottom, leading to **Ripper Chair**.

ADVENTURE

Capow Canadian Powder Guiding (capow.ca) chief guide Troy was one of the first 10 employees at Revelstoke and the ski patrol's head avalanche forecaster – he knows the terrain backwards and it's well worth booking a tour with him.

OFF-MOUNTAIN MUST-DO

- Hot spring hop! Catch a ferry over Shelter Bay to **Halycon Hot Springs** (halcyon-hotsprings.com) or **Halfway River Hot Springs** via a logging road (weather dependent).

EAT UP & DRINK DOWN

- **Chubby Funsters** (chubbyfunsters.com) has a funky vibe, cocktails and cosy wood-burning stove.
- **Nico's** (nicospizzeria.ca), with daily deals in the late afternoon, has pizzas named after the Revy runs and seven types of Quebecois poutines.

APRÈS SKI

- Start before leaving the mountain at **Mackenzie Common Tavern & Food Truck** (aka Mac's Tavern; revelstokemountainresort.com) at the gondola base for street-inspired bites and a unique tater-tot poutine.
- **The Village Idiot** (thevillageidiot.ca) is the epicentre of mountain culture and stories about sweet stashes and huge hucks. It's the sister eatery of Chubby Funsters (*see* above).
- Prioritise a pew at **Monashee Spirits Distillery** (monasheespirits.com) for a bespoke cocktail made from spirits distilled by hand.

STAY

- The **Sutton Place Hotel** (suttonplace.com/revelstoke) is the only ski-in, ski-out property at Revelstoke Mountain Resort's base, and the location is unbeatable.
- Downtown, the boutique **Eleven Revelstoke Lodge** (elevenexperience.com/revelstoke-lodge) in a 1911 building has retained heritage features like rustic bricks and exposed beams in a chic renovation.

ALTERNATIVE: KICKING HORSE

Tame the horse. Kicking Horse Mountain Resort (kickinghorseresort.com), home to the only North American stop on the Freeride World Tour, is another Powder Highway calling card. With 60 per cent of the terrain black and double black, it does kick, with unexpected fine dining at Eagles Eye on the mountaintop at 2336m (7700ft) and cool ski town Golden nearby.

Below left Don't miss the curated craft brews at The Mackenzie Common Tavern & Food Truck *Below right* Skiers enjoy some unexpected art mid-run as part of ROAM, part of Revy's thriving art scene *Opposite* Revelation Lodge (Rev Lodge) mid mountain fulfils all your needs cafeteria-style

Phenomenal national park vistas, a mountain of tasty powder pockets, and the game-changing addition of 'wild' West Bowl make Alberta's largest ski area sweet like (maple) syrup.

Banff & Lake Louise

THE LOWDOWN

People sometimes mistake Banff for one ski area, a 90min straight shoot down the Trans-Canada Highway from Calgary. But there are two mountain towns, bustling Banff and genteel Lake Louise, providing a home base to three ski resorts tucked within the boundaries of UNESCO-listed Banff National Park: Mount Norquay, Banff Sunshine Village and Lake Louise Ski Resort.

Mount Norquay, visible as the bookend of Banff's Main Street, is the local's racing hill (home to the Banff Alpine Racers) and only a 15min drive away, with perfectly groomed, shorter, wide runs. A 20min drive from town is family-friendly Banff Sunshine Village – excelling as a spring ski spot where you park and travel to the base above the tree line by gondola.

And then a 45min drive away is Lake Louise Ski Resort, where the views are unlike almost anywhere else. Situated in 6475sqkm (1.6 million acres) of unspoiled national park wilderness, vistas are of peak after peak of pristine snow, jagged-edged crags and silent trees untouched by mass development as far as the eye can see. And the Fairmont Château Lake Louise (*see* p. 63) is iconic – this word is truly merited here.

Staying in Lake Louise's hamlet a few minutes from the ski area boasts gourmet surprises, twinkly night skies and non-ski diversions. It also cuts out the 40min slope commute. In Banff there's a thriving mountain culture with art galleries, museums, and over 150 restaurants and bars. Take your pick.

The townsite of Banff is on traditional Treaty 7 territory, a gathering place for the Niitsitapi from the Blackfoot Confederacy, which includes the First Nations of Siksika, Kainai, and Piikani; the Îyârhe Nakoda of the Chiniki, Bearspaw, Wesley; Tsuut'ina and Métis Nation of Alberta, Region III.

Mountain stats
- Elevation top: 2637m (8650ft)
- Elevation bottom: 1646m (5400ft)
- Vertical drop: 991m (3250ft)
- Skiable terrain: 17sqkm (4200 acres)
- Longest run: 8km (5mi)
- Beginner terrain (green): 24 per cent
- Intermediate terrain (blue/red): 45 per cent
- Advanced terrain (black): 30 per cent
- Lifts: 11

Run
Paradise Bowl, especially the far rider's right lines, holds powder and is a perfect area for laps. A run here isn't complete without some turns through the Pika Trees glades filled with nicely spaced larch trees that seem to hold powder even during a dry spell.

Experience
Ice-skating on stunning Lake Louise with Victoria Glacier views is a once-in-a-lifetime opportunity.

Local's tip
This is the deep-freeze section of Canada's snow supermarket. Wear a face mask to cover exposed skin on those ultra-cold days. Jan is the coldest month with average lows of -15°C (5°F), but the thermometer can drop to -30°C (-22°F).

Opposite The Aurora Borealis waltzes with Banff's Canadian Rockies peaks

THE MOUNTAIN DEBRIEF

Lake Louise Ski Resort has over 17sqkm (4200 acres) of diverse terrain with 164 runs over four mountain faces, glades, cruising runs, remote areas and challenging back bowls. It can be divided into four areas – Front Side and Larch have a taster menu of terrain with easier sections, including long tree-lined, groomed runs. Meanwhile, the West Bowl and Back Bowls offer alpine-style skiing with steep chutes and cliff bands. Due to the standard north-westerly prevailing winds, those back bowls often receive more snow than other areas of the resort, even when it's not snowing.

This ski area has some unique features. Firstly, there are beginner, intermediate, and expert routes from nearly every chair so everyone can score those famous Lake Louise views and ride together. Even a beginner can head to the Top of the World Express chair and absorb the Allen, Fay, Bowlen and Babel peaks across the Bow Valley (a view so striking it once featured on the C$20 note) and take green Saddleback down amongst a minefield of black runs.

It used to be business in the front, party in the back – but then the West Bowl opened in 2021, adding an enormous 1.95sqkm (480 acres) of powder playground – the equivalent of 240 Canadian football fields – and wilderness skiing. There are seven 'zones' instead of cut runs (the longest is 4.7km/3mi), giving endless possibilities of natural routes and fall lines through steeps, powder bowls and gladed tree areas.

Although considered in-bounds terrain, it's recommended you ride with a buddy, carry avalanche safety gear, and know how to use it.

A RIDING ITINERARY

Start with the **Glacier Express Chair** for warm-up blues like **Juniper** and **Cameron's Way** (and maybe a play in the terrain park). From the **Glacier Express Gondola**, take **Top of the World** quad, where you feel exactly that on an exposed ridge, and drop backside into a maze of blacks like **ER 6**.

Take a tasty break and pull in at **Temple Lodge** for the smokehouse downstairs or head upstairs to **Sawyer's Nook** for a real deal emmental/gruyère fondue. And then head for one of my favourite runs – **Rock Garden**. Located off the Lark Quad skiers' right, the trail opens into a wide basin peppered with boulders that turn into pillows or white-topped rock moguls to slide between and around.

The finale of the day is up to **Summit Quad**. Choices – drop backside into **Boomerang Bowl** (there are multiple options) or traverse across to the hectic chutes of **Hector Ridge** (boarders keep speed as it's a green traverse back out to **Ptarmigan Quad**) or circuit them all and take blue **Boomerang** down.

If your legs aren't burning after this itinerary, you're made of steel.

ADVENTURE

Do an intro to ice climbing class with an ACMG-certified guide from **Alpine Air Adventures** (alpineairadventures.com/ice-climbing). Another highlight is caving the Rat's Nest Cave with **Canmore Cave Tours** (canmorecavetours.com), crawling past prehistoric bones – the Adventure option includes an 18m (59ft) rappel.

Dog sledding through the national park wilderness
Opposite Going steep and deep in Lake Louise Ski Resort

OFF-MOUNTAIN MUST-DO

- **Banff National Park** is Canada's first national park, and the third oldest park in the world. Get into it by renting a fat bike and pedalling along the river to the **Cave and Basin National Historic Site**.

EAT UP & DRINK DOWN

- Farm-to-table **Bison Restaurant** (thebison.ca) is a foodie favourite using local suppliers like Noble Farms Bison.
- **Park Distillery** (parkdistillery.com) is all about locally sourced campfire-inspired cooking with small-batch spirits distilled in-house (try the smoked tomato chilli vodka soup).

APRÈS SKI

- Start on slope at Lake Louise's **Powder Keg Lounge** or **Kokanee Cabin** (skilouise.com), then continue in Banff at **Three Bears Tavern and Restaurant** (threebearsbanff.com), complete with patio tabletop fires and a 'winter warmer' cocktail menu.

STAY

- **Fairmont Château Lake Louise** (fairmont.com/lake-louise) is one of the world's most famously situated - and iconic - hotels on the pristine shores of Lake Louise.
- **Fairmont Banff Springs** (fairmont.com/banff-springs), a castle-like hotel is just 7min from Banff, and fit for a princess.

A warm water wallow in Banff Upper Hot Springs is a perfect ski day bookend *Opposite* Gripping by a pick point and hanging while ice climbing in Johnson Canyon

One hundred per cent ski-in, ski out accommodation, hot tubs galore, signature 'snow ghost' trees and rockstar intermediate runs make this a family stand-out.

Big White

THE LOWDOWN

Riding powder through snow ghost trees – those frozen landscape stalagmites – while your husband and kids ride the parallel groomers, before busting into the condo for a hot-soup stop, then rolling out again to keep on trucking. This is how riding should be: hassle-free. No one's parking cars. No kids are face-planting on stairs carrying skis.

That Big White is entirely ski-in, ski-out is not the only magic. At 29.5sqkm (7300 acres) it's not that far off the monolithic 33sqkm (8171 acres) of Whistler Blackcomb (*see* p. 43), and its 7.5m (295in) of powder is enough to bury a house. That Okanagan powder is so dry you can hardly pack a snowball, and it's not uncommon for super-sized, fat flakes to float like slow-motion mini frisbees.

Big White boasts the biggest night-skiing area in Western Canada (0.15sqkm/ 38 acres), as well as the second largest lifting system, highest elevation resort village and highest ice-skating rink in the country. And in case that isn't perfect enough for families, from every lift summit there's a green-run option so mixed abilities can ski together. The ski school GPS-tags students so you can always find your kids ... for a fee they'll even pick them up from the condo with the 'door-to-ski' shuttle service.

The Village's main road is listed as a piste – everywhere is by skis or feet. Footpaths wind their way between the Village Centre Mall with fairy lights strung between brightly coloured buildings and the surrounding pines. There's a festive feel for that extra sprinkle of ski-holiday fairy dust.

Big White is built on the Traditional Territory of the Okanagan Sylix People.

Mountain stats
- Elevation top: 2319m (7606ft)
- Elevation bottom: 1755m (5757ft)
- Vertical drop: 777m (2550ft)
- Skiable terrain: 29.8sqkm (7355 acres)
- Longest run: 7.2km (4.5mi)
- Beginner terrain: 18 per cent
- Intermediate terrain: 54 per cent
- Advanced terrain: 28 per cent
- Lifts: 16

Run
The longest run at Big White, the 7.2km (4.5mi) Around the World from the top of Alpine T-Bar to the Gem Lake Base via Whitefoot Trail, Powder Bowl, Blue Sapphire and Ogo Slow.

Experience
Due to the unique climate and snow conditions, the tops of buried evergreen trees become covered in a thick blanket of snow, giving them a 'ghost-like' appearance - a top photo op for an only-in-Big White experience.

Local's tip
On a powder day, the Powder Chair is your pin drop. The Powder Keg and Powder Gulch are dynamite on even just a 20cm (8in) dump.

Opposite Dancing in between the snow ghosts is a Big White highlight

THE MOUNTAIN DEBRIEF

Amongst the glorious groomers, there's enough for thrillseekers – 6.2sqkm (1525 acres) are alpine and glades. Most of the mountain funnels down to the areas around the Village Center or the Ridge Day Lodge. The mountain's western side features long runs off the Gem Lake Express – the chair is sometimes closed due to high winds, but it can get some of the best powder after a storm.

On this note, the nickname Big White Out isn't for nothing as all that snow must come from somewhere. When this happens, stick to the trees, or head over to the Black Forest Express, which is less exposed to the extremes. On a powder day, you'll find the locals at the bottom of the Ridge Rocket or Snowghost Express Chair; follow them to the Powder Chair for the insider lines.

A RIDING ITINERARY

Head to **Black Forest** – it's warmer in the morning as it's on the east side of the mountain – and play around **Cougar Alley** and **Whiskey Jack**. It's also a one-size-fits-all area, with a great selection of easy greens, cruisy blues and snow-stashed glades.

Head back down to the **Village Center** for lunch – a burger and beer at the **Woods** is the go.

For an afternoon session, work your way west to **Gem Lake** for loads of rolling blues and untouched glades. Keep an eye peeled for the **Beavertails food truck** for a sugar hit. At the top of the **Gem Lake Express**, you'll score a handful of trickier black runs like **Black Bear** and **Cann Cann**. On the other side, **Cliff Chair** serves four black double diamonds which flow into the gentler blue **Cliff Ski Out**.

For beginners, **Serwa's** off Ridge Rocket or **Snowghost** are favourites with lots of groomed rollers. Usually beginners are confined to the bottom of the mountain, where gorgeous greens like **Whitefoot Trail** and **Sun Run** flow down from the 2319m (7608ft) summit.

ADVENTURE

Leave the mountain for the excitement of a Canadian **ice-hockey game**. Head to the activities desk in the Big White Village Centre Mall and they'll organise bus transport and tickets to watch the local Kelowna Rockets at their home stadium of Prospera Place.

Big White is ski in, ski out, making it a firm family favourite

OFF-MOUNTAIN MUST-DO

- The **Happy Valley adventure area** has a spectacular ice-skating rink with a rink-side bonfire. Or experience the thrill of **mushing** through Big White's famous backcountry after being introduced to the sled, the harnesses and the hyper-friendly Canadian sled dogs.

EAT UP & DRINK DOWN

- Snuggling under blankets and exploring enchanted forest trails while being pulled by Clydesdales is half the fun of getting to a gourmet dinner in the cosy cabin of **Dinner & Sleigh Bells**.
- In fine weather, say olé to **Cantina Del Centro** for more-ish Mexican street food and margaritas with a side of the best patio views on the mountain.

APRÈS SKI

- **Globe Cafe** (globedining.com) has live music every Friday and Saturday night and Sunday afternoon.
- **Snowshoe Sam's** (snowshoesams.com) has been voted the best ski pub in North America, with regular bands, DJs, karaoke nights, and other theme nights - it's the local's favourite.

STAY

- Choose between condos (apartments), townhomes, mega chalets and a few hotels.
- For families, **Sundance Resort** (bigwhite.com), just above the Bullet Express near the Village Centre, has a pool and hot tub.
- The three-bedroom **Eagles** condo (bigwhite.com) with a bevy of beds is perfect for a gang. Tip - stock up with **Vacation Foods**, a grocery and delivery service.

ALTERNATIVE: SILVER STAR

Okanagan Valley neighbour Silver Star (skisilverstar.com) is a 90min drive away. Big White and Silver Star are equidistant either side of Kelowna and its airport. The brightly coloured mid-mountain village is nothing short of breathtaking. This family favourite has a deceptively large, world-class ski area, including a backside filled with deep, steep double-black terrain.

Top Soaking up some solitude *Bottom* The ski-in, ski-out resorts mean families and friends can connect before and after skiing *Opposite* The top of the Ridge Rocket Express, drop skiers left for blue runs, or right to black

Chris Davenport the big mountain skier

There's a mere handful of skiers or snowboarders with the career longevity of two-time World Extreme Skiing Champion and ski mountaineering pioneer Chris Davenport. Unlike others, 'Dav' moves through all facets of the ski industry from alpine ski racing and competing, to filming and ski mountaineering (including ski descending Everest's Lhotse face). Now he skis far-flung corners of the globe from Antarctica to under the Lofoten island's Arctic midnight sun.

Along the way he's become the first to ski all 100 of Colorado's 14ft peaks and inducted into the United States Ski and Snowboard Hall of Fame. But it hasn't been enough to *just* ski. Business savvy, he's also engineered equipment with sponsors and creates bespoke guiding trips to places you've never even heard of. Peers use the words 'legend', 'humble' to describe him and others may do elements of what he does, but nobody does it all.

Where did your story begin?

I was very fortunate to be born into a skiing family. My grandparents were skiers, they built a small ski cabin in the White Mountains of New Hampshire in the late 1940s and raised their children skiing. Consequently, my father raised his children doing the same thing. I was a third-generation skier in the same ski cabin, we were all alpine ski racers.

When did skiing become your career?

When the first competitions were starting in extreme skiing my very good friend from high school and college Shane McConkey called and said, 'Hey, Chris, I'm going down to the US Extreme Skiing Championships in Crested Butte, you should come with me.' I'd never heard of that, but cool, I'll go. And so I competed and just fell in love with the whole scene. I very quickly realized that those decades spent in the start gate as a ski racer, with the mental focus and technical skills, were going to serve me well as a freeskier.

Was that the seed from which big things (and big mountains) grew?

Yes, I got an invitation to the World Extreme Skiing Championships in Valdez, Alaska. And I went up there and I won the world championship. I was literally on the airplane flying from Anchorage back to Colorado, writing out a business plan of how I was going to turn this into something.

You had a freeski career business plan?

Yes, I wish I still had that notebook! It was mainly questions about what brands would I reach out to, how I would work with them, what I could deliver for them. Of course, I wanted the gear and maybe a pay check but like, how can we work together? A constant in my career is delivering for brands, not just expecting things from them.

You filmed legendary big mountain movie *Steep* with your mentor Doug Coombs who passed two weeks later. Did it make you pause?

If this can happen to Doug, who was the person I looked up to the most, with his skills in the mountains, then certainly, it can happen to me. But then you think, 'Well, he would want you to keep going and just be better at what you do.' At the end of the day, it's a dangerous sport. More professional skiers die than in any other sport I know of, I've lost more than 40 friends over the years.

So how do you handle risk?

My attitude is that I think of what I do as professional risk management. I'm constantly thinking about the decision-making process. What are my options? How do I get the best outcome with the least amount of risk? Lecturing about risk management has made me a smarter skier. The summit is not the goal, the ski descent is not the goal. Coming home is the goal.

Why big mountains?

Even as a teenager I loved climbing, I was a hardcore rock climber, and skiing mountains, being back country – that's really where you can test yourself. You can only do so much at a ski area and then you go, 'Okay, well what's beyond the ropes?' You start exploring and that's taken me to all seven continents and to the highest peaks in the USA. As an athlete, you always want to see what you're capable of.

You do a lot of sea-and-ski. Why's the boat and mountain combination a winner?

When you're on a boat, it means you're at sea level, which is great, because climbing and skinning and going up mountains at sea level is a lot easier than being at 5000 meters. The other thing is, a boat can take you to places that you could never access otherwise. Some of the best places are British Columbia's coast, Greenland, Iceland, the north of Norway, and of course Antarctica.

What might surprise people about living in Aspen?

I think people who have never been to Aspen have a preconceived notion that it's this glitzy glamorous town of rich and famous people. And to a small degree, there's an element of that, but that is absolutely not the fabric of the town. It's a ski town through and through, an outdoor mecca populated by skiers and mountaineers and just mountain people. It's also a cultural hub of art and music; basically, it's a small city in a very small package.

You're a global guide, what do you love most about it?

I started around 20 years ago with heli-guiding in Alaska, I love sharing the passion I have for skiing with people. So I take them on adventures to the places I want to go; I want to go powder skiing in Japan, heli in Alaska or sail to a remote location and I'm just gonna bring people along. I'm showing them an awesome time, they're having an incredible ski vacation and I'm in a place I want to be so it's the perfect business model.

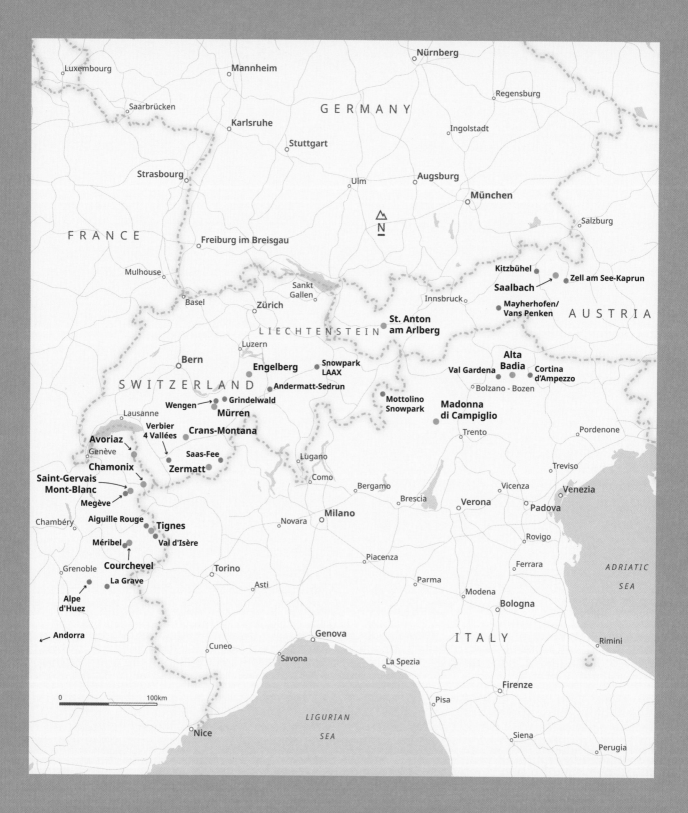

Europe

From gargantuan interconnected ski areas to high-altitude glamour and hidden, charming nooks, each country's snow scene has its own culture-soaked flavour.

FRANCE

If you're packing for a ski trip to France and require mood music, just google 'Ça plane pour moi' by Plastic Bertrand. If this funky-beat toe-tapper doesn't make you visualise the peak-ski 1980s Frenchness of one-piece neon suits and mirrored sunglasses and remind you to toss in some themed outfits, nothing will. This earworm will thrust you straight into the enormous ski areas, big verts, exquisite corduroy and cool après that make you fall head-over-heels for French skiing – on the slopes and off.

France is sexy. Surrounded by lyrical accents, swoon-worthy flavours, heart-thumping mountains and occasional insouciance (oooh, playing hard to get), your inner coquette may be unleashed. It's the most popular ski area in Europe for non-Europeans, irresistible with seven of the ten largest interconnected ski areas in the world, and sophisticated lift systems (over €300 million is spent on new infrastructure annually), but it's what's in between the skiing that renders visitors weak at the knees.

Charm bombs are continually detonated, like pausing in gastronomic Avoriaz (see p. 77) to nibble Abondance cheese; basking in a designer sun lounger in Courchevel (see p. 95), with a (real) Champagne in hand (après is a French word for a reason); staying in a Savoyarde village like St Gervais (see p. 89) and submitting to feasts of fondue and raclette, creamy tartiflette (potato, bacon and cheese casserole) and juicy pierrade (barbecue). Tick, tick, tick.

The scenery in Switzerland (see p. 132) can be more spectacular than France, the vibe in Austria (see p. 104) can be more fun, and Italy (see p. 118) can be cheaper, but there's something relaxed and *sympathetique* about skiing in France because you can always find your niche. For beginners, the ski schools are beyond compare; intermediates love Megève groomers (see p. 93), and if screaming down tight couloirs with mandatory airs on the exit is your brand of fun, there's the mountaineering ringmaster of Chamonix (see p. 99).

One complaint about the French Alps is the weather-proof 1960s concrete bunker-like villages built on the high-altitude plateaus. Even observed through champagne-coloured Le Specs, they have a hard time looking good. But they're ski-in, ski-out and are actually masterpieces in disguise, designed to reflect their rocky, snow-sure surroundings. For example, the untreated, chemical-free, wood-clad buildings of Avoriaz are cutting-edge mimetic (landscape mimicking) architecture – each building is unique in size and silhouette and fits into the organic mountain curves. Mais non, this was 60 years ago; it's *brilliant* (avant-garde is *also* a French word for a reason). Merci, you forward-thinking Frenchies.

The country that has *everything* is France, the elements are woven together with an effortless chic that make this destination ripe for a lifelong snow affair.

Coolest winter selfie
Snap the icy flow of the Mer de Glace in Chamonix (see p. 103) from the new viewing areas. Or have almost one-fifth of France as your backdrop from Pic Blanc atop the Sarenne run (Europe's longest; see p. 81) in Alp d'Huez. Capture the eerie insides of a crevasse on the Tignes glacier, skiing behind a horse in Avoriaz (see p. 77), or any La Folie Douce (see p. 81) après shenanigans after 4pm.

Get appy
The Ecole de Ski Frances (ESF) is one of the best ski schools in the world, with multilingual instructors. Or try the Carv app (inserted as a ski boot liner), which measures your pressure and motion 20 times per second and provides personalised audio tips as you ski.

Snow-Forecast.com's app works particularly well in France, and Cheezam (like Shazam, but cheese-focused) identifies a cheese via a photo and suggests wine pairings.

Don't break the bank
The euro can go far in France, especially on non-ski experiences. For example, a 10min paraskiing (taking off on skis) over the pistes in Alpe d'Huez (see p. 81) is ideal for first-timers and a next-level experience for just €50. And you don't need to dine at Michelin-star places for fine fare; a €5 boulangerie baguette with simple jambon cru (dry-cured ham) and a slice of local cheese is gourmet heaven. You can find 'picnic rooms' on-slope; look for 'salles hor sac' signs.

When it snows
The northern French Alps include the Haute-Savoie, home to Avoriaz (see p. 77), the resort with the highest average snowfall in France each season (7.5m/295in), as well as Courchevel (see p. 95) and Alpe d'Huez (see p. 81). Most of the snow comes from the north-west and is associated with low pressure (a storm) centred somewhere to the north of the Alps, typically over the North Sea or in the low countries (Belgium, Holland and Luxembourg). Storms arriving from the north will typically deliver more snow to the northern and western foothills of the Alps; storms arriving from the north-west are more likely to deliver across the entire northern French Alps, all the way down to Courchevel.

This futuristic, snowbound village – smack bang in the Portes du Soleil – was eco-friendly long before sustainability was a 'thing'.

Avoriaz

THE LOWDOWN

They say you never forget your first love. My first cheese love was a melted raclette panini slope-side in Avoriaz, a true obsession that made me accidentally miss a boyfriend's freestyle competition. Suffice it to say the relationship didn't last, but golden memories of that raclette sandwich will live forever.

Avoriaz is in the very heart of the Portes du Soleil, a mammoth ski area of 13 ski resorts with 209 lifts straddling the French–Swiss border, and it's wise not to underestimate the area's gargantuan size. If you like a journey in your ski day, this is the ultimate snow-sure base camp at 1800m (5905ft).

Avoriaz's location seems impossible when you approach from below via cable car (it's snow-locked), perched like a cat about to pounce into the Morzine Valley below. Built as a wild gamble by three architects under 30 (Jacques Labro, Jacques Orzoni and Jean-Marc Roques), the design is unlike any other. It's a collection of acute-angled buildings covered in red cedar-wood shingles, each more bizarre than the last, intended to meld organically with the mountain.

Europe's only 100 per cent ski-in, ski-out resort incorporated eco-principles before sustainability was a 'thing'. For example, the living spaces are south-facing to the sun, delivering passive heating, while the north-facing areas are occupied by utility areas and walkways.

The mountains here are endless – but bite off as much as you can chew.

 Mountain stats
- Elevation top: 2466m (8090ft)
- Elevation bottom: 1800m (5905ft)
- Vertical drop: 1466m
- Skiable terrain: 130km (80 miles), 650km (403 miles) in the Portes du Soleil
- Longest run: 6km (3.7mi)
- Beginner terrain: 54 per cent
- Intermediate terrain: 33 per cent
- Advanced terrain: 14 per cent
- Lifts: 36

 Run
The off-piste, 3km (1.9mi) Les Crozats with more than 1000m (3280ft) of vertical drop.

 Experience
Ski through the tiny Village des Chèvres in Les Lindarets. In winter, the road turns into a ski run, and the tiny collection of buildings is a gastronomic magnet.

 Local's tip
Click off skis at La Crémaillère, run by three generations of the Braize family, for a raclette - if you're willing to risk falling in love with a new food.

Previous Freestylers play in the park at Saint-Gervais Mont-Blanc in the Haute-Savoie *Opposite* Red cedar and larch wood building materials blend into the dramatic landscape

THE MOUNTAIN DEBRIEF

With a seasonal snowfall average of around 7.5m (24.5ft) at resort level, Avoriaz is officially the snowiest ski resort in France – take a guide if you're heading off-piste for that reason alone.

Avoriaz's local slopes are split into several distinct sectors. Immediately above are the open bowls and peaks of Les Hauts Forts, Arare and La Chavanette; on the other side of Avoriaz, just over the ridge around the back of the village, is the heavily wooded Les Lindarets area (home of The Stash, with a sister park in The Remarkables, NZ).

In normal snow conditions, the Portes du Soleil circuit can be easily managed by an intermediate-level skier in a single day, and can be skied in either direction. Hit the nearby Le Pas de Chavanette, known as the Swiss Wall – on a powder day, ride it into Switzerland early before moguls grow to the size of small vehicles.

A RIDING ITINERARY

Tackle a Portes du Soleil circuit: from the top of **La Chavanette**, attempt the **Swiss Wall** (or take a chair down if icy) leading into Swiss **Champéry-Les Crosets**. Beyond Les Crosets, continue to **Morgins** via **Champoussin** and back to Avoriaz via **Châtel**. An intermediate can complete it in a day; the only place to remove skis is in Morgins (if skiing the circuit anti-clockwise from Avoriaz, which is through Châtel first).

Alternatively, many flock here for the four parks. If that's your jam, beeline to the **Stash park** built from naturally fallen trees in the forest. Some features are massive, others more forgiving for mere mortals (and **Li'l Stash** is for kids).

Avoriaz is great for beginners with ultra-convenient nursery slopes both in and above the village and the long, gentle green run (**Proclou**) for progression.

ADVENTURE

Just arriving at your accommodation is an adventure – either by horse sleigh, sled or skis (luggage arrives via piste basher). Also, sign up for ski-jöering – being pulled along on skis by a running horse.

Explore the snowbound, car-free village on E-fat bikes
Opposite top The otherwordly cliff-top architecture is a sight to behold *Opposite bottom* Try Scandinavian-style ski-jöering: skiing through a forest being pulled by a galloping horse

Europe

OFF-MOUNTAIN MUST-DO

- Aquariaz! It may seem bizarre (like many things in Avoriaz) to ski in freezing weather and then swim in Jamaica-esque surrounds with over 1500 tropical plants and 183 tropical trees, but it's definitely worth taking the time to check out.

EAT UP & DRINK DOWN

- Michelin-recommended **La Réserve** restaurant (la-reserve-avoriaz.com) is serious date night territory.
- **La Ferme** (laferme.ski), located in an 1860s Les Lindarets farmhouse building, is a pick for gourmands.
- On a chilly day, tuck up by the fire at cosy **La Fangle** (lepetitdru.com) on the descent to Morzine.
- **La Cabane** (lacabaneavoriaz.fr) is where you'll find pot-au-feu (boiled beef and vegetables) but also sushi and prawn dumplings.
- **Le Cookie Café** (cookie-cafe.com) at the border with Switzerland is the area's highest dining at 2300m (7546ft) and has books to curl up with, plus a view of the Swiss Wall for entertainment.

APRÈS SKI

- The **Folie Douce** (lafoliedouce.com) strikes again, but rather than being up the mountain like the original in Val d'Isère (*see* p. 87), it's located on the main piste in town. Ski patrol love that it's a walk, not a slide, home and the action goes until 6pm.
- If you make it beyond this, **Le Shooters**, with a selection of over 50 shots, is sure to compound any damage.
- You'll probably wind up at Avoriaz's sole nightclub **Le Yak** (avoriaz.com), which closes at 5am and is guaranteed to interfere with your ski day. Find winter events online (avoriaz.com/en/discover/the-essentials/events).

STAY

- **Hotel Les Dromonts** (hoteldesdromonts.com) was the first building in the resort by architect Jacques Labro. Shaped like a pine cone, it's a skier cocoon with 35 recently renovated rooms (don't miss **Le 67** cocktail bar - a nod to the year the resort was founded with a trendy '60s decor).
- At the other end of the spectrum is the chic **Hotel Le Mil8** (hotelmil8.com) by Morzine architect Hervé Marullaz. It opened in 2020 with an outdoor pool.
- If you're travelling with a tribe, **Club Belambra** (belambra.fr) has an all-inclusive formula with an easy club, ski rentals, an open bar and snacks.

ALTERNATIVE: ALPE D'HUEZ

In a sun-blessed situation, Alpe d'Huez (alpedhuez.com) basks on a fully south-facing plateau at 1860m (6102ft). Access is not by cable car, but via 21 hairpin turns (recorded on one of the famed stages of the Tour de France). Its skiable area has maximum *soilel* exposure - the French weather bureau has recorded an average of 300 days of sunshine per year here. With 236km (147mi) of riding, the star is the Sarenne run, which is 16km (10mi) long, with 1830m (6000ft) of altitude drop. It's simply in a league of its own as the longest ski run in Europe. Plan ahead, it takes an average skier an hour to descend.

Stop in at La Ferme de Seraussaix for local Abondance cheese made on site *Opposite* The wonderfully snaggle-toothed Dents di Midi overlook the ski area

To most high-altitude, 1960s-built French resorts, we say 'non'. But glacier-accessible Tignes, linked to Val d'Isère, is an exception, with 300km (186mi) of pisted terrain.

Tignes

THE LOWDOWN

Most of the purpose-built, high-altitude resorts built in France during the 1960s and '70s (Val Thorens, Flaine, Les Arcs, Les Deux Alps) are so charmless they would make their mothers weep. It's arguable that the Brutalist apartment-style architecture of these resorts doesn't quite fit in such a chic country. But Tignes is the dark horse worth visiting.

I'm not high-fiving all of Tignes, which cascades in a series of five disjointed villages, only Tignes 2100 (the highest). And even then, just the top of the village, Val Claret, separated by a frozen lake from Tignes-Le-Lac. The amount of ski-in, ski-out accommodation is phenomenal, there's an unexpectedly spellbinding snowbound village centre, new (more aesthetically pleasing) buildings are sprouting, and there's summer glacier skiing.

The ski area is so well integrated with neighbour Val d'Isère (*see* p. 87) that the pistes in the Tignes–Val d'Isères ski area (formerly Espace Killy) seem like one of the world's largest ski areas. If you're serious about skiing, at some point you'll arrive in Tignes.

 Mountain stats
- Elevation top: 3456m (11,338ft)
- Elevation bottom: 1550m (5085ft)
- Vertical drop: 1900m (6234ft)
- Skiable terrain: 300km (186 miles) in Tignes/Val d'Isère ski area
- Longest run: 10km (6.2 miles)
- Beginner terrain (green): 12 per cent
- Intermediate terrain (blue/red): 63 per cent
- Advanced terrain (black): 25 per cent
- Lifts: 17 in Tignes, 38 in Val d'Isère (total 55)

 Run
La Sache, an exhilarating, knee-quivering 10km (6.2-mi) black run descending from L'Aiguille Percée via a spectacular valley to Tignes-les-Brevières (escape routes are via Echappatoire and Pavot).

 Experience
Book ESF instructor Theo Lejeune, a former Olympic moguls skier from a multi-generational Tignes family (the Henri piste is named after his grandfather).

 Local's tip
At the Val Claret cinema look for VOST or VO ('version originale') for English-language films.

Opposite Getting grabby in Tignes

THE MOUNTAIN DEBRIEF

With a base of 2100m (6890ft), Tignes soars up to La Grand Motte glacier at a gasp-worthy 3450m (11,319ft), accessed via an underground 3.5km (2.2mi) funicular that climbs 920m (3018ft) in 7min. Tignes is snow-sure and has access to the perma-peak on the La Grand Motte Glacier with a vibrant summer ski scene. It boasts 150km (93mi) of pistes, plus Snowpark DC, Easy Park and a 1200m (3937ft) Le Palet boardercross course attracting race teams, freestylers and freeriders.

Like much of the French Alps, snowfall blows in from the west with Atlantic depressions, but Tignes double dips with retour d'est, a Mediterranean low-pressure system dumping copious amounts of snow like a powder-filled dump truck on the nearby Italian Alps. Skip school-holiday and weekend crowds if possible.

A RIDING ITINERARY

Tignes can be split into four ski areas: **La Grande Motte Massif glacier**, mid-bowl **Palet/L'Aiguille Percée**, **Tovière** linking to Val d'Isère, and lower **Tignes-les-Brevières**.

Warm up on the main chairlift of **Palafour** (which locals call 'P4'), ascending the **L'Aiguille Percée** side of the mountain. GS turn the long and wide blue piste runs (with fun side jibbing) back down to **Tignes Le Lac**.

Once warmed up here, head up **L'Aiguille Percée** and hit four blue runs – **Corniche**, **Rhododendron**, **Melezes** and **Myrtilles** – cruising all the way down to **Tignes Les Brévières** at 1550m (5085ft). This little morning sun trap is also an inviting place to stop for lunch.

Beginners are happy on the easier runs down in the valley towards **Tignes-Les-Brévières**, where shorter chairlift runs keep legs fresh.

ADVENTURE

Unique to Tignes is scuba diving under the 2m (7ft) thick ice of Lac Tignes (with an instructor). Take it a step further and learn how to fall through the ice and survive, set up a tent mid-storm, build your own igloo and more survival antics on a full-day **Extreme Explorer course** with North Pole skier and Tignes local Alban Michon (albanmichon.com).

Tignes is the perfect place to taste test an off-piste adventure

OFF-MOUNTAIN MUST-DO

- **La Banquise** has a sledging run - whizz down the 3km (1.86-mi) Expedition Cobra. There's a curling rink, an igloo village, a fun snow labyrinth (and the Insta-famous red Tignes sign).
- **Tignespace** has 3500sqm (almost an acre) of activities, including a skateboard ramp, golf simulator, climbing wall and even pole-vault pit.

EAT UP & DRINK DOWN

- Even stalwart Val d'Isère lovers will venture across to eat at **La Ferme des Trois Capucines** (ferme3capucines.com). This working farm makes its own cheese in wintery dishes (like tartiflette) that retain rural French charm.
- **Le Caveau** is one of Tignes' best-loved restaurants with a buzzing little bar.
- **Basuto** (ynycio.com/restaurant) serves traditional Columbian hacienda-style food, including moreish empanadas.

APRÈS SKI

- The craziness at the original Val d'Isère (practically Ibiza on ice) **Folie Douce** (lafoliedouce.com) has to be embraced; the last lift back is at 5pm.
- Val Claret has vibrant base-area bars; kick off the afternoon après-ski at **Drop Zone** (tignes.net) and **V Bar.**
- The cosy **L'Embuscade** is a hidden gem with funky music and a pool table.
- Bust moves at nightclub **Blue Girl** which revels in Euro-trash cheesy tunes.
- The **Avant Garde** is where you'll find the seasonaires at 4am.

STAY

- Club Med has a habit of choosing the best locations, and the fact that it recently chose Tignes to build its French Alps flagship, **Club Med Tignes** (clubmed.com) is proof Tignes is no longer Val d'Isère's ugly stepsister.
- The recent **VoulezVous** (etincelles.com), built of steel and glass to mimic the glacier, has a funky atmosphere.
- For something out-of-this-world, stay at the **Wild Nest** (evolution2.com). The luxurious, solar-powered, translucent dome, on the edge of Lac de Chardonnet in the heart of the Vanoise National Park at 2384m (7822ft), is accessed by an hour-long snow-shoe hike.

ALTERNATIVE: VAL D'ISÈRE

If the altitude and architecture are too much, swap Tignes for Val d'Isère. The village is prettier, there's off-piste galore, and it's home to the world-famous downhill course, the Face de Bellevarde.

ALTERNATIVE: AIGUILLE ROUGE

For more thrills, conquer the famous Aiguille Rouge with spectacular mountain amphitheatre views. This is a bucket-list run for experienced skiers: a vertical drop from the peak of 3226m (10,583ft) to 1200m (3937ft) over a leg-burning 7.4km (4.9mi).

Tignes offers an exciting array of off-slope action, even ice diving *Opposite top* Val Claret by night *Opposite bottom* Dog sledding is a fun Tignes experience

The real deal with Savoyard soul, this is where to find the French on the 'other' lesser-known side of Mont Blanc.

Saint-Gervais Mont-Blanc

THE LOWDOWN

Rated as the Ultimate's quiet achiever, Saint-Gervais Mont-Blanc is the unsung gem of the French Alps wedged between the bright lights of Chamonix and the chi-chi fur coats of ritzy Megève. This idyllic low-key mountain playground is as French as it gets; while you may have glimpsed it amongst a blizzard of lycra on the Tour de France route, it's in winter that it takes centre stage.

Driving up from Sallanches, you'll discover that the turn-of-the-century spa town, nestled in a gorge at the foot of towering Mont d'Arbois and Mont Blanc, has retained lots of romantic character. A snow globe of a village, the main street is lined with Baroque churches, medieval touches and gourmet restaurants that excel in farm-to-fork fare in the most unpretentious manner. Also, head to the neighbouring village of Saint-Nicolas de Véroce and its 10th-century parish.

Located on the doorstep of the Evasion Mont Blanc (EMB) ski area, the third largest in France, with a whopping 445km (277mi) of terrain and 107 lifts, it's possible to ski for an entire week and never ski the same run twice. The pass accesses Saint-Gervais Mont-Blanc, Megève, Saint-Nicolas de Véroce, Combloux, La Giettaz, Les Contamines Montjoie and Hauteluce. The vibe is French family, but with all the trimmings of an international heavyweight ski area.

 Mountain stats
- Elevation top: 2353m (7720ft)
- Elevation bottom: 1400m (4593ft)
- Vertical drop: 950m (3117ft)
- Skiable terrain: 236km (147mi)
- Longest run: 5.5km (3.4mi)
- Beginner terrain: 20 per cent
- Intermediate terrain:66 per cent
- Advanced terrain: 14 per cent
- Lifts: 263km

 Run
Prime those legs of steel! La Grande Epaule (named after the shoulder-shaped summit) is a stunning 1000m (3280ft) descent red run facing Mont Blanc.

 Experience
Take a stylish splash in the L'Oreal-managed Les Thermes Saint-Gervais Mont-Blanc (thermes-saint-gervais.com). The mineral-rich water is drawn from the heart of Mont Blanc at a constant 34°C (93°F), travelling for 60 years before reaching the baths.

 Local's tip
Catch the fourth highest train in Europe, the 1912 cog wheel *Mont Blanc Tramway* that stops in the village (the carriages bear sweet first names like Anne, Jeanne and Marie).

Opposite Sant-Gervais displays its alpine history proudly

THE MOUNTAIN DEBRIEF

Don't be surprised if something on the mountain feels a little odd. The snow can be excellent, the sun shining, jagged mountains posing – but you're alone. Just over each side of the valley, slopes bustle in touristy Chamonix and foreigner-filled Megève, but *voila*, here you're singing 'All By Myself' by mid-run. That's the drawcard of St-Gervais Mont-Blanc. Sure, the elevation isn't as high as others, but there's still great skiing above the mid-stations of La Princesse or Le Bettex at season's end. Plus, Mont Blanc creates its own weather pattern, resulting in proportionately high snowfalls; under your skis are summer pastures requiring little snow depth. The more people avoid the sub-2500m (-8202ft) peaks, the better.

A RIDING ITINERARY

Start the day with the mountain workers at **Aux Petits Gourmands** for a cosy coffee on comfortable couches. Caffeine ready, take the **Bettex cable car and gondola** and warm up around the 1958m (6424ft) **Mount Joux** and 1840m (6037ft) **Mont Arbois** (where you'll also find the best freeriding back side). For first runs, **La Croix** snow softens quickly in the sun and is ideal for carve turns and avoiding chilly mornings.

In the afternoon, head to the highest point of the EMB at **St Nicolas de Véroce** and from the top of the **Epaule** chairlift towards **Croix du Christ**, swoop the multiple red or blue runs. Or drop down to **Megève** on cruisy **Milloz**.

Given Saint-Gervais Mont-Blanc is predominantly a family resort, powder lovers can score fresh tracks between the trees days after a fall. My pick is **St Nicolas de Veroce**: it's quiet with east-facing slopes and tree skiing. In short, everything except the crowds.

Beginners can start with the very playful forest track of the **Princess**, and **Le Bettex** mid-mountain has all the beginner facilities, plus restaurants for breaks.

ADVENTURE

Located on the flanks of Europe's majestic Mount Blanc, this is a prime locale to dip a toe into **mountaineering**. With prior crampon and crevasse training, consider a two-day summit climb with a UIAGM guide from La Compagnie des Guides de Saint-Gervais/Les Contamines.

Where'd everybody go? Finding a feeling of solitude within a variety of vistas

Europe

OFF-MOUNTAIN MUST-DO

- Check with the **tourist office** (saintgervais.com), as there are concerts, shows and weekly experiences aplenty. It can hook you up for **twilight skiing** with a mountain guide at Saint-Nicolas de Véroce, free **village walks** with a passionate volunteer, **snow yoga**, **igloo building** with a specialist, **dog sledding**, introduction to **ski-touring** and school-holiday events.

EAT UP & DRINK DOWN

- Book ahead at one-Michelin-star **Le Sérac** (3serac.fr) by the church for fine fare.
- **Restaurant L'Eterle** (eterle.com) has drool-worthy and family-friendly three-cheese wood-fired pizza (chèvre, reblochon and raclette).
- Just near the Baroque footpath and the fishing lake is **Chèverie Au Coeur de Montjoie** (saintgervais.com) goat farm producing yoghurts, Tomme cheese, fromage frais and goats cheese spread.

APRÈS SKI

- It's inconceivable I'm writing about another **Folie Douce** (lafoliedouce.com), but here we are. It's simply because their audacious formula of table dancing, DJs and fine fare works.

The cluster of cafes at Le Bettex *Opposite* A paraglider swoops over empty pistes

- In general, there isn't a manic après scene. The pick is the friendly **Les 3 Mousquetons** bar where you'll find a melange of locals and visitors and a range of beers, and trendy **Pur Bar** (pur.eatbu.com) with top-tier creative cocktails.
- A shout-out to **BJ's Café** (degeneve-classicscars.com) in nearby Contamines with locally brewed Brewhouse74 and Marmotte Beer, adjacent to a classic-car workshop.

STAY

- The elegant, four-star **Le Saint-Gervais Hotel & Spa** (accor.com) is just what the village needed. The Art Nouveau—style building has been constructed with modern alpine interiors and a spa, including pools, and is now a luxury landmark with a chic bar.
- **Hôtel Coeur Des Neiges** (hotelcoeurdesneiges.com) is a charming boutique hotel mid-village that feels like a tasteful chalet belonging to a wealthy friend.
- If seeking ski-in, ski-out, stay at the three-star **La Flèche d'Or** (hotel-laflechedor.com).

ALTERNATIVE: MEGÈVE

Less than 20min up the road is Megève, better known amongst the fur-wearing set. Most runs have incredible views of Mont Blanc - the medieval village - and the central square with its historic church is picture-book pretty. The spa at **Les Fermes de Marie** (en.fermesdemarie.com) is one of the best in the world.

This glamour-puss poses like a movie star in the world's largest ski area, Les 3 Vallées, with serious room to move.

Courchevel

THE LOWDOWN

It comes down to splitting hairs, choosing a Les 3 Vallées favourite. Méribel or Courchevel? (Sorry 1970s-built Val Thorens, you may be a ten in the snow-sure category, but in looks you're sub four). The Three Valleys and 600km (373mi) of runs comprise the world's largest lift network. So, where to set up base camp?

Méribel, despite being purpose-built, retains a quaint main village in the Savoyard style. The deal-breaker is the aspect – Courchevel has more north-facing slopes than south-facing Méribel, meaning the snow stays longer and in better condition. So Courchevel it is.

More decisions – which Courchevel? The four villages were renamed Courchevel 1850, Courchevel Moriond, Courchevel Village and Courchevel Le Praz, respectively.

The hero village is Courchevel 1850. The altitude and prices rise in synchronicity, so it's no surprise this, the highest of the villages, hosts three of France's few six-star palace hotels and 16 five-star hotels. A hotel room for US$16,000 a night? It happens.

Chinese, Middle Eastern, Brazilian, Mexican and Indian skiers (or non-skiers, as the case may be) have replaced the Russian oligarchs and their entourages once known for their outrageously extravagant behaviour. Many have welcomed the change.

 Mountain stats
- Elevation top: 2738m (8982ft)
- Elevation bottom: 1100m (3608ft)
- Vertical drop: 1738m (5374ft)
- Skiable terrain: 150km (93mi)
- Longest run: 5km (3mi)
- Beginner terrain: 19 per cent
- Intermediate terrain: 71 per cent
- Advanced terrain: 9 per cent
- Lifts: 58

 Run
L'Eclispe is *the* superstar, specially designed for the Courchevel-Méribel 2023 FIS Alpine World Ski Championships.

 Experience
Courchevel Aquamotion, arguably the Alps' best water facility, has snow-fringed outdoor pools (heated to 32°C/90°F) and a plethora of indoor action.

 Local's tip
Put Les Chapelet on your dance card, one of the ski area's most picturesque slopes overlooking the little-known Avals Valley.

Opposite Summit seeking in Courchevel

THE MOUNTAIN DEBRIEF

Even without its siblings, Courchevel would satisfy any skier with 150km (93mi) of terrain, including superb off-piste skiing, steep terrain (including Europe's steepest black run), wide, open groomers for beginners and intermediates and, rare in the Alps, even some tree-lined runs. That it's also well linked to the rest of Les 3 Vallées (two access points lead to Méribel Valley, one at the top of Saulire and the other at Col de la Loze) means endless opportunities for exploring a wide selection of ski runs on the daily.

A RIDING ITINERARY

After grabbing a pocket pain au chocolat to eat on the gondola, head straight to the rolling beauty of **Combe de la Saulire** before 9.30am. Why? Both Méribel and Mottaret gondola lifts deliver skiers here earlier than the Courchevel lifts, so make this the first run of the day.

If you're keen for a wake-up challenge, take on the **Grand Couloir** that claims the crown as Europe's steepest run. From here, it's possible to ski down to **Le Praz**, with over 1400m (4593ft) of descent.

This area around the **Saulire** and the serious terrain in the **Creux Noirs bowls** provide plenty of advanced skiing – there's no shortage of black pistes with steep and tough moguls around the Susses lift. Slightly mellower red runs fill the space between Courchevel 1850 and Courchevel Moriond with **Jean Pachot** (the alternative black Chanrossa can ice up) and **Park City**.

For a well-earned lunch break, head for the 2112m (6929ft) **La Cave des Creux** (cavedescreux-courchevel.com) with Savoyard specialties and some Thai dishes.

For beginners, the gentle descending slope of **Jardin Alpin** is like a leisurely stroll between the beautiful chalets and hotels for which Courchevel 1850 is renowned.

ADVENTURE

Adventure abounds – test your skills through the snaking zig-zags of the 3km (1.9mi) **Moriond Luge** (seecourchevel.com), take charge of your own pack of huskies (or let the professional musher drive for a more relaxing ride) and, once the lifts close, there's the option to switch skis for a snowmobile.

OFF-MOUNTAIN MUST-DO

• Time a trip with one of Courchevel's events. There's the **La Folie Douce Festival** (lafoliedouce.com), bringing the best DJs and singers to Courchevel 1850, the **International Festival of Pyrotechnical Art** (courchevel.com), run since 2003, which is fireworks-tastic, or watch the **FIS Alpine World Ski Championships** when the ski area buzzes with professional athletes and amped spectators. Visit courchevel.com/en/events for the latest.

———

EAT UP & DRINK DOWN

• At Courchevel Le Praz, at the foot of the slopes, you'll find the Michelin-starred restaurant **Azimut** (restaurantazimut.com).
• **Le Caveau** (caveaucourchevel.com) is a fondue and raclette haven located between the Grangette gondola and the slope of Les Tovets)].
• **Bel Air** (belair-courchevel.com) at Moriond has an outside terrace with sensational views and good food, leaving spare change.

———

APRÈS SKI

• You will likely find your chalet host or ski instructor at **La Boulotte** (courchevel.com) or **Le Schuss** in Courchevel 1650.
• **Le Catérail** (courchevel.com) is ideally located in the heart of Courchevel Village with DJs and concerts (and 2am finishes).
• The **Seven Kings** has a sharp selection of seven English and Scottish draught beers (and sports screens).
• Don't miss the new headquarters of flamboyant gourmet chic, the **Ferme Saint-Amour** (lafermesaintamour.com).

———

STAY

• Most Courchevel 1850 activity is centred around La Croisette; the area above is called Jardin Alpin, where you'll find the most expensive hotels and chalets scattered amongst the woods with direct slope access.
• In the heart of Le Praz, **Les Peupliers** (lespeupliers.com) has modern and cosy rooms 100m (328ft) from the ski lifts. Or, if you're determined to stay at Courchevel 1850, book early for the four-star **Les Sherpas** (hotel-les-sherpas.com) at the Jardin Alpin, as it's especially good for families due to direct access to beginners' slopes (and great views of the Saulire and Loze summits).

Top Courchevel 1850 village *Bottom* A hut room with a view *Opposite* The dynamic slopes are a magnet for keen skiers

ALTERNATIVE: MÉRIBEL

If a laid-back atmosphere is a priority over ultra-high elegance, go Méribel. The 2500m (8202ft) **Folie Douce** (lafoliedouce.com) bar is sweet madness for still-in-your-ski-boots après, and there's a recent cache of new hotels, including **Le Coucou** (lecoucoumeribel.com) and **Refuge de la Traye** (refugedelatraye.com).

*La grande dame of mountaineering,
there is no mightier name in Europe.*

Chamonix

THE LOWDOWN

Millions of years ago, a gargantuan glacier inched away from Mont Blanc (4808m/15,774ft), carving a deep valley below. The glacier has long gone, but nature's brute force is evident in the soaring valley walls, on top of which lie some of the best off-piste ski areas in the world.

The town of Chamonix is hunkered down in the valley, often in the shadow of the surrounding cliffs and mountains. It's bursting at its high-tech-outerwear seams with adventurous skiers and boarders drawn to test their skills on seriously gnarly terrain. There's also the cobblestone, car-free main streets, the shops for gear fanatics, the Belle Époque architecture, the bubbling Arve River, and the statue of Jacques Balmat pointing excitedly and eternally to the summit he first reached with Dr Michel Gabriel Paccard in 1786.

Chamonix has never lost its pioneering epicentre cache. The world's oldest guiding association – the Compagnie des Guides de Chamonix – began here in 1721. The first Winter Olympics were held here in 1924. And in the 2000s, long-term residents, like former freeski World Extreme Champion Andrea Binning, began ripping on the daily.

Today's elites are drawn not just by the staggering terrain but the easy access to high mountains, year-round town amenities, and the location, just an hour from Geneva airport. But – here's the but – only the top, most experienced riders can access the areas that made Chamonix famous (without a guide). Otherwise, it's a linear valley. The pistes are in small-to-medium ski areas involving a crowded bus schlep and powder pilferers.

Soaking up the vibe of Chamonix and ascending the Aiguille du Midi cable car 3842m (12,605ft) up Mont Blanc (*see* p. 89) are life experiences – but if you're a piste rider, the real magic may lie just out of reach.

Mountain stats
- Elevation top: 3842m (12600ft)
- Elevation bottom: 1042m (3400ft)
- Vertical drop: 2805m (9200ft)
- Skiable terrain: 170km (106mi)
- Beginner terrain: 15 per cent
- Intermediate terrain: 36 per cent
- Advanced: 48 per cent
- Lifts: 67

Run
The 3343m (10,968ft) Men's Downhill World Cup (one of only two in France) Kandahar on the La Verte des Houches.

Experience
The valley's four introductory touring routes offer novices a taste of skinning uphill (chamoniarde.com).

Local's tip
If the arête (ridge) accessing the Vallee Blanche (with 50 degrees to free fall on either side) is making you reconsider, there's easier access via Courmeyer's Skyway Monte Bianco.

Opposite Roping up on the arête for the legendary Mer de Glace

THE MOUNTAIN DEBRIEF

Chamonix can be confusing: it's one town, plus multiple villages. There are four major ski areas (plus additional pocket-size beginner areas) and the Aiguille du Midi cable cars.

Brévent and La Flégère

The only connected resorts in Chamonix (not by ski trails but by a cable car, the Liaison) have staggering Mont Blanc views. Brévent starts from a cable car atop a steep hill in Chamonix, while south-facing La Flégère's base is in the village of Les Praz. Both have groomed runs, powder bowls and small off-piste hikes that yield great runs.

Grands Montets

Rising above the village of Argentière, Grands-Montets is for strong riders. The slopes face north and north-west, so it's often the best place in the valley for powder, especially since its aspect combines with steep, wide, mostly off-piste runs.

Domain de Balme

Stretching above the villages of Vallorcine and Le Tour, the snow-covered mountain pastures of the Balme ski area are best for beginners and intermediates.

Les Houches

At the start of the valley lies family-friendly Les Houches with Mont Blanc and Aravis range views.

Aiguille du Midi

There's also Aiguille du Midi, which isn't a ski area, just two sensational cable cars travelling from 1035m to 3840m (3396ft to 12,600ft) in 20min for the world-famous 20km (12mi) Vallée Blanche off-piste run. The free 'Step into the Void' glass-floored cage suspended over a 1000m (3281ft) drop is an agoraphobia-triggering experience.

A RIDING ITINERARY

The **Col De Passon** has breathtaking views among granite peaks and gigantic glaciers. The route travels from the top station of the Grands Montets to the village of Le Tour with one ascent and two large vertical descents.

The **Brèche Puiseux** route is one of the finest in the Alps, the highlight being the descent right beneath the huge north face of the **Grandes Jorasses** (one of the three great north faces of the Alps). Starting from the **Aiguille di Midi**, it concludes on the **Vallee Blanche**, **Mont Mallet** and **Leschaux** glaciers.

From the top of **Les Grands Montets**, you can launch into the multi-day **Haute Route** connecting the Chamonix Valley and Zermatt (*see* p. 135), running along the highest and most famous peaks as well as over the widest and longest glaciers in the Alps.

ADVENTURE

Riding the **Vallee Blanche** from Aiguille du Midi is a bucket-list descent and the world's longest lift-served vertical descent. There are myriad routes – the classic Voie Normal (available to intermediates), and more technical Le Vrai Vallée Blanche, Petit Envers du Plan and Grand Envers du Plan. It requires full safety equipment (including a harness and crampons); crevasses on the glacier can alter daily and a guide is required.

There's more than one way to head from valley to summit in Chamonix *Opposite top* The mountaintop Aiguille du Midi *Opposite bottom* The spine-tingling Step into the Void is free, included in the price of the Aiguille du Midi cable car ride

OFF-MOUNTAIN MUST-DO

- The **Mer de Glace** (en.chamonix.com) glacier-viewing area has received a multimillion-euro facelift with a Glaciorium, the Interpretation Glacier and Climate Centre, as well as a new gondola to access the glacier's current position (having receded hundreds of metres since the Montenvers train station was built in 1909).

EAT UP & DRINK DOWN

- Have an adventure up to La Tour at tiny on-slope Alpage de Balme for both rösti and views by the Swiss border.
- In town try **La Maison Carrier** (hameaualbert.fr), housed in a rustic farmhouse; *c'est une bonne adresse* for Haute Savoie specialities.

APRÈS SKI

- The only place to be for après in Chamonix is **Chambre Neufe** (hotelgustavia.eu) by the station. Summit-fresh mountaineers, party-loving Scandinavians and Brits dance to No Limits (a Swedish cover band).
- Conveniently, **Elevation 1904** opposite can be equally buzzing, so you can flit between the two.

STAY

- One of the best hotels in the Alps is **Le Hameau Albert 1er** (hameaualbert.fr). In cramped Chamonix, this hotel, spa and two restaurants (one with a Michelin star) is an oasis.
- The **Vert Lodge** (vertlodge.com) by Lake Gaillands has had a makeover and now includes stylish capsule pods.

Top Riders arrive from the Aguillle du Midi and pause before descending the arête to the Mer de Glace *Bottom* A skier removes her skins while ski touring *Opposite* Drinking in the majesty, like a tonic for the eyes

AUSTRIA

Pop music blares through the loudspeaker as a bearded macho mountain man prances onto a table, wiggling his hips and swinging his T-shirt overhead. Slope-side at St Anton's MooserWirt (*see* p. 109), one of the wildest après outposts in Austria – if not the world – the the crowd is going crazy, like Eurovision would if the audience were drinking schnapps shots and tankards of beer. It's an outdoor, joyful mass of humanity in various states of undress, and the revellers barely notice as the mountain man adds spraying champagne to his repertoire of moves.

And there you have Austria in a nutshell. Or a shot glass. A fun fest of people living their best lives, dancing like it's 1999 to a playlist that often *is* 1999. And après is *everywhere*; the country reverberates to the clang of ski boots on cobblestones crossing villages at 8pm. There's only one thing as hectic as Austria's afternoon shenanigans: the skiing and boarding.

This is one holiday you might return from needing an actual holiday. Austria is bulging with world-class ski areas. There are cute-as-a-button villages, glaciers galore, pistes for every standard and ski days filled in part by kaiserschmarrn (a deliciously sweet compote pancake). The country is similar in many ways to neighbouring Switzerland, even sharing some peaks and mountain ranges, but it costs less, so you can do more, from sleigh rides in the tongue-twisting Saalbach Hinterglemm Leogang Fieberbrunn ski area (*see* p. 111) to the 11 indoor and outdoor pools at Tauen Spa at Zell am See-Kaprun (*see* p. 115).

There are so many outstanding snow options as riding here is a national sport and they throw everything at it. If the elevation is low, they'll build a matrix of snow guns; if it's high, they'll add chairlifts with weatherproof bubbles and seat warmers (if not a gondola). If there's a series of villages, they'll link them and create an uber ski area like the Arlberg (*see* p. 107), offering the largest interconnected area in Europe.

But on the flip side of all the après madness and efficient infrastructure is the softer side of Austria: old-school hospitality and gemütlich (cosiness or warmth). Most ski hotels were once farmhouses (such as the historic, luxurious Hotel Post Lech, *see* p. 109). They are family-run, often by clans wearing dirndls in a non-ironic manner. These folk take you in as their own; they have long histories of sheltering travellers crossing mountain passes. After a savage slope day in Lech, being tucked under a rug by a roaring fire with a deep glass of Blauburgunder (pinot noir), one can only feel satisfied.

Skiing hard, playing hard, and pausing in an elegant hot outdoor pool after it all – that's Austria.

Coolest winter selfie
When the Aqua Dome debuted in Tirol, it blew up Instagram. Technically it isn't ski-related (although it's an excellent leg recovery), but this thermal-pool complex has an architectural and alpine setting that has to be seen to be believed.

The top of the Valluga (*see* p. 108) in the Arlberg has 360-degree views over multiple countries and a shot from the balcony of the MooserWirt (*see* p. 109) overlooking the people-pit is a must.

Get appy
iSKI Austria - Ski and Snow, with Austrian ski resort rundowns and a ski and GPS tracker for run activity.

The ÖBB app will help you plan the cheapest trip from airport to ski area, and the Ortovox Alpine Touring App is designed to be used in the German, Austrian and South Tyrolean Alps for anyone thinking about venturing off-piste, with a topographical map of the mountains and marked freeride routes. Unbelievably, there's no dedicated Austrian après ski app - I smell opportunity.

Don't break the bank
Austria is sandwiched between Switzerland and Italy, both geographically and in price point. The biggest saver is to book half-board at hotels. Meals are usually three-course affairs of homemade schnitzel and kilo-adding dessert treats.

In a country as well connected as Austria, eschew private transfers for public transport between airport and slope. And a €6 lunchtime gulaschsuppe (goulash) will keep you going until lifts close.

When it snows
The Austrian climate can be quite temperamental, with the valleys and peaks causing an internal matrix of climate zones. But as with much of Europe, the snow bringer is the Genoa Low, a low-pressure system that develops south of the Alps drawing in water from the Gulf of Genoa, Ligurian Sea, Po Valley, Gulf of Venice and northern Adriatic Sea. It then heads north, hits the Alps and fire hoses the contents out like, yes, an overenthusiastic après drinker. In a good way.

Often called the 'cradle of skiing', St. Anton has four Arlberg siblings tempting you to play the field.

St. Anton am Arlberg

THE LOWDOWN

The facts: St. Anton is part of Ski Arlberg, the fifth largest interconnected resort in the world. It's blessed with one of the best snow records in Europe, 305km (190mi) of runs, 200km (124mi) of freeride terrain, a seamless lift system with 88 lifts and cable cars, and a huge range of accommodation. This is where modern skiing began; resident Hanne Schneider's ski techniques remain the blueprint for ski schools globally. Oh, and it has the wildest après on the planet. Settle down already, St. Anton, you chronic over-achiever.

Combined with its siblings St. Christoph am Arlberg, Stuben, Lech and Zürs, as well as the attached Warth-Schrocken ski area, it's part of an entourage you can't ignore – a line-up of top-shelf Austrian shots. So do what foreigners have always done when faced with impeccable Austrian hospitality – surrender and accept the schnapps.

All the Arlberg areas are unique. St. Christoph is a white-skirted debutante; riding her groomed pistes is like a smooth Viennese waltz. Tiny Stuben is a snow globe of a village, with traditional buildings sporting high-brimmed, white-trimmed bonnets. Discrete Lech and Zürs seem restrained, but they are total bombshells when it comes to world-class skiing.

And sporty St. Anton (nicknamed 'St Man-ton' due to it being a popular destination for 'boy's trips') is the high-octane Las Vegas of the siblings, with the most challenging runs, epic off-piste a stone's throw from groomed slopes, and legendary bars.

While Austria exported ski culture to the world, no place on the planet has captured the atmosphere of St. Anton.

Mountain stats
- Elevation top: 2811m (9222ft)
- Elevation bottom: 1304m (4278ft)
- Vertical Drop: 1507m (4944ft)
- Skiable terrain: 305km (190mi)
- Longest run: 9km (5.6mi)
- Beginner terrain: 34 per cent
- Intermediate terrain: 42 per cent
- Advanced terrain: 24 per cent
- Lifts: 88

Run
On a powder day, take Skiroute 51 from Galzig down black Osthang through the trees. For intermediates, Piste 85 from Schindler down to Ulmerhütte is Insta-worthy scenic.

Experience
Squeeze the most out of the Arlberg with guide, instructor and former professional freestyler Geli Häusl who knows the secret spots (geliskiing.com).

Local's tip
Purchase the Arlberg Safety Card at a Ski Arlberg ticket office. The €15 insurance (for up to eight days) covers recovery costs after a ski accident - which includes helicopter.

Previous A rooster tail of powder in the Arlberg *Opposite* Out of the Arlberg ski areas, St. Anton is the cool, sporty sibling

THE MOUNTAIN DEBRIEF

The best thing about St. Anton (with many to choose from) is the 200km (124mi) of marked powder runs; orange-diamond signs on groomed runs indicate areas that are not maintained but are safety controlled. So, you can venture 30m (100ft) to the right or left of a diamond sign, follow the markers and have an easily accessed off-piste experience, inbounds.

While St. Anton has a variety of runs for every level of skier, the steeps, cliffs, bowls and couloirs have made it famous. If you have the right equipment and a guide, the possibilities are endless.

The more challenging terrain is in the huge bowls off the Valluga and Schindlergrat mountains. Strong intermediate skiers will enjoy the terrain in the Rendle area and at St. Christoph. Less confident intermediates may be daunted by many of St Anton's blue runs, which morph into moguls. Aim for the friendly, cruisy runs in the Galzig area.

A RIDING ITINERARY

Always follow the sun east to west. In the morning, take **Piste 44 Gstans** from Kapall down to **Gampen** for early rays. Then over to **Zammermoosbahn** and up **Galzig** with a pit stop at the **Patriolbar** (arlbergerbergbahnen.com) for the best coffee on the mountain.

Have a play here, then ski down to **St. Christoph**, stopping at the **Hospitz Alm** (arlberghospiz.at) for a Tyrolean-style lunch (visit the incredible underground wine cellar). Then up **Schindlergratbahn** and down to **Rauz**. If time allows, take the lift up to **Albona** in Stuben and return to St Anton.

ADVENTURE

If the digital ski race at the **Hall of Fame** (*see* p. 109) whets your appetite, sashay around the **Run of Fame** (skiralberg.at), an 85km (53mi) circuit with an 18,000m (59,000ft) altitude difference tracing the big-star ski tracks from St. Anton/Rendle to Zürs, Lech, Warth and back again.

OFF-MOUNTAIN MUST-DO

- For ski (and history) lovers, the interactive **Hall of Fame** (skiarlberg.at) is an extraordinarily curated area devoted to Arlberg ski history, heroic pioneers and glamorous celebrities.
- Stretch out in **Arlberg WellCom** (arlberg-wellcom.at) with pool, sauna and massages.

EAT UP & DRINK DOWN

- If there's one place to eat in all of Arlberg, it's at **Museum Restaurant-Cafe** (museum-restaurant.at), in the mansion home of a former German industrialist. Head upstairs for ski history and downstairs for lamb that falls from the bone (don't miss their kaiserschmarrn pancakes).
- At Lech, even if you're not staying at the eclectic boutique hotel **Kristiania** (skisolutions.com), dine at their restaurant for creative cuisine and arty surroundings.
- In Stuben, **Mondschein** (mondschein.com) serves village-specific schlutzkrapfen (ravioli with burnt butter) that won't be found even in St. Anton.

APRÈS SKI

- The party atmosphere in St. Anton is phenomenal. Note: park your skis somewhere memorable among the hundreds of similar-looking skis - you'll need them to get home.
- Après ski starts on the bar crawl along Piste 1, beginning at relatively tame **Heustadl** (heustadl.com) and culminating at the full-tilt schlager music fest, the **MooserWirt** (mooserwirt.at).

STAY

- The **MOOSER** Hotel (mooserhotel.at), with a secret door directly into the MooserWirt, is so incredible it requires capitals. It's the definition of ski-in, ski-out with only 17 guest rooms, a pool and après-to-bed efficiency.
- Tucked in quaint St. Christoph on the site of a medieval refuge, **1800 Hospiz Arlberg Hotel** (arlberghospiz.at) is half historic, half cutting-edge contemporary.
- The Eggler family-run **Alberghaus** (haus-stanton.at) has a bullseye location by the cable car in Zürs.
- Lech's family-owned **Hotel Post Lech** (postlech.com) is a former farmhouse turned exceptional luxury hotel with next-level personalised service and a glorious 15m (50ft) outdoor heated pool.

ALTERNATIVE: KITZBÜHEL

For pure historical cache, Kitzbühel is a winner. As home of the World Cup Hahnenkamm, its twists, banking turns, flats and jumps make it one of the gnarliest on the World Cup circuit. Apart from a vast ski area (although with low altitude), it's a vibrant and busy town - morphing into a monster party when 70,000 descend for the Hahnenkamm. Its centre is blessed with ancient architecture, car-free, cobblestone streets and restaurants and bars galore.

Mountain hut lunches are an Austrian highlight
Opposite It's easy to get a little existential beholding the beauty of such a behemoth

One of the partying capitals of the Alps, you'll find the steeps are as hard as the shots, and the slopes – like a 1am dance floor – are all about endless choice.

Saalbach

THE LOWDOWN

Saalbach, the OG, already had a posse when it took on a new gang member in 2016, when it was linked to Fieberbrunn in Tyrol via a gondola to make Skicircus Saalbach Hinterglemm Leogang Fieberbrunn (say that ten times after a Jäger), a giant circuit.

It's the addition of Fieberbrunn, a mixed family and cult freeride resort, that's catapulted this area off the reserve bench and into the major players – it's a stop on the Freeride World Tour. Polyamorous Saalbach Hinterglemm Leogang Fieberbrunn has also been linked to Zell am See-Kaprun (*see* p. 115) via the ZellamseeXpress bubble since 2020.

Saalbach is a great base option – it's at the heart of the Skicircus with designer shopping, a pedestrian main street and traditional buildings. And if you're into après, you've come to the right place. The Austrians know how to party even if it's 2pm in the afternoon – if you're going to wake up with a hangover somewhere, it may as well be here.

Mountain stats
- Elevation top: 2100m (6890ft)
- Elevation bottom: 795m (2608ft)
- Vertical drop: 1097m (3599ft)
- Skiable terrain: 270km (168mi)
- Longest run: 8km (5 miles)
- Beginner terrain: 50 per cent
- Intermediate terrain: 42 per cent
- Advanced: 8 per cent

Run
The appropriately named run The Challenge ranks among the Alp's top ski routes in stats: 65km (40mi), 32 lifts, and 12,400m (40,680ft) of altitude difference. It takes around seven hours, schnitzel stops not included.

Experience
Kaiserschmarrn! There are over 60 mountain huts in the Skicircus and most will have a variation of this dish - shredded pancake with apple sauce or stewed plums, with or without raisins. Spend a week finding your favourite (a tip - try the one at the Westgipfelhütte; westgipfelhuette.com).

Local's tip
Try the local Bartl Enn schnapps, distilled in Hinterglemm and widely regarded as some of the best schnapps in Europe.

Opposite When a north-north-west storm blows in, Fieberbrunn is one of the snowiest spots in Austria

THE MOUNTAIN DEBRIEF

For enormous daily mileage, this area ticks all the boxes. In Saalbach, head around the Hochalm peak for carving; if seeking sunset vistas, the Kohlmais area delivers; and for a challenge, there are the black pistes on the Zwölferkogel peak's north face (site of the FIS World Ski Championship 2025) or the Schattberg peak's north descent.

The ski circuits' blues and reds are a darker hue than other resorts, with true blacks like the Nordabfahrt from the top of the 2020 Schattberg Ost dropping back into Saalbach with 1000 vertical metres.

Saalbach Hinterglemm Leogang (as it was) wasn't a hardcore off-piste destination until Fieberbrunn came to the party throwing shakas. It doesn't look like much on the map – 35km (22mi) of runs – but it boasts a labyrinth of ski routes, tree runs, couloirs and powdery meadows and is one of the snowiest spots in Austria.

The one issue is a lack of altitude, as the slopes are mainly under 2000m. In spring, start on south-facing slopes in the morning and, after midday, switch to the north. This is also when Leogang, in the next valley north, comes into its own – these runs are north-facing, so they hold their snow well, and are much quieter than the main circuit.

A RIDING ITINERARY

'Easy up, wild down' is the motto of the Skicircus, and you'll find the area's a well-connected machine. Back off on après for a day to catch the 8.30am early-bird gondola – **Hintergemm's Zwölferkogelbahn** takes you straight up to 1984m (6510ft). From the Zwölfer summit, pause for the stellar views across the **Glemmtal valley** before taking some turns down to the **Westgipfelbahn**. If you're feeling chipper, try the **World Cup route**. Then head up the Westgipfelbahn to the second greatest view of the day (cue: photo stop) and cruise down the blue valley route to **Vorderglemm**.

After such a vista-laden start, you can buzz your way up the **Schönleitenbahn** for a hot chocolate at the **Wildenkarhütte**, with more 360-degree Alp views. Use **Slope 66** to return to Saalbach with another wide valley view in time for 2pm après.

If heading into the other ski areas, launch your day from Saalbach, taking the **Schattberg X-Press** up the mountain. If you're planning on the **Skicircus Challenge**, study the piste map closely for the entire route with its 65 slope kilometres.

ADVENTURE

There are vast freeride routes catering to all levels of difficulty. Grab a guide to explore them, or join a Freeride Camp from Freeride School Saalbach. For anything backcountry, the **UIAGM** guides have unmatchable local knowledge (mountainguides-saalbach.at).

Fine lines for fine days *Opposite* The Challenge, a 65km circuit, is a skier's must-do in the Alps

OFF-MOUNTAIN MUST-DO

- It's hard to carve out time between the riding and the après-ing, but try the 3.2km (2mi) toboggan track at the **Reiterkogel** (accessed via the D1 Reiterkogel lift in Hinterglemm), particularly for their night sessions down to the twinkling village lights.

EAT UP & DRINK DOWN

- Within the Skicircus, try **Wildalpgatterl** (wildalpgatterl.at) in Fieberbrunn for Austrian fare.
- Ride the super-fun Amsel piste to the **Spielberghaus** (spielberghaus.at/en) for the best deer burger in town.

APRÈS SKI

- There are over 30 bars, many on the slopes, just in Saalbach. Start at **Hinterhag Alm** (hinterhag-alm. at) atop the Turmlift T-bar for tabletop dancing and a live band (it's full by 4.30pm) - remember it's still a few hundred metres of riding back to base, straight into the arms of the **Bauer's Ski Alm** (bauers-schialm.at), open until 3am.

STAY

- Just above Saalbach is the ski-in, ski-out, glass-and-reclaimed-wood **Art & Ski-in Hotel Hinterhag** (hotel-hinterhag.at). Inside are paintings and sculptures by owner Evi Fersterer and other international artists.
- **Hotel Saalbacher Hof** (saalbacherhof.at) is located right in the heart of Saalbach, just a 2min walk from three main lifts (with nightclub Castello cocooned below, you won't even hear a bass beat).

ALTERNATIVE: ZELL AM SEE-KAPRUN

Since the ZellamseeXpress bubble lift opened in winter 2019/20 (the last season before Covid times), it's a no-brainer to access Zell am See-Kaprun. It just involves a 5min bus ride at the bottom. On a down day, explore Zell am See itself, a picture-perfect medieval town nestled between Zell Lake and the Schmittenhöhe mountain.

Top Try specialities like kaiserschmarrn *Bottom* Old traditions lovingly linger in Austria *Opposite* The bright lights of Hinterglemm

SNOW PRO
Hedvig Wessel the freeskier

Technique en pointe, head game dialled, watch Hedvig Wessel on a Freeride World Tour line or in a Warren Miller movie and she'll be smoking towards a huge cliff and hucking a gigantic backflip. This Oslo native has been pushing the freestyle side of freeskiing to a new level with a deep bag of skills. There's the discipline and technique of being a two-time Olympic mogul skier, years of aerials training, and a healthy drop of Scandinavian Crazy.

After years of World Cup competing, Wessel transitioned to freeride skiing and won the Scandinavian Big Mountain Competition four times. When not showing the others how's it's done and hitting spines for breakfast, this fierce competitor can be found climbing, surfing and filming.

How did you begin your moguls career?

My background was in alpine racing, gymnastics and cross-country skiing. I was introduced to moguls when I was 11 and Kari Traa (Norwegian Olympic mogul champion) invited girls from all over Norway to camps, and luckily I became part of it. We were 20 to 30 girls who travelled around Norway, and started competing. Kari Traa's goal was to get someone to the Olympics, and that was me.

What made you decide to switch to competing on the Freeride World Tour?

After 2014, my first Olympics, I remember my coach telling me if you want to become a better moguls skier, you should actually ski more. And he made me try this freeride competition. I had no idea what I was doing at all – I borrowed some fat skis and I loved the vibe, it was so much fun. I won a few Scandinavian Big Mountain Championships and thought, wow, this is really fun. And maybe I could be pretty good at this. Right after the Olympics in 2018, I got a wild card to Verbier Xtreme and got invited to ski the whole Tour the next year.

Does your technical background give you an edge?

Being a mogul skier you get really good balance and good air control. So mogul skiers come in with a lot of skills. I think growing up in Scandinavia and always skiing on really hard pack snow is an advantage. I didn't really start skiing powder until just a few years ago and being used to landing on hardpack means I haven't been afraid of crusty conditions.

Which is your favourite Freeride World Cup stop?

Fieberbrunn in Austria is for sure my best memory with my first Freeride World Tour medal in 2019. It was my first year on the Tour and I felt I really pushed myself and I skied the best I could. And that was just an amazing memory and such a beautiful day. So Fieberbrunn definitely has a special place in my heart.

What do you love about riding in Europe?

I love skiing in Europe because it's so accessible, I love the big mountains that are right there in the resort, it's more exciting and fun maybe than other parts of the world. This year I've been skiing quite a bit in Whistler and Revy (Revelstoke) and Japan as well and there's more powder. But I do really love Europe and the European vibe.

Where's your home mountain?

Engelberg is my home mountain. I love Engelberg so much, there's so many amazing runs just right from the gondola or from the lifts. A lot of Swedish freeride skiers do their winter season in Engelberg and the community is amazing. It's a small town and that's why I also love it because it's not that busy and it's not that hectic compared to Verbier or Chamonix, where it's so crowded. Here you can actually get pretty good skiing the whole day or even multiple days without it being such a push. It's a low-key vibe and everyone is friends and there's a really chill open environment.

Do you prefer competing or filming?

I love competing, and I love filming! I've been competing for eight years in the World Cup in moguls and straight into four years on the Freeride World Tour so it's been a lot of years competing. So for now I'll focus on filming. And I'm really excited to have a different focus and see if I can make something really special when I don't have the competition stress.

Any advice for those wanting to get into professional skiing?

Ski a lot and ski everyday, ski in bad conditions, ski in good conditions, and go out and ski with your friends. And hopefully try to find someone who's better than you so you can sweat a little bit and learn from others. Try to have fun out there and know why you're doing it and if it's because you love it don't stop.

What do mountains bring to your life?

Honestly, I love just being out in nature. And some of the best days of my life have been on the mountains in the sunrise or a sunset, it's just such a beautiful atmosphere. And feeling small; the mountains are so huge and we're so lucky to be there you know, it's just a very powerful place. And I love that feeling.

ITALY

Ahh, bella Italia! This is the ski-topia of la dolce vita (the good life) with startling scenery, heartfelt hospitality and over 400 gourmet mountain huts housing restaurants in the Dolomites, meaning you're never far from one, and local variations mean it's rare to eat the same dish twice. I doubt anyone has ever starved in an Italian ski area; the fare costs less and tastes better than in most other countries. Italy's north-western border is studded with some of Europe's most famous ski resorts, and with over a dozen peaks exceeding 3000m (9843ft), snow is as sweet as a hot, whipped-cream-topped bombardino (eggnog) at après ski. The maraschino cherry on top is that Italy has the best value in the Alps.

There's the sky-piercing peaks of Val d'Aosta, where Zermatt (see p. 135) and Breuil Cervinia straddle the Swiss-Italian border, and medieval town Courmeyer shares Mont Blanc (ahem, Monte Bianco, per favore) with Chamonix (see p. 99). But don't click off skis just yet – there's another Italian riding area that's out of this world, and this is (drum roll) the Dolomites. For scenery that makes you feel like you're skiing on a James Bond film set, this is it (and a film set it was, *For Your Eyes Only*). Even among the world's most jaw-dropping ski scenery – looking at you, St. Anton (see p. 107) – there is nothing as unique as the dramatic Dolomites. Formed by a giant prehistoric coral reef 200 million years ago, the mountains are streaked in a myriad of hues that earned a UNESCO World Heritage listing in 2009.

The Dolomites boast the largest ski area in the world, with over 1200km (746mi) of ski trails and runs that can each take several hours, starting at mountain summits and taking you to a galaxy of towns. The helpful Italians have put them under one pass, the Dolomiti Superski (see p. 128).

The ski circuit you must do at least once in your life is the 25km (15.5mi) Sellaronda (see p. 127), which can each be completed in a day without removing your skis. Running over the four Dolomite passes around the Sella massif, the circuit passes through the Ladin valleys of Val Gardena (see p. 131), Alta Badia (see p. 127), Arabba and Fassa (see p. 128). Just remember the lifts shut at 5pm and après ski socialising waits for no one.

For the ideal base, there's the screen siren of the Dolomites, Cortina d'Ampezzo (see p. 125), home to the Milano Cortina 2006 Olympics, riveting jet set fashion, and where half the stellar slopes are intermediate, pairing well with the Italian flair for relaxation. Alternatively, there's Val Gardena with three authentic Alpine villages; say 'si' (yes) to the local grappas made from forest-fresh hay or pine cones. Alta Badia is a gastronomic haven with over 40 mountain huts and Ladin culture, while Madonna di Campiglio (see p. 121) is a nature-bound beauty.

Whether seeking glitz and glamour, quiet serenity, endless riding or the perfect family outpost, there are fantastic spots in this corner of the globe – the only problem is choice.

Coolest winter selfie

This culture has fully embraced the selfie, down to reapplying lipstick mid-slope. Whatever. But it's the background that counts: keep those cathedral-like mountains in focus, especially for enrosadira, the pink-blazing glow of the rocks at sunset. For more incredible light, get in the frame on a dawn or sunset ski run in Madonna di Campiglio (see p. 121) and on Val Gardena's First Tracks up the Seceda lift (see p. 131) for when the first sunny rays dive into the Sassolungo.

Get appy

The Dolomiti Superski app (see p. 128) will help you sort through the Dolomiti Superski Pass area of 12 ski resorts with real-time information and resort rundowns.

The Meteo Trentino app is excellent for localised weather, as is ARPA - its meteorological office is based in Arabba, mid-Dolomites. If there are fronts moving around, these forecasts will keep you in the know.

Don't break the bank

No strategy or tips are needed here - precious euros stretch a lot further in Italy than at other ski destinations; everything is cheaper, from an espresso to a mountain-hut lunch, as well as lift passes and equipment rentals. Rather than looking for ways to save money, the advice is to spend it. Have the dessert, the ski lesson, the one-more-star hotel. It'll never be better, for cheaper.

When it snows

Thanks to their location on the southern side of the Alps, Italian resorts are also less affected by the warming effect of the Gulfstream. They benefit from lower humidity and better snow preservation than many resorts at the same altitude in the north-western Alps.

The Dolomites are not especially high and have an erratic snow record. Still, few places do artificial snow better than here - perfectly illustrated a few years back during a run of particularly snowless Decembers, which prevented many resorts across the Alps from opening early. In Madonna di Campiglio and Alta Badia, it was business as usual.

This world-class resort surrounded by UNESCO wilderness combines traditional Italian flair with value for the ultimate skiing 'la dolce vita'.

Madonna di Campiglio

THE LOWDOWN

View, views and more views. Madonna di Campiglio occupies a rare alpine position on the border of the Alps, nestled at the feet of the Dolomite's Brenta group in the UNESCO Adamello Brenta Nature Park, with sharp, young mountains on one side and the rock walls of the Dolomites on the other. The subsequent variety of larch, pine and wildlife makes this an adventure nella natura (in nature) as much as on the slopes.

And there's more than a twinkle of glamour in the quaint pedestrian main street that's retained its Italian heritage flavour with elegant buildings dating back to the 19th century. During the heyday of the Habsburgs, the village was a brief summer extension of the Viennese court of Emperor Franz Josef and famed Empress Sissi.

Here, all runs flow back down to the village, the lifts are high speed, the snow-making is high-tech (for lower slopes), and the views of the Brenta Massif and the Adamello glacier offer high-impact visuals unlike anywhere else. And all this world-class goodness can be accessed for more palatable prices than many other alpine areas, certainly when compared with those of similar calibre in Switzerland or Austria.

Mountain stats
- Elevation top: 2504m (8215ft)
- Elevation bottom: 770m (2526ft)
- Vertical drop: 1248m (4094ft)
- Skiable terrain: 154km (96 miles)
- Longest run: 5.8km (3.6 miles)
- Beginner terrain: 33 per cent
- Intermediate terrain: 45 per cent
- Advanced terrain: 22 per cent
- Lifts: 59

Run
Canalone Miramonti is one of the most famous pistes in the Dolomites, home to the 3Tre slope of the World Cup Night Slalom every December, a flood-lit event for alpine racers, attended by thousands and watched by millions.

Experience
Four times a season, you can gondola to a mountain rifugio (hut) for a Dawn Ski at 6.15am with a sunrise breakfast and descent with an instructor as the mountains turn pink. Too early? Instead, lay carves with the fiery spectacle of the Brenta Dolomites during a Sunset Ski, with torch in hand (capigliodolomiti.it).

Local's tip
It would be a crime to ski here without trying a Bombardino, a hot cocktail of milk, whiskey, and zabaglione (an egg-based custard). And enjoy the nightly passeggiata, that wonderful Italian pastime of strolling nowhere in particular.

Previous Cross-country skiing watched by spectacular spires in Alta Badia *Opposite* The geological masterpiece of Madonna di Campiglio

THE MOUNTAIN DEBRIEF

There are three areas; Madonna di Campiglio, Folgàrida-Marilleva and Pinzolo. With 150km (93mi) of well-groomed slopes, beginner and intermediate skiers thrive here with long blue runs on perfect confidence-boosting corduroy stretching from northern Folgàrida to Pinzolo to the south. Even though there are fewer black runs (19 pistes) for expert skiers, don't yawn just yet. Head to the blacks on the 5 Laghi area and Spinale.

A huge drawcard is the Ursus Snow Park (ursus means 'bear', an animal that's still endemic to the area) on the Passo Grosté, one of the best freestyle areas in the Alps. There are three other parks, with the instantly identifiable Dolomites backdrop making them photographer favourites.

A RIDING ITINERARY

Start in the **Pradalago/5 Laghi**; the south-east-facing slopes are mostly tree-lined and sun-drenched with beautiful village vistas towards the Brenta range. The pistes stream effortlessly down the 600m (1968ft) vertical back to town (boarders keep speed, there are some long traverses in the lower sections).

Begin with the scenic **Pradalago Facile** (Trail 50), a 3.7km (2.3mi) run starting with Brenta views that travels across a forest before reaching the bottom. Or if you've had an espresso perk at **Rifugio Viviani** (rifugioviviani.it), head straight for the 1.6km (1-mi) **Amazzonia** with a 67 per cent incline (one of the first slopes scoring morning sunshine).

After playing here and at **Cinque Lagi**, take the **Pinzolo–Campiglio express** (with staggering Brenta-cliffs views, like being in an 11min IMAX movie) to **Pinzolo**, home to the valley's most glorious Presanella and Adamello glacier views (the Tulot ski slope is a must).

After a Pinzolo spin, switch sides and head up **Spinal**e to lash out on a meal at **Chalet Spinale** (chaletfiat.net); tip – continue past the self-service restaurant into the à la carte restaurant with dramatic views.

In the afternoon, head to the higher **Grostè** area, a north-facing snow hole that's *the* place to hit in spring, to play in the park, or swoop the blacks at **Spinale** – it's best to split this itinerary into two days.

ADVENTURE

There is epic ski mountaineering to be had, especially in **Val Rendena** bordered by the rocky spires of the Brenta Dolomites to the east and the peaks of the Adamello-Presanella group to the west. Popular routes (with a mountain guide) include Cima Serodoli, Cima Ritorto and Cima Roma.

The rockstar runs are wide and smooth *Opposite* Ursus Snowpark

OFF MOUNTAIN MUST-DO

- The top activity is the 3km (1.9-mile) toboggan run (one of Europe's longest) starting at 2070m (6791ft) at Spinale.
- On a full moon, go snowshoeing in the **Adamello Brenta Nature Park** (campigliodolomiti.it) with a mountain guide, with optional wi-fi headphones to listen to moon-oriented music and poems in between forest silence.

EAT UP & DRINK DOWN

- Taking a snowcat to a traditional dinner at **Rifugio Boch** is a highlight.
- Michelin-starred **Gallo Cedrone** (ilgallocedrone.it) in the atmospheric cellar of Hotel Bertelli has creative cuisine prepared by talented chef Davide Sabino Fortunato.

APRÈS SKI

- On slope, stop for a Bombardino at **LAB Après-Ski**.
- In town, **Shane at Bar Maturi** (shaneatbarmaturi.it) in Piazza Sissi is the first choice.
- Continue to a sophisticated *aperitivo* in **Bar Suisse** (cantinadelsuisse.com), the oldest bar in Madonna di Campilgio dating back to the 19th century.

STAY

- Relative newcomer five-star **Lefay Resort & Spa Dolomiti** (dolomiti.lefayresorts.com) in the satellite eyrie of Pinzolo boasts seven saunas.
- The **Hotel Spinale Campiglio** (hotelspinalecampiglio.com) tucked next to the Spinale Chairlift, a short walk from the town centre, is dripping in elegant glamour from lake views to rustic mountain touches.
- Or soak up nature in **Chalet Fogajard** (chaletfogajard.it), winter access is by chalet pick up.

ALTERNATIVE: CORTINA D'AMPEZZO

The craggy charisma of the Dolomites is at its most in-your-face stunning here, and unlike the Austro-Germanic influences in Trentino and Süd-Tirol, is undiluted, especially on weekends with Venetian and Milanese weekend home-owners descending to shop. And maybe ski.

Top Partake in the aprés ski passeggiata, or stroll *Bottom* Getting out in nature is a huge drawcard of Madonna di Campiglio *Opposite* In between pauses for scenery appreciation, find your torque

Ancient Ladin culture, Michelin-starred mountain huts, sommeliers on skis and the Sellaronda ski route are the ingredients that super-boost this flavoursome Dolomite dish.

Alta Badia

THE LOWDOWN

Food lovers unite! Just reminiscing about Alta Badia makes me hungry for more – more of the distinctive Dolomite cliff bands burning gold and rose in the afternoon light, more mountain-hut meals, more endless skiing on Sellaronda carousel routes, and more languages: Italian, German and Dolomites-only Ladin.

The ancient Ladin culture is unique to these mountains, and dates back thousands of years with its own language and traditions. Alta Badia has the distinction of being a Ladin Valley (along with Val Gardena, Val Badia, Val di Fassa, Livinallongo and Cortina d'Ampezzo) and its location, in the kernel of the South Tyrolean Dolomites, denotes it as an epicentre of heritage.

If getting from A to B via valleys, cols, villages and even dialects makes you wag an invisible tail, you'll love that Alta Badia's 130km (80mi) of skiing is merely an entrée to the Sellaronda ski circuit where there's a whopping 500km (310mi) of pistes. Wag away.

Finally, Alta Badia's slopes access a handful of towns, from the hamlet of San Cassiano to the largest, lively Corvara.

 Mountain stats
- Elevation top: 2778m (9114ft)
- Elevation bottom: 1300m (4265ft)
- Vertical drop: 1226 m (4022ft)
- Skiable terrain: 139km (86mi)
- Longest run: 6km (3.7mi)
- Beginner terrain: 53 per cent
- Intermediate terrain: 33 per cent
- Advanced terrain: 10 per cent
- Lifts: 53

 Run
Feeling plucky? Try the Gran Risa slope, where top international athletes straight line during Ski World Cup races the weekend before Christmas.

 Experience
This area is known for Skifaris (village-to-village skiing), but how about a Wine Skifari with accompanying instructor and sommelier, stopping at seven mountain huts (altabadia.com)?

 Local's tip
On a powder day, hire a mountain guide for the descent from Val Mezdì, an off-piste Dolomite classic.

Opposite The ski areas seem like a stage set starring the rugged peaks of the Dolomites

THE MOUNTAIN DEBRIEF

With a position on the sunny side of the Alps where South Tyrol meets Italy, Alta Badia has some of the best skiing in the Dolomites, partly due to access. To the east is the mainly intermediate Alta Badia ski area. To the west is the Val Gardena area, which has some of the area's more advanced ski runs, and to the south is Arabba – another area for more advanced skiers.

Direct links within the Dolomiti Superski ski carousel afford you unimpeded access to 500km (310mi) of pistes where you can ski to your heart's content.

A RIDING ITINERARY

Buckle up for one of the ski journeys of a lifetime, the **Sellaronda**, a 40km (25-mi) ski tour circling the huge limestone formation of the Sella massif, dipping in and out of several different resorts with skis and board permanently attached.

Warm up on the **Col Alto** slope, site of Italy's first chairlift in 1946, and ride onto the **Boé** to start the Sellaronda, heading off clockwise to maximise the sun. Pause for a coffee at the **Piz Boé Alpine Lounge** (boealpinelounge.it) for après mission preparation. Continue onto **Arabba**, down to **Val di Fassa** (a quiet fairy-tale locale), through the **Val Gardena** and you should reach **Jimmi Hütte** (jimmyhuette.com) at the Passo Gardena for lunch.

This is a strategic stop as you'll be enjoying the work of Michelin-starred chef Ciccio Sultano (from Sicily's two-star Duomo Restaurant fame), and odds are lunch will be long. All that remains is skiing down the final run from the Passo Gardena to **Colfosco** to complete the Sellaronda.

Beginners can purchase the local Skipass Alta Badia to explore the valley with an instructor and not miss a second of dazzling scenery.

ADVENTURE

The **Skitour Lagazuoi** (First World War Tour) is longer than the Sellaronda, including a 7.8km (4.8mi) run with horses at the bottom to pull skiers to the next lift. World War I remnants, including barbed wire, trenches, parapet walks and forts, are reminders of the heavy fighting and loss of life that took place here.

Corvara is one of Alta Badia's villages, nestled at the foot of the imposing Sassongher mountain

Alta Badia, Italy   129

OFF-MOUNTAIN MUST-DO

- Dive head-first into the local culture with **Nos Ladins** (email: info@altabadia.org). Fascinating locals take you into their world to reveal secrets from schüttelbrot (bread-making) to perfect ski-waxing - participants include a young baker, ski-making expert, local gamekeeper, sommelier, snow-groomer, goat farmer, young weaver, and a mountain guide.

EAT UP & DRINK DOWN

- No one is ever going hungry here. **Club Moritzino** (moritziano.it), **Ütia de Bioch** (bioch.it), with a spectacular terrace, and **Ütia La Crusc** (lacrusc.com), one of the oldest mountain huts in the Dolomites and situated near a magnificent rock mountain wall, are standouts among the dozens of superb mountain huts.
- If you're in Corvara the one-Michelin-star **La Stüa de Michil** (in La Perla hotel) is a destination in itself, or dine at gourmet **Cocun**, which has a cheese-and-chocolate room.
- Our pick is **Maso Runch**, a traditional Ladin restaurant in a working farmhouse with hearty valley specialties, including woodstove-cooked shank.

APRÈS SKI

- You'll hear it before you see it - the 2000m (6562ft) **Club Moitzino** (moritzino.it) après ski with a daily DJ from 2pm to ski-lift close.
- Keep those ski boots dancing down in Corvara's **L'Murin** (altabadia.org) from 4pm to 9pm.
- If you're focused more on quality drinking than dancing, perch at **Iceberg** (colalto.it) cocktail bar in Corvara's centre.

STAY

- The **Movi Family Apart-Hotel** (movifamily.it) is a parent's dream as the valley's first family-focused apartment hotel, with two-storey Acqua Fun World (complete with waterslides), an airport-hangar-sized playroom, and full fridges upon request.
- Conversely, soak in silence surrounded by steam tendrils in the rooftop pool at boutique **Badia Hill** (badiahill.com) with spectacular Santa Croce mountain views.
- Corvara's quaint **La Perla** (aperlacorvara.it) is an absolute gem with an in-house spa.

ALTERNATIVE: VAL GARDENA

South Tyrolean Val Gardena valley also sits within the legendary Sellaronda. The three villages of cosy pedestrian Ortisei, lively Santa Cristina and Selva Val Gardena, the largest, create a vast snow bowl. The area is historically fascinating with the combination of cultures, from Ladin to Austrian to Italian. Riding the Seceda sector is particularly special with dazzling views of Mount Sassolungo, the characteristic rifugios (huts) with valley-specific cuisine and lovely wide cruising slopes under the Odle Mountains. And don't miss the area's longest run, the 10km (6.2mi) long La Longia, for the stunning variety of terrain, including a natural canyon with a frozen waterfall.

La ciliegina sulla torta (the cherry on the cake) is indulging in the stupendous Italian produce and hospitality *Opposite* The Sas dla Crusc - Sasso di Santa Croce massif dominates the scenic La Crusc - Santa Croce ski area

SWITZERLAND

It's impossible to schuss past Switzerland, beckoning with her 4000m (13,000ft) pointy-finger peaks, where 70 per cent of the country is mountainous. Switzerland has never drawn the short straw. When Mother Nature doled out the world's most spectacular mountains, she over-gifted this tiny country with beauty.

Here, mountains are laser-cut against endless skies, and parallel worlds exist on plateaus and balconies far above deep valley floors. It would be fair for Switzerland to complain in true supermodel fashion, 'people only like me because of my looks', but dive deeper, and there's more than spires cut like chiselled cheekbones.

These mountains hide a catwalk of cultures; each valley has its own traditions and dialects, the result of evolving in geographical isolation. Hence, despite the unifiers of 20th-century developments, you'll still find hyper-local, traditional identifiers like Schmutzli (Santa's sinister sidekick) sneaking into Mürren (*see* p. 149) at Christmas time, the ancient time-blackened chalets of Zermatt (*see* p. 135), the 450 types of cheeses and the regional languages of Swiss German, French, Italian and Romansh (and scores of dialects).

Selecting these Swiss resorts was like being unfairly tasked with choosing a favourite child – the Bern, Valais and Graubünden cantons boast mountains above 4000m (13,000ft), the latter two sporting over 100 mountain peaks, while the Bernese Oberland is an undisputed skier's Disneyland. There were topographical-map debates and whispered apologies to those on the cutting floor, even Ski Arena Andermatt-Sedrun (*see* p. 139), one of Europe's hottest up-and-comers only just scraped in this list.

It's clear Switzerland is one country that needs not just a chapter, but its own book. So why ride anywhere else? Cost – pure and simple. But while you will forget the price of the CHF25 plain omelette (or not), you'll never forget these Alps.

Coolest winter selfie
Anywhere, literally anywhere. The scenery is the stuff dreams (and film sets) are made of. Just when you've captured the best shot, a run twists and turns, revealing yet another new angle of the Matterhorn - or any other mountain.

Get appy
SwissTopo is a handy local app for route planning. Tourenatlas is another location-specific app from the Helvetic Backcountry's *Tourenatlas* book on ski-touring and splitboarding. Thirty of the book's ski tours across the Swiss Alps are featured in digital form.

While technically not a ski app, turn on Freedom to block specific apps and websites to keep your phone available for emergencies and all the photo ops while dialling down the distractions.

Don't break the bank
Swiss retailers Migros and Aldi sometimes offer discounted ski passes (peek on their websites). Getting a Snow'n'Rail deal from the SBB train company is cheaper than buying a railway ticket and ski pass separately. Some banks, including Raiffeisen, offer discounted ski passes.

Some regions offer heavily discounted ski passes to hotel guests - look for Sleep + Ski deals, including almost half-price tickets. A Zermatt day pass nudges CHF100, but in smaller areas dynamic pricing tickets start for early birds at CHF50.

When it snows
With labyrinthian mountains causing a maze of micro-climates, weather is an hourly game. The top tip is to check landi.ch (ch denotes a Swiss website), the forecast service for the Swiss agricultural sector (use Google translate).

Meteoblue.ch is a good source but tends to go all in with optimism (excellent when looking for a good news forecast).

SLF.ch doesn't provide forecasts but updates its sites in the morning with accumulated snowfall over 24- and 72-hour periods, so you can adjust your pow expectations. Plus, it's a top source for avalanche information - both long-term trends and regional avalanche bulletins.

The one and only car-free Zermatt sits head and shoulders above the rest on its mid-Alps throne.

Zermatt

THE LOWDOWN

In a game of word snap, you say 'Zermatt', and I say 'gold bars.' Bring them – this isn't just Switzerland, not known for budget travel; this is Zermatt in Switzerland, where oligarchs' eyes have watered over dinner bills. Even for the Swiss, where spectacular mountain towns are a dime a dozen, Zermatt sits head and shoulders above the rest, figuratively and literally. Why? There's nowhere else like it.

Zermatt is car-free (bar a few electric luggage buggies) and is an amphitheatre with 38 peaks above 4000m (13,123ft). It includes that supreme joy: cross-border skiing – in this case, down to Italy. Plus, its microclimate creates 300 sunny days a year.

There's also that authentic and, in true Swiss fashion, efficient hospitality. Many hotels have been in the same family for generations, and those lucky locals (surnames Julen and Perren are synonymous with the town) can be easily identified by their hyper-local Walliserdeutach dialect. Girls may run the world (thank you, Beyoncé), but farmers-turned-multimillionaires own Zermatt.

Long before royalty visited with diamond-encrusted Piagets, mountain royalty was here – climbers. The Matterhorn looms over the town; its crooked, witch-hat profile is an all-knowing, all-seeing beacon.

Mountain stats
- Elevation top: 3899m (12792ft)
- Elevation bottom: 1620m (5315ft)
- Vertical drop: 2375m (7792ft)
- Skiable terrain: 365km of pistes
- Longest run: 25km (15.5mi)
- Beginner terrain: 17 per cent
- Intermediate terrain: 61 per cent
- Advanced terrain: 22 per cent
- Lifts: 53

Run
Tufternkumme, with the Matterhorn perfectly framed at the end (piste 15).

Experience
Click in for an almost 1500m (4921ft) moonlight descent with a full-moon fondue at Restaurant Rothorn (zermatt.ch).

Local's tip
Sit on the right of the Gornergrat train for the best views - catch the 8am service with the lifties and restaurant staff to get early tracks.

Previous Identifying the dozens of surrounding mountains is a favourite pastime - you'll need your instructor to help!
Opposite The omnipresent Matterhorn

THE MOUNTAIN DEBRIEF

Zermatt is way more than the Matterhorn. Apart from boasting the highest lifted European piste terrain, it's one of only two resorts with 365 days of skiing (the other is Austria's Hintertux Glacier). It has 360km (224mi) of slopes on the Matterhorn Ski Paradise pass (200km/124mi in Zermatt, connected to 160km/100mi in Cervinia/Valtournenche, Italy), three peaks in Switzerland (Sunnegga-Blauherd-Rothorn, Gornergrat, Matterhorn Glacier Paradise) and sparkly new facilities.

Skiing spans three main ski areas; the Klein Matterhorn-Schwarzsee area is the largest, with mainly north-facing snow-sure slopes and a massive vertical of 2279m (7477ft). The Sunnegga-Rothorn zone has more forgiving, diverse terrain. Gornergrat-Stockhorn is where to go for beginner and intermediate riding, while adjacent Stockhorn boasts freeride terrain.

There's no single base here; the different sectors must be accessed via transport services. You may want to chew on one sector at a time rather than gobble them all in a day.

A RIDING ITINERARY

The early bird gets the groomers, and while others are pulling socks on, you'll be meeting a patroller at 7.30am at the **Matterhorn Glacier Paradise valley station** before heading up to the hub of **Trockner Steg** at a lofty 2939m (9642ft). After descending to **Furi**, head back up for breakfast at **Glacier Paradise Restaurant** with astonishing views from its 3883m-high (12,739ft) sundeck.

Take the **Matterhorn Glacier lift** to the highest point, and from here it's a never-ending 20km (12.4mi) ski slope all the way to the Italian town of **Breuil-Cervinia** (2000m/6562ft) or, if burning thighs allow, **Valtournenche** (1524m/5000ft). Crossing the border, the **Rifugio Testa Grigia** (rifugioguidedelcervino.com) makes a great stop for la prima (the first) Italian espresso.

Adventurous intermediates will revel in the long **Kelle** from the top of Gornergrat and the **Kumme** from the top of Rothorn. Both get you well away from the lift system and offer magnificent views.

ADVENTURE

Switzerland is one of only a few European countries allowing **heli-skiing**, and the Valais area (the canton of Zermatt) has heli-ski thrills galore.

Husky sledding with a peak panorama *Opposite* There are four mountain heli-ski drop points around Zermatt

OFF-MOUNTAIN MUST-DO

- The fast and furious toboggan (sledging) ride from Rotenboden to Riffelberg takes 10min from top to bottom.
- Or visit the excellent **Matterhorn Museum Zermatlantis** (zermatt.ch/museum). Seeing the broken rope from the first Matterhorn summit ascent in 1865 is chilling.

EAT UP & DRINK DOWN

- Zermatt has the greatest density of gourmet restaurants in the Alps. You can never put a fork wrong in Findeln, part of the Gourmetweg, with restaurants dribbling down the mountainside towards Zermatt like tumbling crumbs from a table.
- Don't miss the penne with truffles and ceps at **Adler Hitta** (adler-hitta.ch) or a typical fondue or raclette at **Whymperstube** (whymper-stube.ch) or **Zermatterstübli** (legitan.ch).
- Given Zermatt is located right on the Swiss-Italian border, it should be no surprise there's plenty of good Italian food here - **Ristorante Capri** (montcervinpalace.ch) is il migliore (the best).

APRÈS SKI

- You won't miss the **Hennu Stall** (hennustall.ch) below Furi as it's loud and lively, perfect for a quick drink on the final descent into town.
- The charming **Elsie's Bar** (elsiesbar.ch) attracts a mature, sophisticated crowd, both early and late in the evening.
- **Grampi's** (grampis.ch) and the **Schneewittchen** nightclubs are for late nights if you have any energy left or have found someone who earns CHF to buy you drinks.

STAY

- Several stellar ski-in, ski-out options exist high above the town for a range of budgets.
- **Cervo Mountain Resort** (cervo.swiss) is a wellness sanctuary with its own Ashram spa.
- **Riffelalp Resort** (riffelalp.com/accueil) at 2222m (7290ft) has the best pool view in the Alps.

ALTERNATIVE: SKI ARENA ANDERMATT-SEDRUN

Not mentioning super-snowy Ski Arena Andermatt-Sedrun, which has long flown under the radar but is in the process of going gangbusters thanks to a €1.6-billion development, would feel like leaving a puppy in the carpark. It gets hit by storms from all directions making it legendary for serious backcountry riders, and the north-facing 1500m (4921ft) brooding vertical face of the Gemsstock looming over Andermatt is a freeride magnet. Andermatt is still a traditional Swiss mountain village but the opening of swanky five-star Chedi Andermatt in 2013 was a game changer and Vail Resorts bought a majority mountain share in 2022, proving it may bit be Switzerland's newest power player.

ALTERNATIVE: VERBIER 4 VALLÉES

Verbier 4 Vallées is the largest ski area in Switzerland, with 410km (254mi) of linked pistes and a whopping 93 ski lifts climbing between 1250m (4101ft) and 3330m (10,925ft) elevation.

Have a meal with a side of the Matterhorn *Opposite top* Ski mountaineering and touring enjoy long legacies in Zermatt *Opposite bottom* The town shimmers as alpenglow fades to night

Once under the radar, until pro skiers put it on the social-media map, this laid-back and thriving town is home to hard-core locals and international off-piste pilgrims.

Engelberg

THE LOWDOWN

Chamonix. La Grave. Engelberg. Back up, where? For Europe, Engelberg is to off-piste skiing what Crans Montana, LAAX and Stubai Zoo are to freestyle. Until a few years ago, this destination in Switzerland's central Uri Alps had been a well-kept secret. However, the recent influx of Instagramming pro skiers and filmmakers capturing its mountains have seen Engelberg rise in popularity with a cult-like status.

It's partly due to the absence of celebrities, but in their places are the equivalent of ski royalty here for the challenging terrain, legendary 6m (20ft) snow and a dose of charm in the form of the 12th century monastery. Plus, there are the 2000m (6562ft) descents from 3292m (10,800ft) Titlis (reached by a revolving cable car, the Titlis Rotair).

The Rotair journey is happily shared by avalanche-beacon-carrying skiers and swags of first-time snow-seekers, mainly from China and India (Titlis has featured in numerous Bollywood blockbusters). At the summit is a tourist destination complete with ice caves, a suspension bridge and, of course, a chocolate-and-watch shop.

Unlike other Swiss ski towns, which excel in high glamour, high prices and high-end everything (like Verbier, Davos and Klosters), Engelberg is an authentic little farming village. It's like a mini Chamonix, minus the attitude (no offence Chamonix, you do you), and still offers some fun for those who don't wake up thinking couloirs instead of coffee.

Mountain stats
- Elevation top: 3028m (9934ft)
- Elevation bottom: 1050m (3444ft)
- Vertical drop: 2000m (6561ft)
- Skiable terrain: 82km (51mi)
- Longest run: 8km (5mi)
- Beginner terrain: 33 per cent
- Intermediate terrain: 57 per cent
- Advanced terrain:10 per cent
- Lifts: 20

Run
The off-piste runs served by the famous Big Five lift: Laub, Galtiberg, Sulz, Steintäll and Steinberg. The Laub is a football-pitch-wide 1000m (3281ft), 35-degree, off-piste, perfect run designed by nature. The second, the 8km (5mi) Galtiberg, involves more work, with glacier skiing, powder bowls and forest, but there are dangerous sections with cliffs and tricky tree exits, so a guide is essential.

Experience
You can't miss the hyper-local älplermagronen - a pasta dish layered with cheese and potato, topped with caramelised onion.

Local's tip
Take a UIAGM-qualified guide off-piste or an on-piste guide like Kili Weibel (kiliweibel.com), your local in the know.

Opposite The mountain station project (designed to mimic a snow crystal), TITLIS 3020 is a prime example of Swiss engineering and design

THE MOUNTAIN DEBRIEF

Located on the north edge of the Alps, Engelberg has excellent snowfalls and one of Switzerland's longest ski seasons (around 200 days) from October to May.

There are two main ski areas: the adrenaline nirvana of the shady, north-facing Mount Doom-esque Titlis and the smaller, sunny, south-facing family-friendly Brunni. The latter is lower (top elevation is 2040m/6693ft), which means tree skiing (Titlis tops out at 3238m/10,623ft) with a handful of intermediate and beginner runs. A couple of off-piste runs terminate near the town, often requiring a taxi pick-up at the end, or a long walk. If you're thrill-chasing on this side, ride the 48 per cent incline of the Schonegg (Switzerland's steepest T-bar) on an icy day.

There are only 82km (51mi) of pistes, but the action is off-piste. That's the drawcard – and it involves danger, having so a guide to help navigate the area is worth every penny.

A RIDING ITINERARY

Arrange your guide for the day ahead of time. Start your day with treats at **Dossenbach bakery** (beckdossenbach.ch), then take the gondola up to **Trübsee** for a couple of laps down the valley run **Kanonenrohr** (or cruiser **Stanndart**). Then head to the top of the glacier at **Klein Titlis**, where the main attraction for advanced skiers lies just underneath in the form of an off-piste glacier run (including open crevasses and avalanche dangers). The on-piste ski area around this section consists of a few short chairlifts and groomed runs.

For on-piste skiers, the better skiing is over in the **Jochpass** area with sweet off-piste runs that don't require any hiking, especially not sure what this means, extra clarification may be needed. Those willing to work for it will be rewarded with great runs, particularly heading from the top of Jochstock back towards the base of the Engstlenalp lift. At the end of the day, ski back to the village without downloading.

ADVENTURE

Go **night sledding** on Gerschnialp or brave the Cliff Walk; it's Europe's highest suspension bridge at 3041m (9977ft).

OFF-MOUNTAIN MUST-DO

- The **snow park** has electric snowmobiling, epic sledging, snow tubing and ice-skating inside a huge igloo. Then there are 38km (24mi) of cross-country trails, an evening descent by snooc (snowshoe that turns into a mini-toboggan) and a cosy **cinema** in town.

EAT UP & DRINK DOWN

- **Alpenclub Engelberg** (alpenclub.ch) is all your Swiss foodie dreams come true (it's hard to choose between the rustic indoor decor and the outdoor terrace).
- The **Hoheneck Bar** (hotelhoheneck.com), just by the monastery, offers good food, a cosy bar and live music.
- All roads end at the Ski Lodge Engelberg, where the **Konrad Brasserie** (skilodgeengelberg.com) has creative, delicious French/Nordic dishes with farm-to-table produce.

APRÈS SKI

- The **Chalet** bar (titlis.ch) at the base of the Titlis Xpress is a good place to kick off après.
- If stamina allows, you can drink at the **Yucatan Bar** (bellevue-terminus.ch) from après to close at 5am.
- However, it's all about the **Ski Lodge Engelberg** (skilodgeengelberg.com/de), where people yell 'let's get the party staaaaarted' and adventure-loving locals swap stories. They also host live music and ski movies.

STAY

- A sophisticated ski-bum vibe permeates at the **Spannort** (spannort.ch) and **Ski Lodge Engelberg** (skilodgeengelberg.com/de) - apart from bar shenanigans, it's an excellent hotel in its own right. Both are old hotels bought and renovated by Swedes and sold back to Swiss.
- Fresh from a five-year renovation, the **Kempinski Palace Engelberg** (kempinski.com) is the only five-star accommodation in town with a rooftop spa and staggering pool.

ALTERNATIVE: LA GRAVE

France's La Grave is the only place that comes close, with one lift serving off-piste terrain that attracts international skiers in droves. It shares a similarly laid-back, skier community vibe with more stoke and less ego. Like Engelberg, it's all about the riding.

Top The ultimate thrill, the 100m (328ft) long TITLIS Cliff Walk is Europe's highest suspension bridge at 3041m (9977ft) above sea level *Bottom* A snow globe village — just shake for flakes! *Opposite* This little town with the big mountain has produced local legends like Denise Feierabend, an Olympic gold medal-winning alpine racer

This once-staid and conservative Swiss resort is having a huge renaissance as riders flock to the parks and pipes.

Crans-Montana

THE LOWDOWN

Adam Bonvin, the age 20-something founder of Alaïa Chalet, clearly believed in the 'build it and they will come' approach, and he was right. Well known as the home of James Bond actor Roger Moore, Crans-Montana, in the French-speaking Valais canton, was two independent villages until 2017 – upmarket Crans and Montana. It's now experiencing a cultural makeover: fur-wearing is out and froth is in. Froth is a deliberate word choice; the low-pant-wearing, yo-bro brigade has moved in, bringing GoPros and fresh energy with them.

This is all thanks to Bonvin's Alaïa Parks, close by in Lens, the first indoor–outdoor action sports centre in Switzerland. It's a one-stop freestyle spot with over 5000sqm (1.25 acres) of trampolines, indoor skate ramps, foam pits, bowls, an outdoor skatepark, and – wait for it – a mechanical surf spot known as Alaïa Bay. It's closed from Nov to Feb; the rest of the time you can ride in the morning and the surf is always up in the afternoon.

The snowpark is a drawcard, but this is also a gentle resort with graceful red and blue pistes and some black options. The general air of civility is thanks to the absence of tour operators – they simply can't get the space amongst the holiday homes – and the result is an uber-Swiss enclave without a tonne of British accents, which even the few Brits enjoy.

Crans-Montana boasts one of the most beautiful panoramas in the Alps, with 180-degree views of 18 peaks above 4000m (13,123ft), including Mont Blanc and the Matterhorn. As it's also a plateau at 1500m (4921ft) with south-facing slopes, it is sun central with 300 days of sunshine from dawn to dusk.

Mountain stats
- Elevation top: 3000m (9842ft)
- Elevation bottom: 1484m (4868ft)
- Vertical drop: 1500m (4932ft)
- Skiable terrain: 160km (100mi)
- Longest run: 6km (3.73mi)
- Beginner terrain: 22 per cent
- Intermediate terrain: 70 per cent
- Advanced terrain: 8 per cent
- Lifts: 33

Run
Kandahar (19), of course. From the Plaine Morte glacier, it's 8km (5mi) of mixed black and red runs down to Barzettes.

Experience
International artists have dabbed Crans-Montana in around 80 murals, some of the highest in Europe, as part of summer's Vision Art Festival (visionartfestival.com), the sole mountain-based urban art festival.

Local's tip
Crans-Montana has dynamic lift-pass pricing; booking early pays dividends.

Opposite Whether seeking frozen water or liquid, Crans-Montana has you covered

THE MOUNTAIN DEBRIEF

Crans-Montana has 150km (93mi) of perfectly groomed runs and 1500m (4921ft) of vertical drop; for its size, the variety of terrain is applaudable. There's high altitude on the 3000m (9843ft) Plaine Morte, large slopes, tree line, and a swathe of freeriding possibilities.

Alaïa Parks by Tudor is the largest snowpark in western Switzerland, boasting a main park stretching 100,000sqm (25 acres) over two sites. Its scalable infrastructure is some of the best in Europe for beginners through to advanced.

A RIDING ITINERARY

Start your day with coffee on the go at **1900** (cafebar1900.ch). Head to **Cry d'Er**, explore **Pas du Loup** and dive into the **National piste** to **Barzettes**. Back up to **Violettes** to ski **Cabane de Bois**. Shift to **Aminona** for some open carving on **Tsa and Toula**, then back to National intermediate and lunch at **Cry d'Er Club d'Altitude** restaurant. Voila, morning circuit sorted; you've earned one of their juicy burgers à la minute (prepared to order). Or go all Euro for a long lunch and settle in at **Merbe** (merbe.ch).

A full afternoon of skiing after lunch can be tricky, but buckle up. From Bellalui, head to **Violettes** via the **Col du Pochet**. Take the gondola to **Plaine Morte** and ski the famous **Kandahar** all the way down to **Barzettes** or **Cabane de Bois**. Then it's back to **Cry d'Er** restaurant to ski the **Chetzeron** all the way down to the town and stumble straight into **Zero Dix** (zerodix.ch).

Beginners are happiest at **Ballesteros** golf course, where three beginner lifts await; otherwise, head to **Arnouva** on the mountain.

ADVENTURE

The flat-topped **Plaine Morte glacier** means a taste of polar adventure is available even to pedestrians; it's impossible to be indifferent to the immensity of this snowy landscape.

OFF-MOUNTAIN MUST-DO

- This is the most unlikely spot to find Australian First Nations art, but the **Fondation Opale** (fondationopale.ch) aims to make it accessible to Europeans with exhibits and workshops.
- For post-ski romance, stroll the 2km **Lantern Path** (Chemin des Lanternes) at night between Lake Moubra and Lake Etang Long or sled with husky dogs.
- Pause in one of 18 wine cellars for a rare taste of Cornalin, Petite Arvine, Humagne Rouge – grapes you won't find anywhere but here.

—

EAT UP & DRINK DOWN

- The raclette flight (like a wine flight) at Alpine rustic **Le Mayen** (mayen.ch) will take your tastebuds across Switzerland (the Liddes variety is punchy).
- **Viva Vocce** (vivavocerestaurants.com) is a trendy pasta and pizza place as good as in Roma.
- On mountain, the croute au fromage trois étages (oven-baked bread with ham and local cheese) at **Cabane des Violettes** (cabanedesviolettes.ch) is reason itself to ski here.

—

APRÈS SKI

- For the best views in the Valais, it's straight onto a blanket-lined chair on **La Terrasse** (cransambassador.ch) at the Crans Ambassador.
- Beer lovers are in a frenzy at **Monk's** (monkis.ch) with a wide range of brews.
- There'll be a party at **Absolut Club** (crans-montana.ch) and **Bar Amadeus** (baramadeus.ch).

—

STAY

- The five-star **Crans Ambassador** (cransambassador.ch), shaped like a mountain, is funky elegance. It's a mix of Swiss luxe and unexpected art made of solar panels, plus a ginormous graffitied apple lobby sculpture purchased from the Vision Art Festival (*see* p. 145) for charity (claps).
- The three-star **Faern Hotel** (faernresorts.com) is just 150m (492ft) from the ski lifts (with pool).
- **Alaïa Lodge** (alaialodge.ch) has dorms if you're up for mixing with snowboarders born after 2000.

ALTERNATIVE: SNOWPARKS

Vans Penken (mayrhofner-bergbahnen.com), located in Mayerhofen in Austria has one of the best snowparks in Europe and was originally spearheaded by the legendary Ästhetiker crew, with its own chairlift for literal armchair spectating.

Snowpark LAAX (flimslaax.com) is a pro favourite with the world's largest halfpipe, an Olympic-size pro kicker line and over 90 obstacles for all levels.

The Mottolino Snowpark (mottolino.com) in Livigno, Italy, will host the 2026 Olympic freestyle competition (and is a training base for UK athletes) and the place to play on over 50 features or watch the pro line for inspiration.

The Swatch Nines is one of the competitions drawing freestylers *Opposite* Not being a tour-operated destination means more room to move on the slopes

This charmer is the ultimate chocolate-box village, with an almost surreal stage setting and a co-star of excellent skiing.

Mürren

THE LOWDOWN

Boom. That's the sound of your retinas exploding when you arrive in Mürren, perched on a 1650m (5413ft) mountain shelf. It's one of the most charming and peaceful ski villages in Switzerland, *nein*, the world.

Located above the Lauterbrunnen Valley (one of the world's deepest and an Eldorado for base jumpers), this tiny, traditional Walser village of only 410 inhabitants has scored a front row seat to the blockbuster alpine trio of the Eiger, Monch, and Jungfrau mountains. It's an A-list mountain bonanza.

Getting here is a spectacular adventure in itself. You take the cable car from Lauterbrunnen, then the little chugging Murrenbahn train to the northern end of the village, or the Stelchberg cable car to the southern end.

The area isn't huge, but it includes the 2970m (9744ft) Schilthorn peak. It forms part of the larger Jungfrau region extending beyond Mürren-Schilthorn to Wengen Grindelwald on the other side of the valley. And if you're just judging by size, you've missed the point – no statistic can measure the beauty or charm.

 Mountain stats
- Elevation top: 2970m (9744ft)
- Elevation bottom: 1638m (5374ft)
- Vertical drop: 1432m (4698ft)
- Skiable terrain: 54km (33mi); 214km (132mi) in the Jungfrau Ski Region
- Longest run:9km (5.6mi)
- Beginner terrain: 33 per centt
- Intermediate terrain: 50 per cent
- Advanced terrain:15 per cent
- Lifts: 16

 Run
The long, winding piste from the top of the Schilthorn down to Mürren is 1300m (4265ft) of vertical, accompanied by sensational views. It follows in part the legendary Inferno race route (with 1850 competitors, held every Jan since 1928).

 Experience
You can overdose on 007 at Spy World at the Schilthorn 2970m (9744ft) top station. *On Her Majesty's Secret Service* was filmed here in 1969. As you approach the exposed outcrop (with Bond theme cable-car music), it seems a heavily accented, turtleneck-wearing nemesis could appear any moment.

 Local's tip
With few powder panthers around, you'll still find late fresh tracks between the pistes off the lower chairs when it snows.

Opposite Just unleashing the bag of tricks in the Skyline Snowpark

THE MOUNTAIN DEBRIEF

The Jungfrau ski area has 214km(133mi) of pistes and 42 lifts spread over the three areas. Mürren has just 54km(34mi) of those, but don't let the map fool you into dismissing this pocket rocket.

Blue runs are featured throughout the rest of the resort, making it an intermediate's happy place, and there are enough blacks to scare your ski boots off. When snow conditions allow, it's also possible to ski 16km (10mi) and 2175m (7135ft) vertical – from the Schilthorn to the valley floor – with just one short chairlift in the middle.

A RIDING ITINERARY

Dust off the cobwebs on the northerly slopes, which won't have iced up yet with afternoon sunbaking. Start with pistes off the **Winteregg chair**, then progress onto slopes with more southerly aspects on the 2145m (7037ft) **Schiltgrat** (once the sun softens them around 11am).

This would also be the time to hit the **Skyline Snowpark** (skyline-snowpark.ch) with a dozen jumps, rails and boxes, by the Maulerhubel and Winteregg lifts. Also, check out the 650m (2132ft) **Bärgelegg park** with halfpipe over at **Grindelwald First** (muerren.swiss/en/summer).

If you're a cruising intermediate skier, try mid-mountain pistes like the **Engetal** blue. If you're ready, when you exit the Birg station you'll find the **Diretissimma**, a 49-degree *steilste* run, *steilste* being German for steepest and English for mildly terrifying. Pause for a spoonful of cement on the **Schilthorn** taking in the views of the Titlis, Jungfrau, Mönch, Eiger, and Jura mountains, as well as of Germany's Black Forest (and Mont Blanc on a good day).

ADVENTURE

The cable car en route to Schilthorn stops at 2677m (8782ft) Birg. Here the **Skyline Walk** (schilthorn.ch) and the **Thrill Walk** snake around the sheer rock face with glass-bottom floors, fenced-in slacklines, and fence tunnels. Strap into the two ziplines in Grindelwald First; both are included in your ski pass.

Mürren isn't known for its extreme skiing, but there are some big-mountain descents off the back of the Schilthorn. From the summit, drop south into the Sefinental valley or north into the Soustal. Alternatively, the Tschingelkrache involves a tricky descent above a cliff band before you arrive on the wide-open slopes of the Blumental. All of these need a guide or could become grisly quickly.

The Thrill Walk at the Birg middle station has a 200m (656ft) long rock footbridge built along the vertical drop into the rock *Opposite* Alpine trains are crucial for access, like the Wengernalp Railway (WAB) connecting Lauterbrunnen, Wengen and Grindelwald with Kleine Scheidegg

OFF-MOUNTAIN MUST-DO

• At Grindelwald, visit the **Top of Europe** at Jungfraujoch (jungfrau.ch), the highest train station in Europe at 3454m (11,332ft) and one of the most popular Swiss excursions.
• Locally, the **Sportzentrum Mürren** (sportzentrum-muerren.ch) has had a €10 million makeover and has ice-skating, a pool, a 37°C (99°F) outdoor hot tub and a wellness centre.

—

EAT UP & DRINK DOWN

• A highlight is Thursday fondue evenings at the **Allmendhubel** (schilthorn.ch), then ski back to the village (or return by funicular).
• **Stägerstübli** (staegerstuebli.ch), on lower Dorfstrasse, is perfect for local food and local people, with tagesteller (daily specials) of soup, salad and a main course for under CHF20.
• The four-course, half-board dinners at **Hotel Eiger** (hoteleiger.com) are also available to non-guests.

—

APRÈS SKI

• Life is simple up here - you don't come for the après. **Gondel Bar** (hoteljungfrau.ch) at the Jungfrau Hotel (inside an actual gondola) is the best bet.
• Or if you're returning from the other side of the valley, **Grindelwald Terminal Square** makes a great refuel pause with food trucks, a DJ and the legendary **eTron Bar** (jungfrau.ch) with glühwein.

STAY

• There are no more than a dozen places to stay in the village. Choose your accommodation location carefully, as feet are the only transport option.
• **Hotel Alpenruh** (alpenruh-muerren.ch) at the southern end is steps from the valley cable car and the ski slopes.
• The historic **Hotel Eiger** (hoteleiger.com) at the other end of the village, next to the train station, requires a little walk to the closest ski run - many choose to ski down via the village streets.

—

ALTERNATIVE: SAAS-FEE

For another area with a bubble ambience created by a car-free village, Saas Fee also happens to be utterly stunning. Just exiting the train station, you'll feel part of the mountains - not at the bottom of them, like at many other resorts. Eighteen 4000m (13,123ft) peaks tower above the charming village, and the glaciers are so close you can almost touch them. Better yet, there's great skiing from 1400m (4593ft) to 3600m (11,811ft), making these some of Europe's highest, most snow-sure slopes.

Bottom left Tubing in the Snow Fun Park at Jungfraujoch *Bottom right* Do you fondue? A Swiss highlight that'll keep you riding all day *Opposite* Launching into the Swiss-scape, you often feel part of the picture-perfect postcard

EUROPE'S QUIET ACHIEVERS

Europe overflows with bucket-list worthy runs but this section covers some lesser-known cool kids: namely, Finland, Bulgaria and Andorra.

Scandinavia is now the cool kid on the block, literally, from frosty winters where the Northern Lights blaze to where the capitals of Denmark, Sweden and Norway exude chic. Whether you're into traditionalism or minimalism, thriving nightlife or remote scenery so raw it's heart-searing, or if you're just a passionate connoisseur of skiing, at some point you'll dig an edge into Scandinavia.

Sweden's Åre (*see* p. 161), and midnight-sun, freestyle summer slope spot Riksgränsen (*see* p. 161) are well known, and Norway is never one to miss a marketing opportunity to lure people to snowy climes. But take a sidestep to lesser-known, nearby Finland, frequently sitting atop the World's Happiest Country polls and where the world's northernmost skiing can be found in Lapland.

There are some things to know about Lapland though. Firstly, there are no towering mountains like the Alps. The slopes are short, although Levi (*see* p. 157) is no international slouch with a World Cup run and events. The après is stratospherically expensive, oh, and mid-winter there's no sun. In late December above the Arctic Circle, the sun does lazy laps just above the horizon in eternal twilight. But this is what makes it stand out - there's just nothing like it.

Think of a ski trip here as a winter holiday based around skiing, rather than a pure ski trip. Nuzzling reindeer, warp-speed-whizzing huskies and ice plunges add an extra dimension to skiing under the Northern Lights. And it's all far from the crowds of European slopes.

Equally unusual is skiing in Bulgaria. As a bang-for-your-buck bonanza (value being determined by infrastructure, quality of skiing, off-slope action and overall pricing) Bulgaria is the Ultimate in its class. If you're hoping for Veuve and steeps, you've taken a (very) wrong turn, but you can't argue with cheap lift passes. If you're a beginner, or value is a priority, Borovets (*see* p. 163) is worth checking out.

And then there's the sweet, sweet Pyrénées. Tax-free Andorra was once the Bulgaria of Europe in reputation and price. Dismissed by many as 'that cheap place', Grandvalira (*see* p. 167) has been having a renaissance while your back's been turned. Now is the time to have another look at Andorra (except Pas la Casa, some things are beyond change).

This is the quiet achievers' list – all skiing to their own rhythm away from the mainstays of Europe.

Coolest winter selfie
Finland has snow-globe-worthy photo opportunities on steroids. If you manage to get a shot of dog or reindeer sledding, with the Aurora Borealis, while passing a frozen lake plunge hole, you've hit the trifecta. And images of skiing under a 10am pink dawn sky are bucket-list territory.

Grandvalira's tapas après ski with Tostada (a local microbrew beer) in hand shouts 'Hola!' and flashing your receipts in Bulgaria will have wannabe skiers pressing the Stories pause.

Get appy
Aurora Alerts monitors real-time auroral activity and alerts you if there are Northern Lights visible (however the most reliable indicator is going outside and looking up).

VR is Finland's sole train company with tracks running from Helsinki all the way to Lapland - the VR app gives real-time upates.

The App Grandvalira is packed with features, including an audio guide.

The My Borovets app has weather, lift openings and a lift-pass reloading function.

Don't break the bank
We're bank busting all over the place here. Except in Finland: that far north nothing is cheap, but happily the wild nature is gloriously free. Bulgaria already feels permanently on sale - the cost of lift tickets doesn't always tell an entire story, but most other costs fall in line. No-frills Ryanair flies from the UK into Sofia 90min away, but ski-tour operators have by far the best bundles.

When it snows
None of these places feature in any powder pocketbook. There are no snow issues in Lapland - that blanket of Arctic white sticks around until May. And while Borovets and Grandvalira don't win huge snow awards, Borovets has snow guns in the beginner areas and Grandvalira has a sophisticated snow-making system on 60 per cent of the runs, producing at up to +4°C (39°F).

North of the Arctic Circle, this Finnish Lapland ski area offers skiing under the Northern Lights and otherworldly remote wilderness adventures.

Levi

THE LOWDOWN

I'm just throwing it out there: if there's one inbounds adventure you take on skis, make it Finnish Lapland. Lapland (referring to the ancient lands of the Indigenous Samí or Lapp People) wraps from Russia in the east to Norway in the west. Levi, 170km (106mi) north of the Arctic Circle (and just 15min to Kittilä airport), is Finland's biggest ski area and a gateway to one of the most dazzling wildernesses on Earth.

A love of Lapland skiing buds slowly, then blooms spectacularly like the Aurora Borealis. Experiences like skiing in a midday sunrise, sleeping in a glass-domed igloo or hurtling towards a burning sun in a top-speed dogsled begins the infatuation. Then you'll find yourself in a reindeer sleigh, listening to the swishing hooves on muted snow as the sound of the world washes away, leaving only your soft breath and gentle heartbeat. Suddenly, like in a Disney movie, the reindeer looks back with its antler-framed eye and winks (although recollections may vary). Suddenly, you're a Finland fanatic hook, line and frozen-pond-sinker.

And you still haven't even sliced beneath the snow-speckled surface into the soft heat of a sauna, the icy plunges, snowmobile safaris or Northern Lights hunts (if you're lucky). Most people avoid the kammos: the dark period of polar night. But darkness shouldn't be a deterrent, rather part of the once-in-a-lifetime experience. Arriving in December has the added incentive of Santa for a Christmas never to be repeated. No wonder Finland regularly ranks as the world's happiest country.

Mountain stats
- Elevation top: 531m (1742ft)
- Elevation bottom: 196m (643ft)
- Vertical drop: 325m (1066ft)
- Skiable terrain: 38.5km (24mi)
- Longest run: 2.2km (1.3mi)
- Beginner terrain: 45 per cent
- Intermediate terrain: 47 per cent
- Advanced terrain: 8 per cent
- Lifts: 26

Run
Levi Black, aka G2, with a steep-point pitch of 27.5 degrees, is where the Alpine World Cup is held every November. The non-groomed slopes (6.3 and 6.4) at Northeast Slopes work on fresh-fall days.

Experience
Any of the 2000 saunas estimated to be around Levi, followed by an avanto (ice hole plunge). Or go for a no-chill plunge with an Arctic Ice Float (info@visitlevi.fi) - floating in a lake surrounded by ice and trees in a dry suit.

Santa's Cabin on W.3 slope is Levi's most iconic photo spot and the place to capture the pink January skies.

Local's tip
There is no crowd in the morning, so be on the first lifts to have the fresh groomers to yourself. You can also hit the slopes at 3pm when other skiers have moved on to aprés ski - the slopes are under lights and open until 7pm.

Opposite In the world's happiest country, happiness is ... bombing through fresh powder! *Previous* Hiking the stunning snowscapes of Levi *Overleaf* Riding beneath the flowing swirls of the Aurora Borealis is a rare event (they usually appear late at night), but it does happen

THE MOUNTAIN DEBRIEF

Tell it like it is and make it easy – that was the directive when naming the mountain sections Front Slopes, West Slopes, Southeast Slopes, South Slopes and Northeast Slopes. Having exhausted the compass points, the runs are named numerically (the runs near Lift 8, for example, are named 8.1, 8.2, etc). Every now and then, there's an alphanumerical bomb to throw you off your game (for example, a 7B.3). Regardless, it's clear there's skiing in every direction.

Levi skiing is quite the surprise – there really is a mixed bag of blue slopes for beginners, red slopes for intermediate skiers, and black slopes for experts. Freeskiers and snowboarders can enjoy the kilometre-long South Park, Junior South Park, and Fun Park, and backcountry lovers have a swag of ski-touring routes and non-groomed areas.

A RIDING ITINERARY

Right by the slopes, grab a coffee at **Coffee House Levi** or **Café Zero** to warm up. **Front Slopes**, which also forms the centre of the village, is the main gateway. Then head to the **Northeast Slopes**, the best place to enjoy carving-style skiing. The slopes next to **Lift 5** are natural-snow slopes, open mid-Feb. At the lower station of Lift 6, pit stop at **Draivi** restaurant.

Then head onto the **Southeast Slopes** – those next to **Lift 7** are easy runs, but with fun shapes and terrain. Next, onto the happy place – South Slopes. Skiing down **Slope 8.1** is easy next to Levi's biggest 'snow giant' (snow-encrusted) trees. **South Slopes** has the longest slopes of the resort, with the six-seater South chairlift equipped with heated seats and a bubble shell for wind protection.

Head down to **West Point** and find **Santa's Cabin** (*see* p. 157), next to **W.3 slope**. Have a hot chocolate at the little cafe on the top of the Gondola2000 lift – **Restaurant Palovartija** is an old fire-watching guardhouse used during the 1960s and 1970s.

The slopes off **Lift 12** are the place to be on a powder day during spring and **Lift 13** is where you can usually spot alpine skiing teams practising. A stop at the best restaurant on the hill, **Restaurant Horizont**, on Front Slopes, is mandatory for some spicy pulled reindeer pizza, and back to base.

ADVENTURE

Driving a team of huskies (levi.northernlightsvillage.com) over the white, shimmering fells (hills) is an experience that is almost mandatory during a trip to Lapland.

Europe

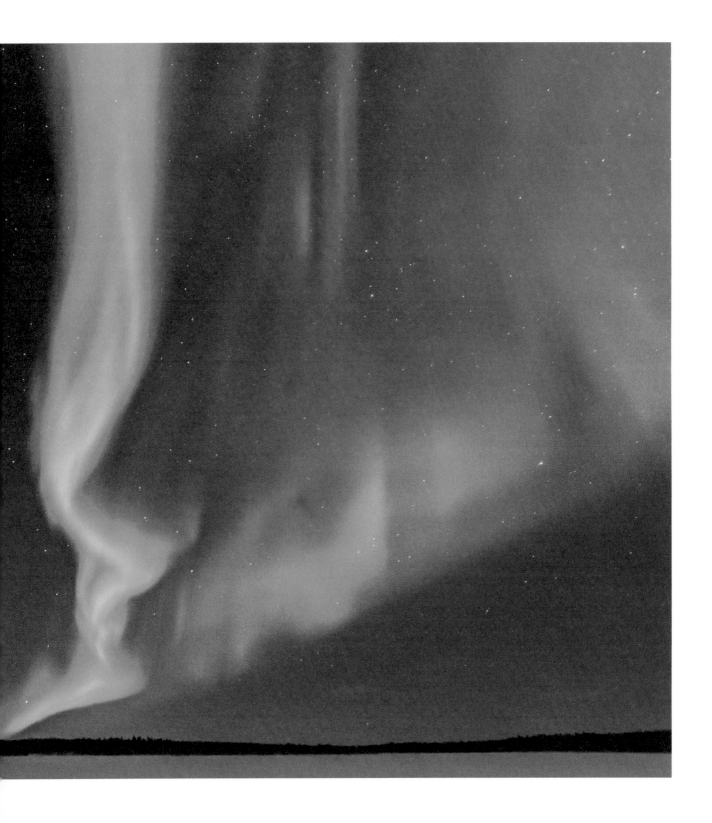

OFF-MOUNTAIN MUST-DO

- So. Many. Options. But a photographic Aurora Chase with **Arctic Frontier** (arcticfrontier.fi) is an only-in-Lapland opportunity. All photography equipment is provided and no prior photography experience is needed.

EAT UP & DRINK DOWN

- A unque dish is sauteéd reindeer with mashed potatoes and lingonberries at **Restaurant Ämmilä** (hulluporo.fi), and you can also try king crab at the northernmost seafood restaurant in Finland, **King Crab House** (kingcrabhouse.fi).
- Enjoying a traditional Lappish menu in the warmth of a traditional Lappish hut is an unforgettable experience. Try it either at **Saamen Kammi**, with *joikh* singing, or at the **Hullu Poro Kammi**.

APRÈS SKI

- Here it's called 'after ski' and it can get wild at on-slope **Restaurant Tuikku** (levi.fi) with glögi (spiced wine) in hand. Then head down where the party continues at **V'inkarri** and nightclub **Lift**.

STAY

- The **Northern Lights Village** (levi.northernlightsvillage.com; with a sister property in Saariselka) has a glass-roofed igloo 9km (5.6mi) from town for minimal light pollution and an Aurora Borealis iPad alert system.
- The lakeside **Scandi House**, owned by an Olympic skier couple (Finnish and Australian), comes with its own ice plunge pool (known as an avanto), hot tub, optional ski guiding and yoga classes.

ALTERNATIVE: ÅRE AND RIKSGRÄNSEN

Sweden's Åre is the obvious choice, another icicle-frosted, storybook land with Swedes, skiing, saunas and schnapps. But Riksgränsen, a freeriding mecca a 16hr drive north of Stockholm is something special too. It opens in February when the sun appears and stays open sometimes until Midsommer with skiing under the midnight sun.

Top Go for the ride, fall in love with the dogs *Bottom* Santa Claus's house mid slope in a 2pm December sunset *Opposite* Frozen trees are one of the many surprises of Levi

Some call it cheap, but that doesn't mean it's substandard. This is one of the best-value ski resorts in the world – you do you, Bulgaria.

Borovets

THE LOWDOWN

Don't dismiss Borovets in Bulgaria. Consistently topping 'cheapest ski resorts in Europe' lists, it's tempting to scratch this as a non-starter and sub-rate it. But if you're yearning for a ski area with solid basics, this budget-friendly bolthole is a winner. The people are friendly, the food portions generous and it's cheap – crazily, undeniably, ridiculously cheap. That's great, but is there still snow? Yes.

Borovets has been an aristocratic playground since 1896, and UK tour-package skiers descended here like locusts in the 2000s. But during the pandemic, Borovet's slopes were rediscovered by independent skiers; it was one of the few options for snow desperados locked out of other European areas. Many were pleasantly surprised after the bad rap Borovets had received due to the budget tag.

With only 5km (3.1mi) of runs rated black – and a Bulgarian black isn't a Courchevel black – this is the place for those who don't actually want to end up on advanced terrain. The cost commitment is low, the value is high, and Borovets has all the trimmings – flights, ski school and rentals. Plus, eating out every night can cost half the price of a catered chalet in France. The con? You're not actually in a catered chalet in France.

Borovets is well-suited to families with small children who won't be on the slopes all day anyway. Affordable ski-in, ski-out accommodation is what sets Borovets apart from the Alps. Regarding the village, think of the main drag of a package-holiday town on snow, and there you have it: a smattering of currency conversion places (we've left euro-ville), English-style bars and more authentic mehana (traditional restaurants) with traditional food, decoration and music.

 Mountain stats
- Elevation top: 2550m (8366ft)
- Elevation bottom: 1350m (4429ft)
- Vertical drop: 1200m (3937ft)
- Skiable terrain: 58km (36mi)
- Longest run: 12km (7.5mi)
- Beginner terrain: 41 per cent
- Intermediate terrain: 50 per cent
- Advanced terrain: 9 per cent
- Lifts: 13

 Run
The Musala Pathway from the Markudjik is an (almost) outer, top-to-bottom, tree-lined, meandering blue run with an 'am-I-even-in-a-ski-area?' feel (watch out though, as it can get icy in the shade at the end of the day).

 Experience
The night skiing from 6.30pm to 10pm, where the bottom half of Sitnyakovo from the Martinovi Baracki chairlift is under floodlights.

 Local's tip
Those on the easy blue run around Markudjik beware - if you descend on Haramia run and continue to skier's right you'll inadvertently arrive on black Fonton. Head skier's left for the intermediate Popangelov.

Opposite Snow-shrouded trees add to the magic at Borovets

THE MOUNTAIN DEBRIEF

Borovets' name is a literal translation of the Turkish word chamkoria (pine forest); the vista of forests and ambience of being among the trees is a real departure from above-treeline skiing in the Alps. There are three main ski areas – Sitnyakovo, where most beginners head (but also home to two short black runs); gondola-accessed Markudjik, the highest ski area with runs concentrated around the mountain crown; and red-runs-only Yastrebetz with the longest 1000m (3280ft) descents. There's also a world-class biathlon and cross-country ski area in Britsita below Yastrebetz.

A RIDING ITINERARY

The **Yastrebetz Gondola** is the main lift; be here by 8.15am to avoid any queues as it can be a bottleneck. Alternatively, start on the more sedate Sitnyakovo side up the **Martinovi Baraki Express**. It can become a little crowded on the Martibovi Baraki 1 and Sitnyakovo 1 runs. If you start using the ski school snakes as slalom poles, it's time to switch over to red **Sitnyakovo 2 or 3**.

When others pause for lunch, jump on the **Yastrebetz Gondola** towards the **Markudjik** area. This highest area keeps the gang together with four parallel runs – **Markudzhik 1** is easy, **Markudzhik 2B** and **Markudzhik 3** are intermediate, and the expert **Markudkin 2A** separates them. It can also be cold and windy up here, as the Markudjik surface button lift will drag you to the 2550m (8366ft) summit, which is considerably higher than tree-protected Sitnyakovo (1780m/5840ft) if the weather closes in.

Head skier's left from the gondola, and you're in **Yastrebetz** where you'll find three long red runs to burn your legs for a satisfying slope day, all accessed by a fast quad, the Yastrebetz Express. Stop for a break at the **Yastrebetz Hotel** at the end of Yestrebetz 3 (the club sandwich is highly recommended). At 4pm it's a wrap.

ADVENTURE

Try **ski touring** the route around Malyovitsa Peak and the Balkans' highest, Musala Peak at 2925m (9596 ft), with a guide.

OFF-MOUNTAIN MUST-DO

• There's plenty for kids to try, including pony rides, husky sledding, snowmobiling and tandem paragliding.

EAT UP & DRINK DOWN

• The **Pappa Mia Steakhouse** at the base of the lifts is the easy (and satisfying) choice when you click off skis.
• Cheerful **Katina Bar & Dinner** (katinaborovets.online) has an Italian- and Bulgarian-inspired menu; smoke signals from the outdoor barbecue will draw you in.
• The **Green King** is one of the cheapest places in town, but that doesn't mean a compromise on great food. This mehana (traditional restaurant) is calm, cosy (it's small, so book) and a small cultural hit.

APRÈS SKI

• Christo Aneglov is a former ski Olympian and national champion whose hospitality is legendary at **White Magic**. Expect a family-like welcome and, as a bonus to wife Janet's full shots and meals, take ski lessons with Christo or his daughter Laura, a Bulgaria GS slalom team member.
• Otherwise, the bowl of buildings where the ski runs finish has options, including instructors' hangout the **Black Tiger** (with karaoke).

STAY

• The **Hotel Rila** (rilaborovets.com), with spa and pool dominating the base area, is such an institution it's used as a navigational aid.
• For a true mountain experience, the **Finish Line** (borovets-bg.com) guest house has two stylish apartments and one double room above an on-mountain restaurant on the Popangelov run.

ALTERNATIVE: BANKSO

Bankso has won Bulgaria's Best Ski Resort multiple times at the World Ski Awards (no mean feat). It's also featured as a stop on the FIS Snowboard World Cup, has banging nightlife (think saxophonists in the snow at après), boasts a cobblestone town and even a Kempinski hotel. It'll cost more levas (the local currency) than Borovets, but the age-old rule applies - you get what you pay for, but Bankso has more action from slopes to bars.

Top Borovets village *Bottom* Pull up a chair in a wondrous winterland *Opposite* Borovets's bang for buck provides good value for beginners and intermediates

Resort areas link together like a series of tasty tapas, and this Pyrénéan area keeps expanding the ski menu with additions more bougie than buffet.

Grandvalira

THE LOWDOWN

'Host a World Cup Final!' they said. 'Things will change!' they said. And they were right. Soldeu, the swishest of Grandvalira's six ski areas, had already hosted World and European Cups, but it was the World Cup, televised globally in 2018/19, that jetted Grandvalira in Andorra up the credibility list. It was such a success that the FIS (International Ski Federation) and skiers have been returning for more ever since.

Grandvalira is like a bipolar octopus. Sedate Soldeu-El Tarter first hooked up with party-town Pas de la Casa and then Grau Roig in 2003. Since then, its tentacles have snagged beginner Canillo (parents love being able to keep an eye on their kids on the seven slopes) and Encamp, the access point from Spain and Andorra. The most recent additions are the Peretol sector (featuring a snowpark) plus in the northern valley Ordino Arcalis, a stop on the Freeride World Tour and epicentre of off-piste skiing (that Engelberg's Swiss haven't colonised just yet) and Pal-Arinsal ski resort.

And between the two largest, Soldeu and Pas de la Casa, select your tribe. Soldeu is prettier, smaller, has the best location mid-Grandvalira and is the focus of investment. While Soldeu is being elevated, not much has changed in concrete Pas de la Casa – larger and ugly even with beer goggles on, it's still the place to party, and if you're a university student (or a family after more amenities), it has appeal.

The Pyrénées offer better value and quieter slopes than the Alps, and you're certainly not being short-changed on that mountain feeling, with 60 surrounding peaks over 2000m (6562ft). And these mountains have a different tone to the Alps. It's not just the Spanish beer and après tapas snackies replacing the glühwein and bratwurst. Half the clients are Spanish (locals speak Catalan), while around 30 per cent are French, so the vibe is distinctly localised, and 20 per cent are British.

 Mountain stats
- Elevation top: 2640m (8661ft)
- Elevation bottom: 1710m (5610ft)
- Vertical drop: 930m (3051ft)
- Skiable terrain: 193km (120mi)
- Longest run: 6km (3.7mi)
- Beginner terrain: 17 per cent
- Intermediate terrain: 68 per cent
- Advanced terrain: 15 per cent
- Lifts: 67

 Run
Tucked away in the furthest corner of Grandvalira is Rossinyol in Canillo. Cruise along the top plateau and soak up the Pyrénées views before picking up speed winding down steep blue curves and fast corners through to a tree-lined finale.

 Experience
An 8am First Snow (like First Tracks) run followed by breakfast at the Pi del Migdia restaurant in El Tarter. Book ahead for the Clicquot Bubble Experience (grandvalira.com), dinner under the stars in a bubble located mid-forest, accessed by SUV.

 Local's tip
Don't be put off at the 'loo with a view' in El Tarter (top of Tosa de la Llasada), as skiers and snowboarders whizz by the full-length window - it's one-way glass. Use the singles lift line at peak times (10am when lessons start and 3pm after lunch), which cuts waiting in half.

Opposite On a Pyrénées high, this distinct area has a flavour all its own

THE MOUNTAIN DEBRIEF

With 210km (130mi) of slopes you'll never tire of riding the same routes – although some pistes like the red Riu Solanelles and Montmallus are so addictive one ride won't be enough.

Expect tree-lined runs, like the cruisy blue Gall De Bosc snaking its way from the top of Soldeu to the base of sleepy El Tarter, to the adrenaline-inducing FIS World Cup black runs of Avet (Soldeu) and Aliga (El Tarter).

The mountains here aren't glaciated, so off-piste riding feels more like a fun flamenco than a serious, crevasse-dodging waltz (guides are still required for avalanche avoidance).

A RIDING ITINERARY

Avoid the ski schools and the busier parts of the mountain by heading to **Grau Roig** (not a common start spot with only one hotel) in the mornings. First, take the **Soldeu gondola** for some blue laps around **Os**, **Duc** and **Fura**, then continue to **TSD Pla de les Pedres**, a blue winding run with wide pistes and a combination of steeper sections that flatten into cruisier twists and turns.

Half the fun of getting to lunch at **Refugi de Llac de Pessons** (a gorgeous bolthole) is approaching via **Cami de Pessons**, a fun cat track wrapping around the side of the mountain and popping out at the lakeside refugio (hut).

After traditional food inside (or oyster bar outside), ride **Grau Roig** to discover the red **Montmallus** run, a hidden gem (you have to brave the steep, dog-legged drag lift, but it's well worth it!). Then après it up in **Pas de la Casa** and return to Soldeu via the **Serrat Pinos** 'motorway', a key highway connecting the Grau and Soldeu sectors. It's a great run with steep undulating drops and rollercoaster feels.

ADVENTURE

Grandvalira is a starting point for **ski mountaineering** to peaks such as Montmalús, Pic Blanc d'Envalira or Pic de les Abelletes.

OFF-MOUNTAIN MUST-DO

- You'll find **snowmobiling** (Grau), **dog sledding** (Grau and El Tarter) and **snowtubing** (Pas De La Casa) on the longest tubing track in Europe (350m/1148ft) with curves, underground tunnels and night lights (grandvalira.com).

EAT UP & DRINK DOWN

- In Spanish style, many eat at 2pm, so sitting at noon guarantees a spot on the decks of the **Terraza Petroni**, **In the Snow Veuve Clicquot**, or the **IQOS Terrace**, with live DJs (grandvalira.com).
- **La Caleta** in Soldeu takes pole position for the best tapas in the entire Grandvalira.

APRÈS SKI

- Start at 2500m (8202ft) **Coll Blanc** (grandvalira.com) watching the sunset over Grau Roig mountains to a DJ base beat.
- **El Tarter L'Abareset** (abarset.com) has one of the best après-ski in Europe.
- At Soldeu, **Fatty's** (Fat Albert's, fat-albertssoldeu.com) has live music most nights by a ski instructor band suitably named the Shambles (continue to the diner downstairs).

STAY

- Spend the night at 2350m (7710ft) at **Domo Lodge** (bordes.epicandorra.com), a spherical luxury accommodation dome for two at Grau.
- The adults-only **Hotel Naudi Boutique** (hotelnaudi.com) is a nod to Soldeu's new, more sophisticated offerings.
- The self-catering **Bella Vista II Apartments** (soldeuapartments.com) are a 5min downhill walk to the gondola (but a 5min uphill walk home) with great views of the runs.

Top An adaptive skier edges on the morning corduroy
Bottom L'Abareset après is where the party's at *Opposite* Soldeu-El Tarter is the site of World and European Cup races

Chemmy Alcott the alpine skier

Snow pro

Britain's greatest-ever skier, Chemmy Alcott is a familiar face to snow lovers. A four-time Winter Olympian, the alpine skier is the first British skier to win a World Cup, is a seven-time British National Champion and competed in all five disciplines – downhill, Super G, Giant Slalom, Slalom and Combined.

She's also an Olympic and Eurosport winter sports commentator and presents BBC Ski Sunday, taking avid viewers to destinations and events around the globe. Dedicated to multiple charities involving children and sport such as Right To Play, SnowCamp and Ski4Cancer, she's created a legacy and inspiration for the next gen of British and female skiers. If you see it, you can be it.

How did you begin your career?

I first learned to ski at 18 months old. My dad was a rugby player and my mom was a swimmer, I say genetically I was made to ski because I got his glutes and her lungs. I did my first race when I was around three and always thought I won that race because I got a teddy bear with a medal.

Finally, after 20 years of telling the press this, my father said, 'I can't read this anymore. You didn't win that race.' I said, 'Well, of course I did. I won a medal.' And he said that everyone under the age of five got a medal!

What stands out as a career highlight?

My career highlight was definitely the second round of Solden in 2008 when I became the first British ski racer to win a run in the World Cup. I had been ski racing for eight years and I was trying to control the outcome by performing at 80 per cent and keeping 20 per cent in my back pocket, to self-validate when I wasn't winning. But that run, I put myself in a position where I had the freedom to charge and go all out and it resulted in me winning the run, a big turning point for my career.

Unfortunately, after that I started getting injured because with a hundred per cent in downhill ski racing, you either win or you get hurt, but it was a much more satisfying way to live.

As a Brit, how hard was it to compete against more developed ski nations?

Of course, it was challenging when you are racing against big winter sport nations who have a lot of funding and backing. But at the same time, I'm always a glass-half-full person and I try and look at the positives and the big positive of coming from Britain is that you were always the underdog. No one ever expects anything of you. And I think because of that, I was able to perform at a really high level once I found that growth mindset. I remember when I won that run in Austria, everyone was like, 'Who is this Londoner beating our Austrian girls?' And it was very satisfying.

Which are your favourite resorts to compete in?

One of my two favourites is Lake Louise in Canada. It is just an incredible experience to go there and all stay in the same hotel and ice skate on the lake and then race. Obviously it's also the site of one of my biggest injuries, but I try not to let that taint my love of it. And the other favourite is definitely Cortina, I feel like the Tofana piste nestled in the Dolomites is the most special piste in the world for women's racing.

What do you love most about skiing in Europe?

I love that every country has a different culture and that really filters into how they view skiing and their rapport with skiing. So, you go to Austria and the pistes are perfect, but you have to be on the first lift to enjoy them because they're so enthusiastic. In Switzerland, I think the views are some of the best in the world. France, I just love the je ne sais quoi, the all-round. In Italy, I love the food and the passion that they have for their sport. So, I think it's just being able to travel. I don't like being in the same place the whole time. I like to travel and experience new things.

If not working, where do you choose to go on a ski holiday?

I've always said I don't think it's where you go, but it's who you go with and how the conditions are. I've had incredible days skiing with people who are better than me, pushing me out of my comfort zones in tiny resorts that just happen to have loads of snow.

What advice do you have for aspiring professional skiers?

The most important thing is to be driven by passion. Don't get into it because you think it'll be an easy ride of travelling around the world to amazing places. It's an incredibly rewarding sport, but there are a huge amount of sacrifices. If you're doing it because you absolutely love it you'll be able to ride the rollercoaster of emotions, the injuries, the disappointment, and keep your heart in the game.

Now you are a parent with small children, any tips for skiing parents?

I think the best thing is to disregard any luxurious accommodation, but prioritise ski-in, ski-out. Also, go somewhere where there's a communal swimming pool. We tend to ski early in the morning and then find somewhere to swim or sledge in the afternoons. It's exhausting, you'll need a holiday afterwards. But having that moment where you are all sitting on the chairlift together is absolutely magical.

Australasia

Eucalypt-lined runs in Australia, pistes with lake vistas in Aotearoa New Zealand and passionate locals; these Southern Hemisphere slopes offers unique experiences like nowhere else.

AUSTRALIA

'Australians can ski?' a bemused Frenchman once asked me. Oh, can Australians ski! They can ski anything. They ski artificial snow clumps, are adept at grassy mid-slope obstacles in spring, and don't mind a bit of ice. Honestly, if you learnt to ski in Australia, you can ski anywhere.

Australia even has some world champions – hello halfpipe snowboarder Scotty James, tragically departed boardcrosser Chumpy Pullin, and gold medal Olympian Torah Bright. And let's not forget Valentino Guseli (*see* p. 196), the young gun who broke Shaun White's world record in 2021 for the highest air out of the pipe – 7.3m (24ft) – which had been dangling for 11 years. For a big country with little snow, the Aussies have long been knocking it out of the park on podiums across the globe.

So it's not surprising that in a good year, the Australian ski fields punch above their weight. But, like a tricky partner, seasons can be unpredictable, fickle and unfaithful. One year they dump lovely frosty flakes on you; the next, you're forlornly chasing snowmelt puddles in the car park while other people say, 'you should have been here yesterday.'

Australia's longest run is only around 6km. But hockey-stop the judgement – they make up for it in atmosphere. For example, take Karels T-Bar at Thredbo (*see* p. 177) and follow the tracks out to Golf Course Bowl located far skier's right on the area boundary. Roaming free and laying fresh tracks among the snow gums here is one of the most unique, beautiful and wildly natural inbound ski experiences. Or head out the back of Guthega (*see* p. 183) to find silence in the gum trees on Schnaxl (named by 1950s Austrians working on the Snowy Mountains Hydro-Electric Scheme, post–World War II).

Australians go wild for skiing and boarding. Wild. It's big business – not only will they pay a fortune to ski at home (local websites melted during Covid whenever they released tickets), but they head overseas as well. Aussies are the number-one international ski market to Aspen, Colorado, they're ichi ban (number one) in many Japanese ski resorts, and they account for almost 30 per cent of those on New Zealand ski slopes.

It all starts on their home turf. Visit them in their native habitat to understand their passion. Australians are, without doubt, some of the most committed, stoke-filled and addicted snow lovers in the world. They've often earned their skiing stripes battling white-out conditions on Australian T-bars, then graduated to the gondolas of America and added a dash of European après for good measure. But after playing the (ski) fields around the world, they come back to the eucalypt-lined runs that are always calling them home.

Coolest winter selfie

If you want to blow up your Instagram feed this winter, pay the super-cute sled dogs at Mount Buller (*see* p. 189) a visit. For other Instagrammable backdrops, artist 'Grassi' Kellaher makes some of the best ice sculptures (seen at the majority of Perisher's events); try by the fireplace at the Denman in Thredbo (*see* p. 177) and outside odd-angled Huski in Falls Creek (*see* p. 193).

Get appy

All ski resorts have their own apps, and it pays to download. For example, the Mount Buller app tells you the moment your favourite lift opens and pings alerts from the resort, tracks runs and help you find your ski buddies. You can also buy lift tickets and rent equipment on Thredbo's app. The BOM Weather app (Bureau of Meteorology) will give you snow forecasts.

Don't break the bank

With lift passes starting at around AUD$150 (€90), Australian skiing is some of the most expensive in the world - and that's just the lift pass, without factoring in the size of the domain it accesses. If peak season (July/Aug) is in your sights, a midweek visit scores serious savings, leaving spare snow dollars for après aperol spritz sessions. Book early online to get the best prices, and follow resorts' Facebook/Instagram socials to catch deals.

When it snows

When it snows in Australia, it's not the fat flakes that waft down in Lapland or Steamboat's trademarked champagne powder. Oh no, these falls arrive horizontally, often roaring up on the back of winds from Antarctica, a wailing, wild weather event that handily exfoliates exposed skin. You'll suddenly appreciate the drag lifts that keep running after chairlifts go on wind hold and your low-light-lens goggles. Leave the down at home unless you have a waterproof shell on top. The truncated season lasts four months, from the long weekend in early June to late Sept. The sweet spots are in late July and Aug. Make sure you sidestep school holiday periods which push prices up. Ski the shoulder season in early Sept (spring), and you'll be surprised at how much you can save.

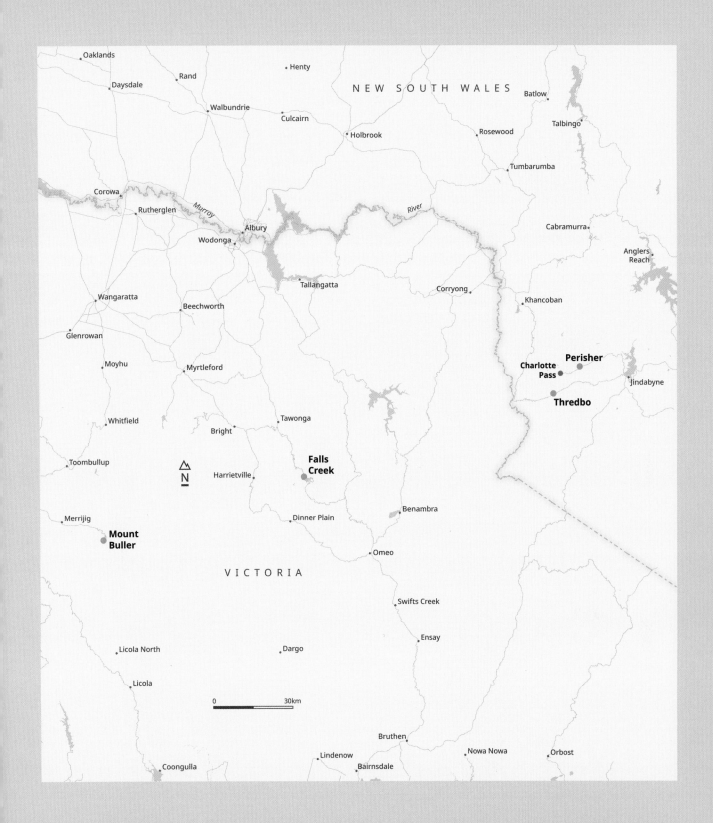

Thredbo is the glamorous, can-can-kicking showgirl of Australia's ski fields.

Thredbo

THE LOWDOWN

Enter stage left, Thredbo. All jazz hands and razzle-dazzle, there's no overlooking this scene stealer. Over 30 bars and restaurants cling to one side of the valley like shimmering snowflakes, while the other valley slope features the lifts. It's the easy transition from ski-time to home-time that makes this quasi-European outpost in New South Wales so attractive.

There's a hint of Euro around Thredbo, and I don't mean neon onesies (although you might find those too). No, it's the legacy of the Czechs and Austrians who came to work on the Snowy Hydro scheme in the 1950s. They brought their skis and knowledge of the slopes with them.

And if you like stats, then you'll like Thredbo's vertical of 672m (2205ft), almost twice the height of other resorts which shall remain nameless ... okay, Falls Creek at 380m (1247ft). Plus, Thredbo has the thigh-burning 5.9km (3.7mi) Karels T-Bar to Friday Flat run in peak season.

A cosy village atmosphere, a cosmopolitan dining scene and the company of the Sydneysiders who ski here make this a top-tier choice. Thredbo is now home to Australia's first alpine gondola (did I mention those drag lifts?), the multimillion-dollar, still-shiny, eight-person Merritts Gondola running from the village to the intermediate Cruiser area.

Thredbo is on the Traditional Land of the Ngarigo Monero People.

 Mountain stats
- Elevation top: 2037m (6683ft)
- Elevation bottom: 1365m (4475ft)
- Vertical drop: 672m (2205ft)
- Skiable terrain: 4.8 sqkm (1186 acres)
- Longest run: 5.9km (3.7mi)
- Beginner terrain: 16 per cent
- Intermediate terrain: 67 per cent
- Advanced terrain: 17 per cent
- Lifts: 14

 Run
The go-to on a powder day is Michael's Mistake.

 Experience
On Tuesday mornings, pre-sunrise, a warm snow cat purrs its way up Karels T-bar (Australia's highest lifted point). The early-bird reward is fresh groomers for breakfast with first tracks on the Supertrail.

 Local's tip
The best windblown powder is found when the wind is strong from the west-north-west, blowing in from the Main Range.

Opener A mesmerising sunset from the view-blessed Mount Buller
Opposite Guided tours take you to backcountry

THE MOUNTAIN DEBRIEF

There's a solid offering of over 50 runs. The mountain is divided into sections – Merritts is ideal for intermediates, Karels is the high mellow bowl, and kids go bananas down in Thredboland, a children's (and beginners') area, so perfect it must have been planned by a parent.

The natural features mid-mountain are the highlights of this resort. Thredbo's upper slopes are lunar (read: exposed and windy), which is why you'll be thankful for T-bars. You might also be thankful for that wind. Or rather, the windblown powder stashes hiding around the resort where boulders and wavy topography come into play. Head to the Bluff or to twin T-Bars Antons and Sponars, and once you've figured out which direction the wind has been blowing and where the loose snow deposits have ended up, hunt them down in the gullies and trees.

A RIDING ITINERARY

On the way to the slopes, kick off with an oat-milk latte at **Central Road 2625** (the best coffee in town). Look beyond the Supertrail, Merrits and High Noon; there's a lot more to Thredbo than those main runs. Start with a wake-up lap on the **Kosciusko Chair**, then head west and ski as much of the off-piste terrain as possible, from the western boundary rope above Golf Course bowl across to the eastern boundary rope at Stanley's Gorge, including the tree runs around **Snowgums and Gunbarrel chairs**.

Stop for lunch at **Kareela Hutte** (*see* p. 181). It's ski-in, ski-out (or tumble out, as the case may be). Best to book ahead.

On powder days, head inbounds from the Bluff cornice into **Cannonball** (which has a long fall line and is usually the last to be tracked out) and then under the old Ramshead lift line through to the bottom of **True Blue** for a fine flake fiesta.

Thredbo is ideal for beginners too: you'll find **Giddy Up off the Burrow** is quieter than the beginner Friday Flat area and has an ideal gradient to get you going (but not too fast).

For intermediates, laps of **Valley View** at the Cruiser are winners, especially at lunch when the slopes are quieter.

ADVENTURE

Push the boundaries – literally – by signing up for a backcountry tour. Courses (thredbo.com.au) range from introduction to advanced and avalanche training.

Eucalypt-lined gums are unique Aussie slope hallmarks
Opposite Thredbo has one of the best snowsports schools in Australia

OFF-MOUNTAIN MUST-DO

- Hit the pool at the **Leisure Centre** (thredbo.com.au), used by Olympic winter athletes.
- Or head to the tiny, tucked-away **Thredbo Ski Museum** (thredboskimuseum.com.au) for historical gems, located below the Kosciusko Room off the Thredbo Village Square, and suddenly a lot of Thredbo makes sense, such as the swinging steins and nods to Europe throughout the village.

—

EAT UP & DRINK DOWN

- Nip down to **Wild Brumby Distillery** (wildbrumby.com) on the way to the satellite town of Jindabyne, where ex-Thredbo Ski School manager Brad Spaulding makes local botanicals into delicious drinkables.
- The bar heaving under bottles at the **Black Bear Inn** has a trio of schnitzel chasers as the house speciality.
- Euro legacies prevail at **Kareela Hutte** (thredbo.com.au) with its cosy, wood-hut ambience. Kareela's lovely lunches are no secret, but capacity is limited - book ahead or go midweek. Either way, keep your eyes peeled for celebs.

APRÈS SKI

- Bring your insulated disco pants - Thredbo hosts more events (thredbo.com.au) than any other resort, from its Corona Sunsets sessions to legendary First Base parties, après at the **Alpine Bar** and **Rainbow Mountain** for LGBTQIA+ powder hounds.

—

STAY

- For self-contained apartments, **Kasees** (kasees.com.au) offers an authentic mountain lodge with hosts Cees (Kasee) and Anne Komen. Kasee will regale you with some epic stories around the lodge fire.
- If you're after a taste of contemporary luxury at a good price, try the **Snowgoose Apartments** (snowgooseapartments.com.au).
- Point your ski tips to the **YHA** (yha.com.au) for possibly the best value in slope proximity in the mountains.
- For five-star alpine luxury, **Rockpool Lodge** (rockpoolthredbo.com) has been named Australia's Best Alpine Chalet at the World Ski Awards for three consecutive years.

Morning groomers off the Cruiser chairlift *Opposite* Bluebird wake-up runs

The Big Kahuna, Perisher is the largest ski area in the Southern Hemisphere with mountains of choice.

Perisher

THE LOWDOWN

Perisher was once Perisher Blue but it dropped the surname and became a family and freestyler favourite. A 6hr drive from Sydney, New South Wales, Perisher has so many integrated areas, the sum of which is supernova-esque and excitingly appealing – to everyone.

The largest resort in the Southern Hemisphere, Perisher combines the linked areas of Guthega, Blue Cow, Perisher and Smiggins Holes, resulting in 12.45sqkm (3076 acres) of riding accessed by 47 lifts. For this part of the world, that's an entire galaxy with serious room to move. Perisher is part of the international Epic Pass system, thanks to the vast network of owners Vail Resorts.

It's also a park paradise, with five terrain parks, halfpipe and two X Rider courses. But even if it's not throwing down corkscrew 540, the many pockets of the resort offer something for all, whether it's the double-black Devil's Marbles at Blue Cow or beginner's Magic Carpet at Perisher. With seven mountains and the convenient 6.3km (3.9mi) Skitube – a Swiss-designed rack rail train helping passengers avoid icy roads by transporting them from Bullocks Flat to Perisher Valley – there's enough to keep you exploring for a week.

But there's a catch (there's always a catch). Perisher misses the magic of the village atmosphere of Thredbo or Victoria's mountaintop resorts, but if it's riding you want, it's riding they've got. Also, the traverses between resort areas will haunt you if you're a snowboarder and don't know back routes. Wax up.

Perisher is located on the Traditional Land of the Ngarigo Monero People.

Mountain stats
- Elevation top: 2034m (6673ft)
- Elevation bottom: 1605m (5266ft)
- Vertical drop: 355m (1165ft)
- Skiable terrain: 12.45sqkm (3076 acres)
- Longest run: 3km (1.9mi)
- Beginner terrain: 22 per cent
- Intermediate terrain: 60 per cent
- Advanced terrain: 18 per cent
- Lifts: 47

Run
After fresh falls, it's the Kamikaze run all the way. For beginners and intermediates, Pleasant Valley is just what it says on the tin.

Experience
Try night skiing and boarding on Tues and Sat nights.

Local's tip
On a snowy day, schuss to Guthega, the most far-flung corner of the resort. Often overlooked, the sheltered, gum-tree-lined runs are tranquil even on the busiest days.

Opposite Blue Cow

THE MOUNTAIN DEBRIEF

If you're not keen to hang at the parks (which have drawn multitudes of winter Olympians, including Torah Bright), the endless variety means you don't have to be an X Games competitor to enjoy the huge variety of slopes. These include undulating, protected runs like outpost Guthega and steep ones like Blue Cow's Zali's. When it comes to T-bars, Perisher's cup overflows. There are more than just a few (21 to be exact), meaning sections of the resorts will keep running even in the wildest weather.

This is the closest you'll get to European-style resort touring in Australia, heading from advanced Mount Perisher to the corners of sleepy Guthega, dipping into beginner's nirvana Smiggins Holes and Blue Cow (where the Skitube also travels directly after stopping at Perisher) en-route.

A RIDING ITINERARY

Instead of starting at Front Valley in Perisher (the bottleneck of the resort despite multiple lifts), take the **Skitube** and start the day at the top in **Blue Cow**. Lap the ridge in the morning – try the trees off **Yarandoo, Outer Limits Chance** and **Rock Garden** (and **Kamikaze** on a powder day), moving along to **Guthega** mid-morning.

Then you're perfectly placed for the secret gem of the resort – lunch at **Basecamp Café** at Guthega (go for the pulled pork burgers alone) tucked in the furthest finger of Perisher with a view of the Main Range. Rip around **Schnaxel, Mother in Law** and **Wombat's Lament**, peaking at **Mount Perisher** in the afternoon with **Side Winder, Hyper Trail** and **Shifty's**, and I'm not adverse to a sneaky hot dog from **Pretty Valley Kiosk** on the way.

ADVENTURE

Head into **Kosciusko National Park**, starting with a half-day trip to **Paralyser** or **Mount Wheatley** (Perisher) with **Wilderness Sports** (wildernesssports.com.au).

Fresh tracks on the way to Mount Perisher

OFF-MOUNTAIN MUST-DO

- A massage at the **Perisher Valley Hotel** (perisher.com.au) is a top-tier indulgence.

EAT UP & DRINK DOWN

- Start your day with breakfast at **Higher Ground** (highgroundcoffeebar.com.au) under the Perisher Manor Hotel, or you can find ski staff at **Aldo's** (aldoscafe.com.au) in the Perisher Skitube, clamouring for bacon-and-egg rolls.
- Eateries are dotted around the mountains for snacks between laps, including **Eyre Hut** at the base of the Eyre T-bar on Mount Perisher, a favourite for a burger and Peroni.
- Succumbing to the hot mini doughnuts at **Lil Orbits Doughnuts** (perisher.com.au) at Perisher's Skitube heading home is a rite of passage.
- Jindabyne is a 30min drive down the hill where the majority of the accommodation is located. It has bloomed with a great range of restaurants, from authentic Japanese at **Takayama** (takayama.com.au) to Mexican at **Cocina Taqueria** (cocina.com.au).

APRÈS SKI

- You will not be partying at Perisher unless the party is with you. **JAX Bar** (perisher.com.au) is the centre of any action in the Perisher Centre.
- Head to locally known bar the Man, actually called the **Man From Snowy River** (themanfromsnowyriver.com.au), or the sunny deck of **Smiggins Hotel** (smiggins.com.au). For an events line-up, check perisher.com.au/events.

STAY

- Pole position for accommodation goes to the **Perisher Valley Hotel** (perisher.com.au). You can't go past perching by the fire at its **Snow Gums restaurant** and admiring the views of the slopes as the entertainment of Front Valley unfolds in front of you, with a glass of wine or a hot chocolate in hand.
- For families, **Smiggins Hotel and Apartments** (smiggins.com.au) has a top Kids' Club with movie nights, dress-up nights, and kids' karaoke.
- Most skiers and workers sleep off-mountain at the satellite town of Jindabyne, where Perisher also owns **The Station.** It's 5km from town but a one-stop budget-friendly place to stay and play.

ALTERNATIVE: CHARLOTTE PASS

This snowbound resort tucked into the foothills of Mount Kosciusko and only accessible by snow cat from Perisher, punches far above its weight. The fairytale valley of club lodges boasts a community vibe where the lift operators call you by name. Families and backcountry lovers are the winners at Charlotte, the latter gathering to bag backcountry bounty on the Kosciusko slopes. If you're not a ski club member, stay at the magnificent, refurbished 1930s' Kosciusko Chalet Hotel. Everything at Charlotte is ski in, ski out, even the pub.

Guthega is the quietest area of the resort *Opposite top* Lessons with views of the Main Range *Opposite bottom* Blue Cow shenanigans

Australia's most accessible resort lives up to its moniker of 'Melbourne on ice', just a 3hr drive from Victoria's capital city.

Mount Buller

THE LOWDOWN

If you like to ride as often as possible, Mount Buller is the pick with the country's shortest route from sofa to slopes. A 3hr drive from Melbourne, Victoria, not only is Mount Buller Australia's most convenient resort but it's outstanding. Its trendy bars are worthy of inner-city status, and there's gorgeous scenery and glam nightlife courtesy of the Melburnians who ski and board here. Did I mention the 3sqkm (741 acres) of riding?

There's another big plus to Buller, and it's visible to the naked eye. It's a real mountain with a pointy peak emerging from lush farmland in pretty north-east Victoria, not part of a ridgeline like its neighbours.

Staying at Buller is like waking up on top of the world (it boasts the most on-mountain beds in Victoria), and gravity is better than caffeine when the wake-up comes via clicking on skis and scoring a downhill run before even getting to a lift.

Off-snow there are over 30 bars and restaurants, so latte lovers have ample choice to schuss into their favourite watering hole. All this means you won't just find Melburnians here – you'll knock poles with Adelaideans, Hobartians and also Sydneysiders who fly down and still find it a quicker mountain option than the resorts in New South Wales.

Mount Buller is on Taungurung Traditional Land.

Mountain stats
- Elevation top: 1780m (5840ft)
- Elevation bottom: 1375m (4511ft)
- Vertical drop: 405m (1329ft)
- Skiable terrain: 3sqkm (740 acres)
- Longest run: 2.5km (1.24mi)
- Beginner terrain: 25 per cent
- Intermediate terrain: 35 per cent
- Advanced terrain: 40 per cent
- Lifts: 20

Run
Drop off the Summit down skiers left for arcing turns with views.

Experience
Book Mount Buller's legendary international ski photographer Harro for your own snow shots or next-level family pics. You can also check out the HarroArt gallery for some inspo.

Local's tip
Listen for rosellas (native parrots) and currawongs singing in the canopy and watch for wombats waddling across the runs around Tirol T-bar.

Opposite Perched on a mountain top, start the day heading downhill at Mount Buller

THE MOUNTAIN DEBRIEF

Buller has distinct northern and southern aspects, so there's always somewhere to ride. In the morning, warm up on the sunny north-facing slopes, then follow the afternoon sun to the south-facing slopes.

An anticlockwise loop will take you from gentle blues and varied terrain up to the summit for hero views, and on to many steeper (and blacker) south-facing runs. The lift network is extensive and quickly delivers you back to the 'spine' of the mountain for an easy green escape route if needed.

For example, head for Standard Run. While it's wide and long for intermediates, there are plenty of options to ski off-shoots, like Wood Run for the more advanced. Easily accessed off Bourke St and Skyline, there's the bonus of the Bull Run Skiosk for post-run snacks. Hot chocolates all round.

A RIDING ITINERARY

Start at **Grimus Grind**, a coffee window at Pension Grimus offering ski-through coffee (and free puppy snacks) where Olympian Anton Grimus may be grinding the beans himself. Then shoot for the gentle blue run of **Shakey Knees** with morning sunshine and fresh groomers, which will have you grinning as wide as the run itself.

The Fox chairlift delivers you to **Tirol Café** to rub shoulders with Ski Patrol grabbing their morning coffee and toasties. Join in or come back for Jimmy's homemade pasta made to order – a bowl will keep you refuelled for hours.

In the afternoon, it's hard to beat **Summit laps** into **Howqua Extension**. If the sun's out, take a break on **Koflers Hutte** deck (try the famous apricot mogul – think 'strudel'), or if it's snowing, tuck inside with a hot toddy between laps. Then it's a seamless segue into après ski.

Beginners, **Burnt Hut** is your sweet spot – the steady pitch and super wide run on the sunny northern slopes is where to build your confidence.

ADVENTURE

Bring your skins and overnight camping kit and take the trail over Howqua Gap to neighbouring **Mount Stirling**, the untamed, un-lifted sister to Mount Buller.

OFF-MOUNTAIN MUST-DO

- Non-skiers win at Buller - take a Siberian Husky tour with **Australian Sled Dog Tours** (mtbuller.com.au/winter) for puppy power!
- Nab a massage in the luxurious **Breathtaker Spa** (breathtaker.com.au/spa-wellness).

EAT UP & DRINK DOWN

- On the mountain, **Bull Run Cantina** is a locals' secret tucked at the base of the Bull Run chair with a 'south-of-the-border' vibe and no phone reception. The empanadas are pockets of deliciousness and make a good one-handed chairlift snack.
- In the village, it's all about the bao buns at newcomer **Jasmine House** (mtbuller.com.au) unless it's the ginger prawn dumplings with chilli at the **Birdcage** (blackcockatoo.net.au).
- Book ahead for the 'Feed me' menu at **Black Cockatoo** (blackcockatoo.net.au) restaurant, inside the Mount Buller Chalet. The interiors are moody and dark, the modern-Australian-Asian flavours are superb, and the share plates moreish.

APRÈS SKI

- For those who like to be seen in the scene, the proximity to Melbourne means Buller is where the city's social set comes to play.
- Rest your hooves at **Snow Pony** (snowponybuller.com.au) for an espresso martini kick, or try their delicious Glühwein (mulled wine) and famous fries.
- Don't miss legendary **Kooroora** (kooroorahotel.com.au). The old weatherboard pub is no more, but the new build has a sleek basement nightclub in action until 3am when they play 'That's Amore' and the ugly lights come on.

STAY

- **Breathtaker Hotel & Spa** (breathtaker.com.au) is the pick, with suite-style apartments, a short stroll to the lift, happy hour for guests in the loft bar, and its own restaurant and lap pool.
- For an iconic village sleep, stay at **Mount Buller Chalet** (mtbullerchalet.com.au) with a ski run by the front door. Choose a view over Bourke Street run or the valley; kids go wild over the lobby moose.
- There's a huge range of apartments here, so opt to live like a local and enjoy cook-ups at home in your PJs at the village square **Kooroora Apartments** (mtbuller.com.au).

Top Grimus chairlift, named after local mountain legend the late Hans Grimus *Bottom* Take a tour with playful Siberian Huskies *Opposite* Pausing in southern powder

A quiet achiever, this snow-bound resort nudges the bewitchery of Zermatt or Chamonix; for Europhiles, the secret weapon is the village charm.

Falls Creek

THE LOWDOWN

There's something about Falls Creek in Victoria. It's the snow-lined, winding lanes and the intimate atmosphere under flake-laden snow gums, but also wandering home late at night and hearing nothing but the crunch of snow underfoot and, on a cold night, the happy hiss of snow guns (snow cannons). In short, it's endlessly charming, a taste of Europe smack-bang in the Aussie Alps.

The other 'thing' about Falls Creek, with its 4.5sqkm (1112 acres) of skiing, is that there's so much to do. Catch the Firework Fiesta on Thursday nights, toast marshmallows over the fire-pit during Twilight Tuesdays, go fat biking (on a specialised bike perfect for riding snowy trails), tobogganing at Windy Corner, snow-tubing or night-skiing.

It's the subtle ingredients here which don't feature in brochures that bubble to the top to become headliners. For example, the streets remain snow covered once the snow settles in, meaning Falls transforms into a ski-in, ski-out village; slide from your accommodation to the lifts and return by following a network of home trails as though on a magic mystery tour to your own door. Another gold nugget – the terrain is progression perfect for all levels. Families are the winners, as most runs funnel back to base.

And then there's the vibe ... being further from Melbourne than other ski areas means skiers stay longer and settle in creating a connected community.

Ridiculously pretty, friendly, without the weekend warriors of Melbourne, Falls gives you a holiday as soft and calm as a lightly falling flake.

Falls Creek is on the Traditional Land of the Jaitmatang People.

Mountain stats
- Elevation top: 2034m (6673ft)
- Elevation bottom: 1500m (4921ft)
- Vertical drop: 538m (1765ft)
- Skiable terrain: 12.45sqkm (3076 acres)
- Longest run: 3.1km (1.9mi)
- Beginner terrain: 17 per cent
- Intermediate terrain: 60 per cent
- Advanced terrain: 23 per cent
- Lifts: 16

Run
If there's powder about, check out often-overlooked Shadow Ridge. The spectacular village views of Roller Coaster win the Most Scenic award.

Experience
Calling all couples! This ski area is romance-arama. Soak up dazzling views of Rocky Valley Dam and alpine peaks.

Local's tip
Click off skis at Snonuts Donuts (snonutsdonuts.com) at Slalom Plaza and pull up an outdoor pew for the best people watching and mountain viewing.

Opposite Night skiing is just one of many activities on offer

THE MOUNTAIN DEBRIEF

Wide open spaces and limited crowds are the hallmarks of Falls across its 90 trails. Separated neatly into areas of ability with different aspects, the result is that you'll find optimum slope to ride any time of day. When fresh snow is about, frolic around Valley of The Moon, Wishing Well and Roller Coaster.

A RIDING ITINERARY

Representing perfect town planning, coffee at **1550** (stfallsresort.com.au) cafe is merely a glove toss from the Halley Comet chairlift – or **Bob Sugar** (bobsugar.com.au) if you decide you need a foot-long bacon-and-egg roll – arriving at the top of **Fast Hoot** with your neurons on fire.

Start with a charging run before any new tracks are made (with top tree off-shoots on a powder day for stashes), then straight back up the chair and follow **Home Trail** to the **Summit chairlift** for speedy turns on deliciously fresh Summit

groomers like **Exhibition** and **Cabbage Patch**. If moving sedately, try laps of **Highway** and **Rapunzel's** or the less busy **Lakeside** to warm up.

As the sun softens north slopes, head backside to **Ruined Castle** for big carve turns on wide-open runs or to the advanced terrain park for airtime before a panini calls at **Snonuts Donuts**.

Beginners aren't left out in the cold either. Committing to Australia's longest green run **Wombat's Ramble** (at 2.2km/1.36mi) is top family fun and a low-risk thrill.

ADVENTURE

You're in the home of Australian cross-country skiing, so unleash on the 65km/40mi of groomed trails. This is pristine High Country at its best, exploring parts of the Bogong High Plains that most visitors rarely see.

OFF-MOUNTAIN MUST-DO

- Mosey around Mount Beauty township, with a quick peek into **Gather + Harvest** (gatherandharvest.com.au) for its handcrafted natural candles and soaps.

EAT UP & DRINK DOWN

- If seeking sensation, you can't put a fork past **Summit Ridge** (summitridge.com.au) for taste, presentation, and a killer wine list.
- The bubbles and shucked-to-order Coffin Bay oysters at **Feathertop Alpine Lodge** (feathertoplodge.com.au) are a *chef's kiss*, and the intimate atmosphere is perfect for an après date**.**

APRÈS SKI

- Party night is Monday when staff hit **The Man** (themanfallscreek.com.au) with bar specials.
- Don't miss **Gay Ski Week Australia** (pointsofdifference.com) when table dancing erupts.

STAY

- **Astra** (astrafallscreek.com.au) is the high-end pick with an award-winning Day Spa, vintage wine cellar and subterranean magnesium pool to soothe sore skiers.
- Runner-up is the boutique apartments of **St Falls Resort** (stfallsresort.com.au), metres from Halley's Comet chairlift.

Top Taking time to appreciate mountain magic *Middle* Finding the tree stashes *Bottom* A family favourite - it's better when we're together *Opposite* A fresh falls day at Falls

SNOW PRO
Valentino Guseli the snowboarder

When you turn up for the LAAX Open World Cup event you know two things: the pipe is going to be perfect, and everyone will be throwing down. In 2021 a then-15-year-old wowed the world of winter sports by taking the top score in qualifying, eventually finishing eighth. Then the day before his 16th birthday, Valentino Guseli broke Shaun White's 2010 7m (22.9ft) World Record for the highest air out of the pipe - at 7.3m (23.9ft). This teenager from Narooma, New South Wales (training on an airbag built by his Nonno, Guido) was hailed as a teenage prodigy.

Guseli has since stomped into history as the first Aussie snowboarder to win a World Cup Big Air event and as the first snowboarder in World Cup competition to stand on a podium in Slopestyle Big Air, Slopestyle and Halfpipe all in one season. This triple threat is set to have career highs breaking records - even if he's the one who set them.

When did you begin snowboarding?

My Dad's been taking me to the snow since before I could walk, and when I was three and old enough to snowboard he got me a set-up. I can't remember it but he said I was just laughing and giggling my way down the hill.

Have you always had a fierce drive to win?

When I first started, I didn't lose very much. And then every time I lost, I would just cry and cry and cry. Because I didn't know what it was like. And I just really always wanted to be the best at everything I did back when I was younger. And if someone was better than me at something, I took it personally.

How was it going to your first open-age event and breaking a World Record?

LAAX in 2021 was my first World Cup event and kind of the moment where I wasn't competing against people my own age anymore. I was competing against the absolute best and I found out that I did have what it takes to compete with those guys. I actually wasn't sure before that competition. I wasn't even sure I'd make finals and was feeling insecure about it and not feeling confident in my riding. And then that was a little bit of a green light.

What were the expectations after that event?

I'd say that lots of people expected a lot of me and I kind of let them down. I didn't get any other decent results that year, I didn't get any results better than eight. I think lots of people thought it was like beginner's luck. And then I started to figure out ways of competing at this level and started gradually getting better and better results. And then finally got my first halfpipe podium at Aspen X Games 2023, which is pretty amazing because it took me three years to get there.

How did you adjust to competing against older competitors?

I started to figure out what was necessary to make finals and not putting everything into qualification and saving some in the tank. And understanding it's pretty tricky to just win straight away when you have to change your level by such a big amount going into that level of competition. I kind of had to learn through trial and error.

How did the decision come about to build you a massive airbag in the backyard?

My Nonno (grandfather) and Dad had the material made in China and then we got it shipped over. We'd been going to the airbags in Japan to work on tricks so we knew roughly how it was supposed to work. It was about probably 9m (30ft) in the air and the length of the deck was around 18m (60ft) long. They didn't want me to have to go overseas to train all the time and it meant I could spend more time at home.

Will you keep all three disciplines of Halfpipe, Slopestyle and Big Air?

It's really popular for people to just choose and only do one. But when I was younger, I was just competing in everything because some wise people told us that it's all snowboarding and that it's very important to be able to do all of it. And then there were certain people that said that I should change to just one. We kind of disregarded that, you meet so many people in this industry and they all have their two cents. And I just kept doing everything.

Why do you think there are so many Australian World Cup and Olympic champions in snowboard?

We don't take it for granted. We have to travel really, really far and be away from our families for so long, so we always have to make the most of being away. I think another thing is the conditions might be a little bit harder where we're from compared to some places in the Northern Hemisphere.

What's great about riding in Australia?

You can ride in a T shirt and it's always a good vibe riding with gum trees in the background – it's totally unique.

AOTEAROA NEW ZEALAND

In Māori, Aotearoa means 'Land of the Long White Cloud'. But for skiers and boarders, it's the 'Land of the Long White Ski Slope'. There are as many reasons to choose a ride in Aotearoa New Zealand as there are peaks in its Southern Alps.

For Aussie neighbours, it's an overseas trip with the added punch of powder – fair conversion rates and cheaper lift tickets, as well as aggressively-priced accommodation and lift pass packages that equal serious savings. For northerners, it's the southern go-to (and the training ground for Swiss, Swedish and Austrian race teams).

There's great diversity in the North Island, volcanoes and lava flows have created topographically fascinating ski fields with unexpected fall lines at Whakapapa, Mount Ruapehu and Turoa. In the South Island, a multitude of ski-resort gems stud the Alps like dropped diamonds. Down here, the mountains are nothing to sniff at, starring Aoraki/Mount Cook as Aotearoa New Zealand's highest mountain at 3724m (12,217ft) and Haupapa/Tasman Glacier. Arriving here by ski plane (a plane on sleds) is a bucket-list experience.

But getting in reveals one of the only downsides of skiing in Aotearoa New Zealand: there is no on-snow accommodation. Anywhere. Well, apart from 15 apartments at Cardrona (*see* p. 202) which are continually booked out. And NZ mountain roads (especially up to Mount Hutt) can put terror into even the hardiest of souls. Also, watch the weather – there are no trees in any NZ ski area, so the slopes are exposed and, like in any mountain zone, weather can change from bluebird to white out in a finger snap.

Take your choice of slopes: you can straight-line for the bright lights of Queenstown (*see* p. 207), head to the pro-rider hamlet of Wānaka (*see* p. 201), take the kids for free to Mount Hutt (*see* p. 213), or absorb the cosy and quirky atmosphere of Club Fields (*see* p. 216). And on a down day, there are wineries and gourmet nooks, legendary lodges, fishing ... you may need a holiday from your holiday.

For a small country with four million people (and 26 million sheep), New Zealanders think and dream as big as their mountains. Whether you're a beginner, a moderate skier returning to the slopes, a teenager who prefers sliding rails, a black-diamond bandit seeking steeps and deeps, or a bi-hemisphere-curious skier – there's a piste here to make you wonder why you've never been before.

The clincher is Aotearoa New Zealand itself, where practical Kiwis have a can-do mentality and the *Lord of the Rings* scenery doesn't disappoint. A ski trip here is never just about skiing; it's the entire experience.

Coolest winter selfie
It's all about the lake views. And the 'things in lakes' views, like 'That Wānaka Tree' in the shallows of Lake Wānaka (for 70,000 tree angles, hit #thatwanakatree). Look out for those rare lake-and-snow views, either with Queenstown's Lake Wakatipu or Lake Wānaka (the view from Treble Cone is particularly stunning).

Off the hill, the rustic towns of Glenorchy, Arrowtown and Lake Hayes are also camera fodder.

Get appy
All New Zealand ski areas are up alpine roads at least a 30min drive from their service towns. Snowriders is a carpooling app that helps drivers find passengers and vice-versa.

Dark, clear skies and unique celestial features make stargazing in NZ an otherworldly experience. There's a Dark Sky Reserve around Mount Cook/Aoraki. With the Star Chart app, point your device to the night sky and virtual stars and planets will appear through the app.

If campervanning, CamperMate offers road warnings and mountain track safety alerts.

Don't break the bank
They may have few, if any, chairlifts, but the Club Fields (*see* p. 216) offer next-level value.

Stay in satellite towns over Queenstown or Wānaka; a solid Q'town savoury pie will keep you going for spare change.

When it snows
Mount Hutt, with its south-east aspect, has a unique microclimate, jutting out from the edge of the Southern Alps with the Pacific Ocean on its doorstep. The flanks catch snow from the south-east like no other ski field in Aotearoa New Zealand and its height means an annual snow accumulation of 4m (13ft). It also gets slammed by the unfriendly north-west wind (it has named its robust eight-seater the Nor'West Express).

Cardrona faces south, so tends to be a few degrees colder than the resorts in Queenstown and Treble Cone. This makes for smooth grooming and light and fluffy off-piste. Coronet, also south facing, tends to ice up after a cold snap.

Nestled at the foot of Mount Aspiring National Park, Wānaka feels like a small bubble with two ski areas 35 minutes equidistant.

Wānaka (Cardrona and Treble Cone)

THE LOWDOWN

Wānaka, on Ngāi Tahu lands, has a vastly different personality from Queenstown and while it's possible to be a fan of both, you'll leave with a preference for one or the other. Where Queenstown is a talker, Wānaka is more of a listener. It's demure, with an equally drool-worthy food and wine scene (albeit on a smaller scale), and within a few days, faces become familiar and you'll feel like a local. Queenstown feels high-octane. Wānaka feels ... real.

Its two ski areas also have different characters. Towards Queenstown is people-pleasing Cardrona with wide groomers, terrain parks and a kids' area. In the other direction is Treble Cone (TC), the South Island's largest ski area with lengthy runs, legendary off-piste, steep and deep natural terrain, and stunning Lake Wānaka panoramas. Water views while on snow are rare in the ski world, and this area outdoes itself.

Wherever you ride, you'll come for a few days and end up looking at Wānaka real-estate windows for the ultimate lifestyle change.

Opposite Powder day at Cardrona

 Mountain stats

Cardrona
- Elevation top: 1860m (6102ft)
- Elevation bottom: 1670m (5479ft)
- Vertical drop: 462m (1516ft)
- Skiable terrain: 3.45sqkm (853 acres)
- Longest run: 4.2km (2.6mi)
- Beginner terrain: 20 per cent
- Intermediate terrain: 45 per cent
- Advanced terrain: 25 per cent
- Lifts: 8

Treble Cone
- Elevation top: 2088m (6850ft)
- Elevation bottom: 1260m (4134ft)
- Vertical drop: 700m (2300ft)
- Skiable terrain: 5.5 sqkm (1360 acres)
- Longest run: 4km (2.5mi)
- Beginner terrain: 10 per cent
- Intermediate terrain: 45 per cent
- Advanced terrain: 45 per cent
- Lifts: 6

 Run
For intermediates, Cardrona's Bowling Alley and Powder Keg are rarely busy and usually groomed top-to-tail for fast laps. Treble Cone's Gun Barrel in Saddle Basin has a gentle pitch with steep walls, offering a playful surf-like descent.

 Experience
Luxe Soho Basin (sohobasin.com) is a 40min drive from Wānaka, and a cat skiing experience with lunch by winery Amisfield.

 Local's tip
Head down Helwick St to find 47Frocks (47frocks.co.nz) featuring New Zealand-designed labels. Wools of Wānaka (woolsofwanaka.co.nz) specialises in possum merino clothing.

THE MOUNTAIN DEBRIEF

Wānaka's two ski areas tend to split the crowd: families and freestylers straight line for Cardrona, while advanced riders and freeriders feel the pull of Treble Cone.

Cardrona

Cardrona is making moves. For a start, it bought Treble Cone. It also added a 'chondola' (NZ's only gondola-chair style lift) and, more recently, a chairlift on the southern face of Mount Cardrona opening two bowls of intermediate terrain in Willows Basin. It has sweet south-facing 1860m (6100ft) slopes, wide-open runs, world-class kids' lessons and facilities, all-level terrain parks and medal-worthy noodles at Noodle Bar – arrive early to snag a window seat for mountain views.

Treble Cone

Treble Cone (TC) has the longest pistes and is the largest ski resort on the South Island. The point-blank lake vistas while riding are something you'll only find in places like Norway's Loftoten or Lake Tahoe in the USA (*see* p. 37). There are natural gullies galore, chutes for experts, insane off-piste-quality grooming on-piste and a buzzing vibe of snow-loving riders. There's nothing not to love about TC – except the 7km (4.4mi) access road, so catch the free shuttle up.

Treble Cone's position in the Southern Alps means it scores some of the more reliable snow conditions and weather in the region, all while being protected from the bitterly cold winds that plague other resorts.

A RIDING ITINERARY

Pick a resort, then lay out your day's game plan.

Cardrona

Get your pass online, park at Valley View, grab a coffee from **Little Meg** (mtcardronastation.co.nz/little-meg) and jump straight onto the chairlift (intermediate-level access only). Ride **Willows** before lunch.

Take a lap on **Skyline** (Main Basin), followed by a Real Journey lap at **Captains Basin**; from these two trails you can see the whole resort. While the resort boasts a lot of friendly riding, **Tulips** and **Secret Bowl** offer solid off-piste adventure.

In the afternoon, ride **Arcadia Basin**, through Arcadia Valley and give the **Chutes** the eye – if you have the experience, access them from the top of Whitestar.

Treble Cone

Park at the bottom of the access road and hop on the free shuttle service to arrive at the resort's doorstep. In the morning take warm-up laps on fresh corduroy in the **Home Basin** on **Triple Treat** and **Main Street**. If **Powder Bowl** is open and firing, outskate everyone along the cat track before diving into the fresh powder below the old tow shed.

Pit stop at **Altitude Espresso** (treblecone.com) at the top of the six-seater in the Home Basin for amazing pizza with even more amazing views.

In the afternoon hike the **Summit** for the best views in the South Island from a ski area, then drop off the back for a few laps of **Gold Rush** chutes until your quads say it's time to go home.

ADVENTURE

Try heliskiing with either **Harris Mountains Heli-Ski Wanaka** (heliski.co.nz) or **Southern Lakes Heli** (southernlakesheliski.com) – they can both access hundreds of peaks in around 11 mountain ranges, from rolling slopes to steep lines.

On terra firma, have an epic adventure tackling the world's highest waterfall cable climb (like *via ferrata*) up sheer rock faces and over suspension bridges with **Wildwire Wānaka** (wildwire.co.nz).

Opposite top Epic views from Cardrona *Opposite bottom* More epic views from Treble Cone ... it's a hard call between mountains

Wānaka, Aotearoa New Zealand   203

OFF-MOUNTAIN MUST-DO

- A personal favourite is **Warbirds and Wheels** (warbirdsandwheels.com), a museum of classic planes and cars by Wānaka Airport.
- Every Easter, **Warbirds over Wānaka** is a spectacular air show for fellow #avgeeks.

EAT UP & DRINK DOWN

- Sustainably sourced food and locally crafted beer abound.
- Go wine tasting at **Maude** (maudewines.com) with a charcuterie platter.
- Funky **Muttonbird** (muttonbird.co.nz) down a lane off Ardmore St is a regular choice for finer bites - book ahead.

APRÈS SKI

- If riding Cardrona, après-ski with a Speight's Ale (a South Island staple) at the iconic 1863 **Cardrona Hotel** (cardronahotel.co.nz), 15min from Wānaka.
- **Wānaka Beerworks** (wanakabeerworks.co.nz) has a craft beer tasting room inside a toy museum for an unexpected combination.

STAY

- The boutique **Wānaka Haven** (wanakahaven.co.nz) on farmland 15min from Wānaka feels like a wealthy friend's holiday house.
- **Cross Hill Lodge & Domes** (crosshill.co.nz) on picturesque Lake Hawaea features luxury geo-glamping domes.

Top Located top floor of the Snow Sports HQ, ski in from Skyline Ridge to Noodle Bar *Middle* The park is stacked with X Games medallists, Olympians and super groms *Bottom* The 'Chondola' (NZ's only gondola chair-style lift) *Opposite* Fast moves on steeper slopes is a Treble Cone signature

Every night is Saturday night in this thumping adrenaline-pumping southern capital, nestled against the shores of sapphire Lake Wakatipu

Queenstown (Remarkables and Coronet Peak)

THE LOWDOWN

Not all ski resorts are created equal when it comes to cosmopolitan offerings and nightlife, but Queenstown, on Ngāi Tahu lands, is synonymous with glitz and glamour. When the slopes cool down, the town heats up – with more than 150 bars and restaurants, the nightlife's as sizzling as any global capital.

And it's a foodie town as much as a skier town, fuelled by incredible local ingredients (the lamb alone with bring you baaaack). It's not just the quality of the food options, it's the density. There's a walk-everywhere matrix of international options from Korean to Mexican to Peruvian, including some excellent no-waste kitchens.

Queenstown's resorts – the more advanced Remarkables and gentler Coronet Peak – are on the same NZSki pass (nzski.com) so double down.

Looking east from Queenstown, the jagged teeth ripping into the skyline is the dramatic border of the Remarkables ski area. A 40min drive from town with its fair share of switchbacks (a ski bus is available from central Queenstown), this tiny slice of NZ has a European alpine feel.

With stunning views, playful rollercoaster terrain and incredible back bowls throwing down a challenge, it's no wonder that some of the best ski racers in the world use Coronet Peak on their international training circuit. Plus it's just a 20min drive from Queenstown … on a sealed road. That doesn't seem like a big deal until you've driven one unsealed mountain road too many.

Why ride one when you can ride two?

Opposite The Remarkables, both in name and nature

Mountain stats

Remarkables
- Elevation top: 1943m (6345ft)
- Elevation bottom: 1586m (5250ft)
- Vertical drop: 357m (1171ft)
- Skiable terrain: 2.2sqkm (543 acres)
- Longest run: 1.5km (0.9mi), 1168m
- Beginner terrain: 30 per cent
- Intermediate terrain: 40 per cent
- Advanced terrain: 30 per cent
- Lifts: 7

Coronet Peak
- Elevation top: 1649m (5410ft)
- Elevation bottom: 1168m (3822ft)
- Vertical drop: 462m (1516ft)
- Skiable terrain: 2.8sqkm (692 acres)
- Longest run: 2.4km (1.5mi)
- Beginner terrain: 25 per cent
- Intermediate terrain: 45 per cent
- Advanced terrain: 30 per cent
- Lifts: 8

Run
First Tracks at Coronet Peak. You'll find local skiers here between 8am and 9am on weekdays, getting a fix before work.

Experience
After a day at Coronet Peak, soak at The Onsen Hot Pools at the bottom of the mountain overlooking the Shotover River. Or, at the bottom of the Remarkables, have 15min rounds of wood-fired steam saunas followed by ice-pool plunges at Wellspace NZ (wellspacenz.com).

Local's tip
One of the best Lake Wakatipu vistas can be savoured from the *Basket of Dreams* sculpture after climbing Queenstown Hill.

THE MOUNTAIN DEBRIEF

The Remarkables
Apart from some pretty impressive freeride terrain, the Remarkables also has up to seven terrain parks, including the only Burton Stash concept park in the Southern Hemisphere, made from natural features and one of only six worldwide; another is in Avoriaz, France (*see* p. 77). It's also home to the Freeride World Qualifier event the North Face Frontier.

Coronet Peak
Coronet Peak is one of the country's most popular resorts and it's easy to understand why. The mountain suits beginners and intermediates, and although it doesn't score high in the snow stakes – just 2m (6.5ft) on average a year – there are excellent snow-making facilities.

On a powder day, venture to the Rock Gully T-bar area where there are fewer crowds. It's often used as the training area for overseas ski teams and it's the place to see some elite-level action.

A RIDING ITINERARY

Both of Queenstown's ski resorts deliver memorable days on the slopes.

The Remarkables
Start the day with a flat white from the **Rastusburn Coffee Bar** (in the Remarkables base building), then ride the **Shadow Basin chairlift** and watch the freeriders shredding Shadow Basin and jumping the infamous Breakfast Cliff. Lap **Shadow Basin**, then hike up to the top of **Alta Chutes** and then ski **Elevator Chute**. It's a 20min hike from the top of the Shadow Basin chairlift, so be sure to know the route before you go and pay attention to all safety and avalanche instructions.

Loop back to Shadow Basin before hiking the **Weather Station** and ski out to **Homeward Bound** (skiers left). This takes you past the ski-area boundary, but you can catch the mountain shuttle back up – usually from 10am to 3pm but check ahead.

Coronet Peak
Grab a coffee from Coronet Peak's base cafe before booting up and heading out to the **Coronet Express**. The appropriately named **M1** is freshly groomed for laying down some arcs. Warmed up, head **to Green Gates Express** or some fast laps. Then over to the **Rocky Gully T-bar** to grab a pizza lunch at **Heidi's Hut** (*see* p. 211).

In the afternoon, take T-bar laps skiing through the **Race Arena** or on **Exchange Drop's** perfect wind-buffed snow. Catch a sunset over the **Wakatipu Basin** and an après before heading back to town.

ADVENTURE

This has been the adventure capital of the Southern Hemisphere ever since Kawarau Bridge bungy jumping took flight in 1988. Now there's also NZ's highest bungy **Nevis Bungy** (bungy.co.nz), indoor skydiving, sky diving from a plane, winter white-water rafting, e-foiling on Lake Wakatipu, the 1600m (5250ft) **Skyline Luge track** (skyline.co.nz) above Queenstown and **Ziptrek Ecotours** (ziptrek.co.nz) that has the world's steepest tree-to-tree zipline.

Opposite Coronet Peak is a winner for views and fun rollercoaster terrain

OFF-MOUNTAIN MUST-DO

- There are six world-class golf courses within a 30km (20mi) drive, including **Millbrook** (millbrook.co.nz), home to the New Zealand Open.
- You're also surrounded by wineries with pinot noir and chardonnay superstars. Grab a glass at longstanding favourite **Amisfield Winery & Bistro** (amisfield.co.nz) or the newer **Gibbston Valley Winery** (gibbstonvalley.com).

EAT UP & DRINK DOWN

- The **Dining Nest** (nestqt.co.nz) at lofty Kamana Lakehouse, with floor-to-ceiling views of Lake Wakatipu and the Remarkables, is Tolkien-inspiring.
- The colourful fare at breakfast/brunch/cocktail bar **Yonder** (yonderqt.co.nz) is as delicious as it is photogenic.
- On Coronet Peak, head to **Heidi's Hut** (coronetpeak.co.nz), a European-style warming hut and restaurant at the bottom of the T-bar with delicious pizza and pasta - some of the best on-mountain dining in Aotearoa New Zealand.

APRÈS SKI

- Pull up a mountainside deck chair or bean bag for DJ tunes and local craft beer at Coronet Peak during Night Skiing or **Cargo Brewery** (cargobrewery.co.nz) on the way back to Queenstown.
- For a speakeasy atmosphere, the below-ground **Bunker** (thebunker.co.nz) is intimate and cosy.
- Head to nearby Arrowtown for a drink at the **Blue Door** (bluedoorbar.co.nz), a cosy bar hiding in an alleyway, before pizza at **Aosta** (aosta.nz).

STAY

- The **Dairy Private Hotel** (naumihotels.com/thedairyhotel) is a character-filled boutique hotel downtown.
- Sustainably designed smart hotel **mi-pad** (mipadhotels.com) has compact, well-thought-out rooms.
- A water taxi will shuttle you between Queenstown and the **Hilton Queenstown Resort & Spa** (hilton.com), away from the hustle and bustle.

Top The hustle and bustle of Queenstown gives the town a vibrant energy *Bottom* Queenstown's lakeside location makes for spectacular scenery *Opposite* Upper alpine gully

Known as Ōpuke in Māori, this can be a moody mountain but, with some of the longest runs in New Zealand, this is the place to 'give it the jandal'.

Mount Hutt

THE LOWDOWN

Give it the jandal. A 'jandal' is a thong or flip-flop in Kiwiland, and to 'give it' means to go fast. Only Kiwis would 'give it' to a wild, wuthering mountain with beach footwear, but this is what you'll hear in the local patois. While half the Queenstown skiers hail from 'over the ditch' (the Tasman Sea separating NZ from Australia), here you'll find mostly locals and the resulting laid-back vibe is Aotearoa New Zealand at its unpretentious best.

And this is no poor cousin - it's a major-player mountain. Owned by NZSki, it shares the same full-service glory as the others in the group (the Remarkables and Coronet Peak, *see* p. 207): high-speed lifts, gourmet restaurants and live weekend music. It's also visually unique, rising like a (very mini) Kilimanjaro from the Canterbury patchwork plains. This is why it sometimes gets weather which can make the access road emotionally traumatising (take a shuttle).

But that's the appeal; with sunshine or wild weather (sometimes both in a day), it gives you a true alpine experience. There's also wide, open terrain with leg-burning runs and spectacular farmland views.

Despite winning New Zealand's Best Ski Resort in the World Ski Awards eight times, the judging reports never mention the welcoming feeling of being greeted with cheery waves from passing cars or the 'I'm-a-farmer' one-finger wave from the steering wheel, but they should. In the satellite town of Methven, 35min down the mountain, you'll find the pace is as wonderfully slow as the riding can be satisfyingly fast.

Canterbury and Mount Hutt lie within the Traditional boundaries of the main South Island Māori iwi (tribe), Ngāi Tahu.

Mountain stats
- Elevation top: 2086m (7618ft)
- Elevation bottom: 1403m (5249ft)
- Vertical drop: 683m (2368ft)
- Skiable terrain: 3.65 sqkm (900 acres)
- Longest run: 2km (1.2mi)
- Beginner terrain: 30 per cent
- Intermediate terrain: 40 per cent
- Advanced terrain: 30 per cent
- Lifts: 5

Run
The Virgin Mile. This intermediate run will take you to what feels like the edge of the earth as the views of the Canterbury Plains and Rakaia River are thrown up in front like a stage set.

Experience
Mount Hutt's 2086m (7618ft) summit and almost coast-to-coast views make first tracks sunrises and fresh groomers almost existential experiences. After an hour of Summit lift lapping power, slip into Ōpuke Kai (*see* p. 214) for breakfast.

Local's tip
Midweek - while residents are back at the daily grind you'll have the mountain to yourself. Also, the resort is cashless, so pack the plastic.

Opposite Giving it the jandal at Mount Hutt

THE MOUNTAIN DEBRIEF

What makes Mount Hutt one of the best? It's the biggest. And the snowiest, with an annual monster snowfall of 4m (13ft) per season. It's also only a 90min drive from Christchurch Airport. Land at 10am and be on the slopes by midday. As the locals might say, sweet as, bro.

With black chutes dribbling down from the mountain ridge, a handful of blues and a base of green, all levels have something to play on, and a powder day is when it comes into its own – which is often.

A RIDING ITINERARY

Catch a coffee at **Alpine Grind** (thealpinegrind.co.nz) on your way up the mountain. You want to start awake, given Mount Hutt's eight-seater chairlift will get you to the top of the intermediate terrain in a few fast minutes. Hone your skills or blow out the cobwebs on **Morning Glory** and **Broadway**. This wide trail is famous for excellent groomed corduroy with heaps of space to shape some nice turns.

If it's a powder day, head for **South Face**, a double-black-diamond run that seems to disappear into the immense Canterbury Plains in a cinematic (too much *Lord of the Rings*?) move. Ride into the big-screen view while picking a line through the many chute and face options.

Your legs will give out before your passion does. Catch the traverse line at the bottom and then enjoy **Monty's** ridge as you pick up the bottom triple chair lift. Then have a pit stop at **Ōpuke Kai**.

In the afternoon, follow the sun and capture the epic view that follows the Rakaia River all the way to the Pacific Ocean while boosting down the **Virgin Mile** trail.

Beginners can do laps on **Highway 72**, perfect for finding ski feet.

ADVENTURE

Hit up the terrain parks. **Gunners Alley** has jump gaps ranging from 10m to 18m (33ft to 60ft), there are rails in the **Jib Garden**, and **Inside Leg** has small to medium rails, boxes, jumps, hips and a park with surface-level boxes and small snow features for freeride novices.

Top You'll pause for the vistas *Bottom* Mandatory selfies with the backdrop of Ōpuke Kai *Opposite* Mount Hutt is on the NZSki pass

OFF-MOUNTAIN MUST-DO

- Soak in the outdoor mountain-sourced, solar-powered **Ōpuke Pools** (opuke.nz) in Methven, catch a flick at **Paradiso** (cinemaparadiso.co.nz), a cute theatre on the main street, or see some pretty fascinating early NZ ski history at the **Methven Heritage Centre** (methvenheritagecentre.co.nz).

___

EAT UP & DRINK DOWN

- Head to **Ski Time** (skitime.co.nz) for that 'who's-who-of-town' dinner experience.
- While an Irish pub wouldn't normally be high on the list, in this case, the Murphy's Stout Pie at the **Dubliner** Irish bar and restaurant (dubliner.co.nz) is a yes from me.

___

APRÈS SKI

- Grab a mountain burger at **Ōpuke Kai** to pair with the live music every weekend on the mountain (mthutt.co.nz/events).
- Methven has two pubs: one imaginatively called the **Brown Pub** (brownpub.co.nz), favoured by local agricultural workers, the other, the **Blue Pub** (thebluepub.com), favoured by everyone else. If the main road seems empty, chances are the Blue Pub is rocking.

___

STAY

- **Ski Time** (skitime.co.nz) is the pick of places to stay with a restaurant and cosy fire.
- There's self-contained apartments at four-star **Brinkley Village** (brinkleyresort.co.nz).
- An alternative to Methven is the golf resort village of **Fable Terrace Downs Resort** (fablehotelsandresorts.com).

ALTERNATIVE: CLUB FIELDS

If you want powder, not poseurs; purity, not partying; and heliskiing options over home heating, then hit the path less trodden. Take a road trip to hit the Club Field areas. Unique to Aotearoa New Zealand and raved about by foreign pro-riders, these hidden gems are strung together like a pearl necklace snaking its way across the 450km (280mi) between the big-daddy ski areas of Christchurch and Queenstown. The families or locals who run the fields aren't focused on profit but on creating a community of soulful skiing with like-minded individuals. Forget chairlifts (although Ōhau and Mount Dobson both have one); it's mainly rope tows and T-bars.

You've probably never heard their names but shovel them to the top of your list for a ski holiday with a twist: Mount Cheeseman, Broken River (Te Waka Ski Awa O Broken in Māori), Craigieburn, Temple Basin (Kaimatua), Hanmer Springs (Te Whakatakanga o te Ngārahu o te ahi a Tamatea), Mount Dobson, Roundhill and Ōhau to name a few. The large commercial resorts of Mount Hutt (*see* p. XXX) and at Wānaka (*see* p. XXX) act as neat bookends. This is not Canada's Powder Highway (*see* p. XXX) but there's an even greater sense of discovery, and the scenery is much more diverse - you'll find ski mountains lost in a different decade.

We're talking bare essentials with lodges that are often of the 'wash your own dishes' variety. The drawcards are the undiluted Kiwi flavour, the wild, raw terrain and the clientele spanning first-timers to hardened vets and drop-ins, as well as staying in the mountain lodges on site, an NZ rarity. You don't have to be an expert to take on the Club Fields, but you do need to be a fan of minimalist conditions and fresh mountain air.

Opposite Sweet, early morning Mount Hutt corduroy

SNOW PRO
Sam Smoothy the adventurer

Born to ride. This is an appropriate tagline for Smoothy, whose mother was skiing Treble Cone in New Zealand the day he was born, and just a few months later he found himself back cruising the slopes in a backpack. A thirst for adventure has followed him ever since.

With a ski racing background, the Wānaka native tried to quench that thirst joining the Freeride World Tour, claiming victories in Chamonix, Fieberbrunn and Andorra in 2015. It was this last competition where it was clear bigger things were in store for Smoothy. His impossible-seeming exposed line had the commentators

exclaiming, 'Where are you *going*?' Was Smoothy lost? No, he stomped one of the gnarliest competition lines ever skied. The clip went viral, the world went wild and Teton Gravity Research called with an invitation to Alaska.

The heady realm of ski mountaineering and the big screen were beckoning. Sam has created movies like *SkyPiercer*, a Banff Mountain Film Festival finalist and he is deep in a project to climb and ski all 24 of NZ's heavily glaciated 3000m (9842ft) peaks.

What was it like growing up in Wānaka?

Wānaka was such a great place to grow up, it was a peaceful little place with heaps of fun activities to get stuck into with a really cool community. I've been all round the world since and it's still one of the most beautiful places I've been. I'm very fortunate to call Wānaka home.

What made you decide to switch over to freeskiing and compete on the FWT?

At the time we were always sneaking off from race training to go jump and ski off-piste, it was just so much more expressive and fun! I could see I was never going to be a World Cup racer, I lacked the skills and funding, so dove head first into freeskiing. After having a go at everything from big air to halfpipe I worked out freeride probably suited me best so I worked away at that, spending years on the qualifying series before finally managing to qualify for the FWT.

Did having a technical background and skiing NZ mountains give you an edge?

From skiing Aoraki Mount Cook, to North Korea, Bolivia, (even skiing an ash volcano in Vanuatu), definitely. I think having that background racing gave me really strong fundamentals and the ability to focus and compete to the best of my ability. NZ has brilliant mountains but a pretty variable snowpack, which helped hone my skills for freeride competition.

What were you thinking on that line in Andorra?

That zone stuck out to me straight away, I was immediately drawn to how exposed and tight those shelves were and I knew if I could dial that line in I'd win. I was having a tough year on the FWT and had given up on placing well overall so I was going all in on this one. I spent more time scoping that line than any of my competition lines, hiking around to get all kinds of angles on it. I knew any mistake on that top section would result in a horror show crash and I wouldn't requalify for the FWT. But I felt good and just tuned it out and dropped.

How did you transition from being heli dropped to actual ski mountaineering?

It was a pretty natural evolution really, while I've done a fair bit of heli-skiing in Alaska, having spent a bunch of time in Verbier and the Alps I'd done a bunch of hiking too. I realised I would need to become an alpinist to be able to ski the big alpine lines I was lusting after so set about developing my climbing. It's been a really great process, I've been really lucky with people mentoring me there as well. Some days I enjoy the climb more than the ski now which is pretty funny.

You've described Aoraki Mount Cook's Caroline Face as 'one of the biggest and baddest faces of New Zealand's Southern Alps'. Was skiing it a career highlight?

Absolutely. That line is the culmination of everything I have been working towards for many years. Aoraki is the centre of my universe, it's an incredible mountain that stands so proud with the Caroline Face as its crown jewel. That bold line was my ultimate homage to its majesty.

When your best friend comes to Wānaka, where do you take them?

I would take them for a day up Treble Cone, touring a couple runs off the back as well as a few fast laps in the Saddle Basin. Swing past the Mount Aspiring lookout beach in Glendhu Bay for a quick cold dunk and a brew before grabbing something to eat at Kai Whaka Pai to finish the day up. A mission up the Matukituki Valley would be on the cards – weather permitting.

What are you favourite places to ride?

I'm currently a big fan of Rogers Pass near Revelstoke, BC, and Verbier Switzerland is my second home, but home is where the heart is with Aoraki Mount Cook taking the top spot easily.

What's your advice for those who want to get into ski mountaineering?

Take your time and do your homework. There are so many different skillsets away from the actual skiing that need time to work on. You need to be able to climb, navigate, manage avalanche hazard, rope and crevasse rescue, understand weather and first aid, there's a bunch to know. Your skiing should be strong enough that it needs no thought freeing you up to work on all the other problems. Start out slow and have a plan for when it all goes horribly wrong.

What do big mountains and skiing bring to your life?

They bring a lot of purpose, joy, challenge, wonder and meaning. The rich tapestry of life.

Asia

Mythical tales of dragon-back mountains, almost supernatural snowfall totals and deep soaks in onsens (hot spring baths) make Asia a riding magnet.

JAPAN

You won't be returning from Japan with a goggle tan – when I say Japan is for serious snow lovers, I don't mean you have to be an advanced skier. But you have to really like snow. Say, 10–18m (400–700in) of it. Snow can fall all day. And all night. And dumping directly from Siberia, it's not just snow, it's *powder*; light, dry 'Japowder'.

Light flakes falling, steaming onsens (hot spring baths), a beguiling, rich and multilayered culture – these are some of the ingredients making the Land of the Rising Sun sizzle. It's no longer the new frontier first snow-colonised by powder-hungry Australians – rather, it has become a dream destination for skiers and snowboarders, with pro athletes from Jon Olsson to Jeremy Jones accurately waxing lyrical about endless, bottomless white lines.

Japan wasn't always the hot ski ticket it is now. During Japan's ski boom of the 1980s, domestic skiers reached 18 million and there was eye-boggling investment, so there was no need to market skiing overseas. But it's amazing what a global recession will do to prompt the welcoming of a new international skier market. When gaijin (foreign) skiers began blowing in 30 years ago, everyone was surprised. Uninitiated skiers were amazed by the potential and the powder. And the groomed slope and mogul-loving locals were like, *you want that annoying powder?*

The locals are another reason to come to Japan. They are exceptionally friendly, openly curious and infallibly polite. Some of the best experiences of a Japan ski trip aren't sliding-related. They range from spontaneous karaoke sessions to riding solo-passenger 'pizza box' chairlifts (it's the box, you're the topping) and stopping in electric-and-eclectic Tokyo.

But which of the 600 resorts splattered across the islands is the one for you? You'll find the bright lights of foreign investment development in Niseko (see p. 225), you can relax among the steamy waters and unbeatable après at Nozawa Onsen (see p. 241), or enjoy the funfair out-there feel at Rusutsu (see p. 235), while Furano (see p. 229) is both an excellent ski area and base for a ski safari. Then there are ski areas you may not have heard about, because they have negligible international marketing – like Shiga Kogen (see p. 233), one of Japan's largest ski areas.

The skiing and snowboarding experience in Japan is different to other countries. You won't find incredibly steep terrain, couloirs and cliffs. Instead, the runs are relatively gentle, skinny birch trees are easy to glide through (some resorts don't allow tree skiing, so choose wisely) and it's all about the powder.

Some tips before diving into the addictive riddle that is Japan: despite cutting-edge technology, cash is king (always carry some), the country-wide Black Cats luggage transport is genius (global-yamato.com, with a black cat symbol) and if you see floating particles in an onsen (hot spring bath) don't panic – it's usually a good sign of watery mineral elements.

Coolest winter selfie

Skiing past a snow-covered rollercoaster in the empty Rustutsu outdoor amusement park (see p. 235) takes primo position. If you go to Niseko and don't take a photo by the Bar Gyu+ 'Fridge Door' (see p. 227), are you even there? Then there's the onsen-soaking snow monkeys (Japanese macaques) at Jigokudani Monkey Park (see p. 245) .

Get appy

Local translation app Yomiwa - Japanese Dictionary - is invaluable when deciphering high tech toilet flushing instructions (also use the Google Translation app).

Tenki.jp is the Japan Weather Association's official app, and used by guides.

HyperDia will help you untangle train travel (including the best routes inter-resort), and find luggage storage with the Eckbo Cloak app - any luggage size accepted (including ski/board bags).

Don't break the bank

To get good value, stay in ryokans (traditional Japanese inns) and eat like a local. Hop on the Ramen Beast app for your closest cheap bowl. The legendary jidōhanbaiki (vending machines), estimated to number 7 million, dispense everything from pastries to hot coffee in a can (a ski-goggles machine seems the only current market gap). If you're riding backcountry, or part-time, some resorts, like Niseko (see p. 225), offer passes with pay-per-lift points. Slower lifts cost less points and gondolas cost more.

When it snows

Jan and Feb is the best time for powder peaks. April brings cherry blossom season, but it's a trade-off for fine flakes.

The weather differs between the islands of Hokkaido (Japan's northernmost island), which can be hit by cold and windy storms with infrequent bluebird days and holds snow longer, and Honshu, which has myriad 'micro event' snow in the varied topography of the Japanese Alps - it may snow in the south one night and not in any other compass direction. But wherever you go in peak season, you'll find more pow than you know how to handle.

RUSSIA

SEA OF JAPAN

Asahikawa

Tomamu

Furano

Otaru
Sapporo

Niseko
United
Rusutsu

Tomakomai

Obihiro

Hakodate

Mutsu

Goshogawara
Aomori

Hachinohe

Odate

JAPAN

Akita

Morioka

Miyako

Sakata

Kurihara

Yamagata
Zao
Onsen
Sendai

PACIFIC

OCEAN

Niigata
Shibata

Fukushima

Nagaoka

Koriyama

Joetsu

Iwaki

Nanao

Hakuba
Valley

Nozawa
Onsen

Toyama

Shiga
Kogen

Kanazawa

Nagano

Utsunomiya

Fukui

Matsumoto

Takasaki

Mito

Tsukuba

Ina

Kawagoe

Tsuruga

Seki

Tōkyō

0   100km

Snow-hungry foreigners and Asia's elite come here for the big reputation and even bigger powder.

Niseko United

THE LOWDOWN

The first thing to know about Niseko (also called Niseko United because of its pass system) is that its mountains act like roadworks for the Siberian air stream powder truck. The frigid north-westerly wind hurtles down from Siberia and over the Sea of Japan, picking up a cargo of moisture en route before firehosing its goodness all over Niseko's Annupuri Ranges in south-west Hokkaido. Depending on who you talk to, Niseko receives 12–18m (39–59ft) of snow each year, and it's some of the driest, fluffiest powder on this earth. If you stay here for a week, you're almost guaranteed to get a powder day (if not seven of them), and a good one at that.

There are also great backcountry opportunities. Niseko has set the standard in Japan for opening boundaries to more advanced skiers looking for fresh tracks and tree skiing, which even beginners can enjoy thanks to gentle gradient runs through the Kitsune Forest. And everyone enjoys the Japowder.

There's an endless selection of restaurants and bars (although as with many smaller places in the Japan snow world, it's lights out at 9pm), while an easy 2.5hr bus ride links to the major New Chitose Airport.

It could be said that Niesko is Japan's Whistler. It's not the most authentic slice of the country but it has all the bells and whistles, and in Jan and Feb, it's famous for powder face shots.

Mountain stats
- Elevation top: 1188m (3898ft), (1308m/4291ft if you hike the peak)
- Elevation bottom: 255m (837ft)
- Vertical drop: 933m (3061ft)
- Skiable terrain: 8.87 sq km (2192 acres)
- Longest run: 5.6km (3.5mi)
- Beginner terrain: 30 per cent
- Intermediate terrain: 40 per cent
- Advanced terrain: 30 per cent
- Lifts: 32

Run
For expert riders, the run off the peak to Hanazono (East Ridge - Jacksons) or Annupuri (back bowl) is one of the longest and best runs on Hokkaido.

Experience
Night skiing isn't just about playing on the groomed runs - rays reach far enough to allow some visibility in the off-piste trees. Riding powder trees in a quiet, eerie shadow zone feels like a surreal VR experience, appropriate for game-crazy Japan.

Local's tip
If you're staying for a longer trip, purchase an hour-based pass (30 or 50) so you only pay for the time you ski.

Opener Fresh track finding in Furano's trees is part of a Japan powder fairy tale *Opposite* Niseko is popular for good reason: a range of accommodation and cuisine when you've had your snow fill

THE MOUNTAIN DEBRIEF

The Niseko United Pass accesses four interconnected ski areas, with the bonus mountain of Moiwa, connected to Annupuri by trail but not included on the pass. While each resort is independent, they all connect near the mountaintop.

Annupuri is on the mountain's south side, with fewer large hotels and a more Japanese vibe, down to the J-Pop playing over speakers on the beginner chair. Choose Annupuri for traditional onsen hotels and a more relaxed feel.

Niseko Village is curiously not much of a village; it's dominated by the shiny silver tower of the hotel, Hilton Niseko Village. There's excellent steep terrain, including the only avalanche-controlled area on the mountain – Mizuno no Sawa (BC gate number 11). This is where to base yourself if ski-in, ski-out convenience is a priority.

Grand Hirafu, the largest of the group, has excellent terrain and a lively bar and restaurant scene. It's great for advanced riders with access to the peak and BC areas and has excellent tree skiing.

Hanazono was previously a base area and little more, but 'Hano' is now the luxury choice. It's recently seen huge investment from its Hong Kong owners, with new lifts, the best hotel in the area (Park Hyatt Niseko, *see* p. 227) and ambitious expansion plans for the future.

A RIDING ITINERARY

Make sure your crew is ready to go first thing: although there's fresh snow almost daily, everyone wants to ski it.

Catch a coffee at **Morning Owl truck** or **Rhythm** (rhythmjapan.com) to get going for the day. In the morning, take **Miharishi laps** followed by a hike up the peak, then down to **Hano. Edge at Hanazono** can be a zoo; instead, there's a semi-secret cafe in the boot room of the **Park Hyatt** (*see* p. 227).

In the afternoon, keep lapping the **BC** until the gates shut around 2pm, then rest and have an onsen (hot springs bath) for a few hours before some **night laps at Hirafu**.

ADVENTURE

Riding **Mount Yotei** is the ultimate Niseko adventure, but be prepared for a slog as the 1600m (5249ft) climb to the 1898m (6227ft) peak can take six (or more) hours depending on your fitness level and conditions. James Winfield at **Hokkaido Collective** (hokkaidocollective.com) has been skiing Niseko for over 14 winters and knows the best lines.

Niseko body shots *Opposite left* Skye Niseko's onsen will relax you after a long day on the powder *Opposite right* Skye Niseko's Kumo restaurant

OFF-MOUNTAIN MUST-DO

- **Yugokorotei** onsen has one of the nicest outdoor pools in the area - there's nothing better than watching the fat snowflakes fall while soothing post-pow legs.
- **Kanronomori** (kanronomori.com) is the only hotel in the district offering private 50min onsen hire.
- **Scout Ski** (scoutski.com) can organise Japanese immersion activities from karaoke to sushi making and tea ceremonies.

EAT UP & DRINK DOWN

- For a blowout, head to Michelin-starred **Kamimura** (kamimura-niseko.com), a French fusion restaurant - go for the tasting menu with wine pairing.
- **Tsubara Tsubara** (niseko-soupcurry.com) has a hearty Hokkaido-style soup curry with a hotness scale rated across 20 points (or order the vegetable with coconut soup, spice level 10, with added egg and mocha).

APRÈS SKI

- **Bar Gyu+** (gyubar.com) is Niseko's oldest cocktail bar, nicknamed the 'Fridge Door Bar' for its iconic vintage Coca-Cola vending machine entrance - it's a portal to unique cocktails and jazz tunes with a classy vibe.
- **Wild Bills** (wildbills.bar) is the eternal Niseko party spot, loose and lit with nightly DJ events, trivia and pool competitions.

STAY

- **Park Hyatt Niseko** (hyatt.com) is the new standard for hotels in the area, with excellent facilities from onsen to concierge (who can make all your dinner reservations), right on the snow at Hanazono.
- The boutique **Sansui Niseko** (sansuiniseko.com) in the upper Hirafu village has a modern Japanese aesthetic and an ideal location with ski-in, ski-out on the family run.
- A luxurious newcomer is **Setsu Niseko** (setsuniseko.com) with yoga, an inhouse ski store, sushi restaurants and a ski shuttle.
- **Skye Niseko** is another super-luxe new hotel, including onsens using mineral-rich hot water drawn from deep below the hotel, and Kumo restaurant celebrating Japanese design, food and culture izakaya (small bar) style.

ALTERNATIVE: HAKUBA VALLEY

Just a 3hr drive from downtown Tokyo, Hakuba Valley is arguably the most popular riding region in Honshu, set against an impressive big-mountain, European-style backdrop and home to ten ski resorts including Happo One, the largest and most popular village. Although the resorts aren't linked by lifts, you can shift easily between them for variety; either from the boarder and terrain-park heaven of Hakuba 47, or the powder stashes and tree skiing at Cortina.

Located in the epicentre of Hokkaido, this dark horse is a powder priestess, balancing on the brink of a boom and blessing visitors with both vertical and culture.

Furano

THE LOWDOWN

Furano, situated mid-region, is known as the bellybutton of Hokkaido , thanks to its location and annual hosting of the Hokkai Heso Matsuri – bellybutton festival – in July. As a notch in your powder belt, it's accessible to resort areas in all directions, including Asahidake, Kurodake, Kamui Ski Links, Sahoro and Tomamu (*see* p. 239).

There's a laid-back, country-town feel here infused with traditional Japanese culture; if you're seeking party central, head further south. The prevalent attitude is that Furano doesn't want to be another Niseko (*see* p. 225) – yet it has begun. Furano's teetering in a transitional space as foreign and local investment increases, yet facilities are not as prevalent as you might expect. Instead of five-star restaurant experiences (they're coming) you'll be served a platter of excellent food in a traditional, sometimes quirky, Japanese izakaya (small bar). The après and ski action is in Kitanomine Village near the ski area.

Down the hill from Kitanomine is vibrant Furano town, with a hot pot of shops, restaurants and bars. It's a genuine, friendly town with a sense of community, where skiers shuffle home from the slopes alongside children snowball-fighting on their way home from school.

Come to Furano to escape the bigger resort areas in Hokkaido and experience authentic Japanese culture, or for visits to Hokkaido's higher peaks and backcountry. And, of course, for vertical.

 Mountain stats
- Elevation top: 1047m (3435ft)
- Elevation bottom: 235m (771ft)
- Vertical drop: 839m (2752ft)
- Skiable terrain: 1.9 sq km (469.5 acres)
- Longest run: 4.5km (2.8mi)
- Beginner terrain (green): 40 per cent
- Intermediate terrain (blue/red): 40 per cent
- Advanced terrain (black): 20 per cent
- Lifts: 11

 Run
First down the Challenge Course on a deep pow day. The link zone between Kitanomine and Furano has some of the best powder and easy navigation.

 Experience
A trip to the Tokachidake range, famous for backcountry terrain with long runs, spectacular views and magnificent village onsens (hot spring baths).

 Local's tip
Come prepared with equipment; it can be difficult to source anything beyond alpine piste rentals. And don't miss the dairies and cake shops - the best crème caramel ever is at Furano Delice (le-nord.com) made from local Furano milk.

Opposite Knee-deep glade skiing

THE MOUNTAIN DEBRIEF

Miles of summer wildflowers and lavender fields made Furano a local tourist destination, then international travellers – powder disciples – began blowing into town, and bowing down to the 9–12m (354–472in) of snowfall and impressive vertical (974m/3195ft). A more technical ski hill on- and off-piste than many in Hokkaido, even advanced skiers will approve of the steep pitches.

Furano is one of the bigger mountains in Hokkaido and while it receives less snow than places like Niseko (*see* p. 225) and Rusutsu (*see* p. 235), it receives drier snow than the resorts further south due to colder temperatures. Yes, this region receives champagne powder.

The mountain is divided into two connected areas on one lift ticket, the Furano Zone and the Kitanomine Zone. Long runs start from either a single gondola ride in the Kitanomine Zone or tram ride (the Furano Ropeway) in the Furano Zone, where there's upper-slope skiing through Golden Week in May. There are large beginner runs in both sections, with many intermediate (and a handful of expert runs) equally distributed on both sides. Small sections of particular runs – and some runs entirely – are left ungroomed all season for powder lovers.

Backcountry and side-country skiing is welcomed through a gate system (sign a form at Kitanomine or Furano base before venturing out). The resort once had a strict policy against leaving the piste but is now proud of how popular Furano is among backcountry snow riders – but make sure you take a guide.

A RIDING ITINERARY

Grab a brew at **BaristArt Coffee** (baristartcoffee.com) in town or **Rojo Coffee** at Kitanomine base. On the Kitanomine side, warm up on F – and later, G – lifts from 8:30am, doing beautifully groomed laps around **G3** and **F2**.

Afterwards, hit the gondola and link to **K1** all the way down to **F5**, or choose a black **K3**, **K2** or **K4** option (K1 and K3 have the best views in the resort). Another option is to go over the Furano side on the **H connecting lift**. Make your way to the **E lift** – if it's a powder day, it's tough to beat the runs and trees off this lift.

Have lunch on the mountain at **Restaurant Downhill** (princehotels.com) at the top of the Ropeway, which is cosy with a fire, or down at the **Shin Furano Prince Hotel** (princehotels.com).

In the afternoon ski **A2**, **A3**, **A4**, explore **H1** linking back to Kitanomine, and finish cruising on **G1** and **F2**.

ADVENTURE

Hit **Asahidake** on a bluebird day and tour up to the bottom of the crater to experience the views and fumaroles (volcanic cracks emitting steam). For the best regional experience, hire a professional backcountry guide like Ross McSwiney at **Whiteroom** (whiteroomtours.com), an Australian national ski patroller trainer and examiner.

Opposite top Furano has some of the steepest slopes in Japan
Opposite bottom The charming shops of Furano's Ningle Terrace

232

OFF-MOUNTAIN MUST-DO

- Go **hot-air ballooning** 1000m (3281ft) over Furano and the Taisetsusan Mountain Range, or **ice fish** nearby, deep-frying your catch with some local mushrooms on the ice (furanotourism.com).

EAT UP & DRINK DOWN

- Have a curry at **Yama No Dockson**, also home to the Furano Beer microbrewery.
- **Cafe Goryo** (goryo.info/cafe) is a very cool little cafe with powder board demos and delicious food in a renovated farmhouse just outside of town.

APRÈS SKI

- Most of the après happens in Kitanomine Village. Nights can end late at **Ajito** (furano-ajito.com).
- You're likely to catch some guides at the **Whiteroom cafe-bar** (the old 7/11 building near the lights at Kitanomine).

STAY

- The luxurious ski-in, ski-out **Fenix Furano** or **Fenix West** (felixfurano.com) steps from the Kitanomine Gondola offer everything from hotel rooms to apartments and penthouses.
- The **Prince Hotel Shin Furano** (princehotels.co.jp) is run by the owners of the ski area.

ALTERNATIVE: SHIGA KOGEN

If you're looking for a similar explorer-like feel to Furano but you're on Honshu island, consider Shiga Kogen closer to Tokyo. Shiga Kogen, the site of alpine events during the 1998 Nagano Winter Olympics, is one of the highest ski resorts in Japan (2307m/7568ft) and provides a classic Japan ski-resort experience due to minimal foreign ownership.

Shiga Kogen is also close to the Hakuba Valley (*see* p. 227), if you're keen for a road trip, and the little-known powder gems of Madarao and Togakushi. Even less well-known is exploring the ancient streets and public onsens (hot spring baths) of Shibu Onsen near Yudanaka - it's like stepping back in time.

Feeling the Furano stoke *Opposite top* Gazing out over the town *Opposite bottom* The patchwork quilt of agriculture tucks neatly into the foothills of Furano's powder pillows

Slide past the large, startling, robotic talking tree and the fun-park vibe at the base to discover Niseko-like powder and a mountain on the move.

Rusutsu

THE LOWDOWN

Rusutsu is a theme park and golf-course resort in summer, which converts to a three-mountain ski resort in winter. Just 40min from Niseko (*see* p. 225) on the east side of Mount Yotei, it's actually Hokkaido's largest single ski resort (given that Niseko is four resorts).

First impressions may be of the talking tree, indoor carousel and robotic animal-character dixie band at the base hotel (this is Japan kitsch unleashed), but beyond this are the discoveries of world-class tree-glade skiing, fewer crowds than at Niseko, epic views of Mount Yotei and Lake Toya, and access to Shiribetsu-Dake for those wishing to bag a major peak in the area.

So who comes here? It's a combination of Japanese school groups, families and people looking for a destination resort with everything in one place. The newer arrivals are from Niseko looking for the next fresh line.

Once off the international radar, Rusutsu now has a slightly more expensive lift pass than Niseko. Accommodation may be cheaper but the opening of the luxe Vale Rusutsu (*see* p. 239) is an indicator that prices are on the move.

Most people stay within Rusutsu Resort Hotel & Convention (*see* p. 239), which has its own bars and restaurants, meaning other nightlife and dining options are limited. However, there is a small village several minutes' walk away with an 'izakaya strip' (small bars) where eateries are small, inexpensive and popular, with friendly owners keen to communicate with foreigners – even when limited to just kampai (cheers). You'll find more exposure to local culture here than in Niseko.

Mountain stats
- Elevation top: 994m (3261ft)
- Elevation bottom: 400m (1312ft)
- Vertical drop: 594m (1949ft)
- Skiable terrain: 2.12 sq km (524 acres)
- Longest run: 3.5km (2.2mi)
- Beginner terrain: 30 per cent
- Intermediate terrain: 40 per cent
- Advanced terrain: 30 per cent
- Lifts: 18

Run
The 1850m (1.2mi) Heavenly Canyon, a wide-open gulley with a fun half-pipe shape and excellent tree skiing off the edges. Situated along a stream, this trail is a natural wind-blown power pocket.

Experience
Skiing through the snow-covered summertime amusement park on West mountain is a unique experience you won't find anywhere else. On Sundays in Jan and Feb, 60 people are shuttled over to Mount Isola for first tracks; purchase tickets in the Rusutsu Resort Hotel & Convention (*see* p. 239).

Local's tip
Schuss to Mount Isola as fast as you can on powder mornings. And if you're driving over from Niseko, purchase passes online as the ticket-office queues can be lengthy.

Opposite Impressive Mount Yotei looms in the background

THE MOUNTAIN DEBRIEF

Most of the lodging is on West Mountain which, while shorter and smaller, has some of the steeper runs and great tree skiing on the (slightly slow) West Tiger Pair. The beginner terrain on this side is also fantastic and the Shin Chan kids area is perfect to get little ones started.

A gondola links West Mountain and East Mountain, which has some dreamy fall line groomers, a small-but-fun terrain park, as well as steep tree-runs heading over towards Mount Isola. From East Mountain, you can connect to Mount Isola, the largest mountain of the three and famed for its tree skiing.

For backcountry, West Mountain extends outside the resort up the ridgeline to Shiribetsu-Dake, which encompasses excellent steeps and backcountry terrain on all aspects.

This resort has a rare feature where the lifts run up the gullies, and pistes run down the ridgelines – with stellar views. You can ski off most piste areas, into the gullies and funnel out back to the lifts.

A RIDING ITINERARY

Catch a coffee at **Daniel Street Cafe and Pastry** (rusutsu.com) – the choux (cream puffs) are particularly delicious! Warm up on the **West Mountain** with Eva and Bambi reds before taking on the steep groomed black of **Dynamic**, which runs from the summit to the amusement park at the foot, giving the unique experience of skiing down the mountain straight toward a Ferris wheel.

Rip through the trees around the black runs **Tiger** and **Natural**. Then take the gondola over to **East Mountain**; the red runs of **East Tignes** along the ridge line and open **East Vivaldi** have spectacular views, and **Super East** double-black bumps are an energy blast to finish the morning.

Pit stop at **Cafeteria Steamboat** (rusutsu.com) which has an independent cafe with great espresso and snacks (avoid the machine coffee at the cafeteria).

In the afternoon, explore the furthest reaches of **Mount Isola** on the cruisey groomers of **Heavenly View;** perhaps challenge yourself with some powder skiing just off the runs. Or try either of the **Steamboat** parallel pistes and dive in between for deep pow skiing into the Steamboat gull.

ADVENTURE

Heli-skiing (hokkaidobackcountryclub.com) on the adjacent Shiribetsu-Dake is one of the ultimate Hokkaido experiences, where slopes are 20 to 40 degrees (a typical Japan black is 32 degrees).

West Mountain is the choice for back country *Opposite* You'll appreciate the gondola on those (many) snowy days

OFF-MOUNTAIN MUST-DO

- Look for local operators to go **snow rafting**, towed in an inflatable boat behind a snowmobile; be your own musher on a **dog sled** around a 250m track.
- Take a dip in the **Westin's Kotobuki onsen** with its 20m (66ft) outdoor bath, plus an indoor bath with floor-to-ceiling windows.

EAT UP & DRINK DOWN

- The main hotel has eateries including a buffet, cafe, izakaya (small bar), French, Italian, and Japanese - for sushi, **Sekkatei** (rusutsu.com) is the pick.
- **Atrium** in the Westin is the best spot for lunch (but requires taking the chairlift) and **Rodeo Drive** (rusutsu.gr.jp) is a delicious independent izakaya close by.

APRÈS SKI

- The **Cricketers Bar** in the main hotel makes its own Rusutsu Love craft beer.
- **Pirateman Izakaya** (stayrusutsu.com) is just along the road from the resort and is the drinking spot of choice for international employees (with an Italian coffee machine).
- **Yotei** is an izakaya that also has karaoke.

STAY

- The **Rusutsu Resort Hotel & Convention** (rusutsu.com) by West Mountain, is perfect for families and offers good value and incorporates a swimming pool, waterslide, bars, restaurants, shopping and indoor theme-park attractions.
- The luxurious **Westin Rusutsu Resort** (marriott.com) is a short chairlift ride to the more challenging East Mountain and Mount Isola (also connected by monorail to Rusutsu Resort Hotel & Convention).
- The new **Vale Rusutsu** (nisade.com) by West Mountain, is spectacular - but with no supermarket nearby, you'll need to stock up in Rusutsu town.

ALTERNATIVE: TOMAMU

Hoshino Resorts' Tomamu will easily entertain families and dedicated power hounds. Located in eastern Hokkaido, there's the Ice Village, Mina Mina Beach, with the largest indoor beach and wave pool in Japan, and cat ski tours over to Mount Karifuri.

Top Sekkatei restaurant is the go-to for fresh local seafood and Hokkaido (wagyu-style) beef *Bottom* Mount Yotei is an island in a sea of clouds *Opposite top* The Westin's Kotobuki outdoor bath has a panoramic view of the mountains *Opposite bottom* Snow rafting and helicopter sightseeing on non-riding days

For real-deal Japan, step back in time at the country's prettiest ski resort.

Nozawa Onsen

THE LOWDOWN

Nozawa Onsen will charm the pants off you, literally. You'll come for the riding, but before you know it you'll be getting naked with strangers in a steam room. This ancient feudal town is recognised as the largest single-mountain resort in the country, with prodigious amounts of powder (12m/472in annually).

It's famed for ryokan (traditional inns) dotting the walk-everywhere village and the way the 13 public onsen (hot spring baths) and soto-yu (outdoor bathhouses) colour a ski trip here. As an example, sitting and soaking your feet at a foot onsen (pants on, just rolled up), surrounded by ryokan, with a vending-machine hot coffee-in-a-can in hand, while women in kimonos and other locals walk by carrying ladles en route to a cooking onsen, is a *Lost in Translation* moment.

There is a huge choice of restaurants here, many with no signage and a red lantern denotes an izayaka (small bar). Local specialities include the famous nozawana pickles or onsen tamago (onsen-cooked eggs with a unique texture – delicious with soy sauce). And while the onsens are basic they'll make you feel like a million dollars, and offer cultural immersion (along with liquid immersion).

Mountain stats
- Elevation top: 1650m (3513ft)
- Elevation bottom: 565m (1854ft)
- Vertical drop: 1085m (3560ft)
- Skiable terrain: 3 sq km (741 acres)
- Longest run: 10km (6.2mi)
- Beginner terrain: 30 per cent
- Intermediate terrain: 40 per cent
- Advanced terrain: 40 per cent
- Lifts: 21

Run
Skyline is a long, well-groomed intermediate ridge run from the peak to the lowest home slope. Take the side trail to Karasawa - on a clear day you're in a vista sandwich with the Japan Alps on one side and the Joetsu coast on the other.

Experience
The unique January Dosojin Matsuri (Fire Festival) culminates in a six-storey wooden shrine being set alight - 42-year-old local men sit on top and 25-year-old men below, the pyrotechnics are intended to cleanse these unlucky ages!

Local's tip
On a down day, snowshoe from the top of the Nagasaka gondola, through the forest to lake Sutakako and onto the Hikage gondola (beautiful and gently downhill). In the centre, you'll find the revered statue of St. Anton am Arlberg's (*see* p. 107) Hannes Schneider, who was invited here in 1930 to introduce ski technique.

Opposite Nozawa Onsen is famed for its waters, but the slopes won't disappoint

THE MOUNTAIN DEBRIEF

The resort topography is an anomaly: the best beginner runs are on top. The Uenotaira (which literally means 'flat area on top') is a gentle 3km (1.9mi) run accessed straight from the gondola, and there are black runs close to town.

The main areas are the home slopes (Hikage, Nagasaka and Karasawa); Yamabiko is at the top of the mountain (and, unlike at some resorts, the resort allows side-country tree skiing); and Uenotaira and Paradise have cruisy runs mid-mountain. There's an Olympic-length ski jump, halfpipe, snowpark with rails, kickers and two cross-country courses. There's also good – and generally safe – backcountry. Heli-skiing and recreational snowmobiling are not allowed.

A RIDING ITINERARY

Get up early with your headtorch and snowshoe over from Maezaka at the bottom of the village to enjoy daybreak at **Lake Hokuryu**. After breakfast, head straight up to **Yamabiko**. If you're a little late getting up the mountain, sneak into the under-skiied areas of **Mizunashi** and **Ushikubi**, where there are always untracked stashes. There's only one entrance to this area, a surreptitious little lane that sidles off Uenotaira.

For lunch, stop on Paradise Slope at **Hakugin** (en.nozawaski.com) for a bowl of miso ramen – the classic Japanese skier's lunch – with a tonkatsu (breaded pork cutlet) chaser.

The end-of-day onsen (hot spring baths) are already calling, but stop and play a little on the cruisy home slopes of **Hikage** or **Nagasaka**.

ADVENTURE

The ski resort is supportive and pragmatic about backcountry, and when your guide files their trip report before you head out, ski patrol might say 'have a great time!' (or 'I wouldn't go there today' – even more valuable). The back bowl is popular with a dedicated access gate; traverse a ridge, then pick one of several gullies to drop into, leading you to the top of Karasawa.

A bluebird day is always a welcome sight in Japan

244

OFF-MOUNTAIN MUST-DO

- Walk up to atmospheric **Ogama** onsen to witness a slice of daily life as locals cook in the 97°F/36°C waters, wreathed in otherworldly steam.
- It's only a 45min drive to **Jigokudani Monkey Park** (jigokudani-yaenkoen.co.jp) to see the **world-famous snow monkeys (Japanese macaques)** relaxing in the onsen like it's a primate country club.

—

EAT UP & DRINK DOWN

- **Sakai** is one of maybe a dozen or more village izakaya (small bars), and they'll happily choose your dishes if you ask.
- Soba (buckwheat noodles) is a local must-try, and **Daimon** is the go-to soba shop.

—

APRÈS SKI

- This is an onsen town, so the main après ski activity is to get naked with the locals in a tub of unbelievably hot mineral spring water.
- **O-yu** (nozawakanko.jp) is the iconic onsen everyone should try once; **Kumanotearai-no-yu** (nozawakanko.jp) is fractionally less hot.

—

STAY

- There are over 200 accommodation options in the village, nearly all family-run.
- **Kawamotoya** (kawamotoya.jp) has the most luxurious apartments in the village.
- **Nozawa View Hotel Shimataya onsen hotel** (viewhotelshimataya.com) offers the best all-round midrange value.

—

ALTERNATIVE: ZAO ONSEN

Zao Onsen is a lesser-known gem combining local immersion with cultural saturation and some great skiing. It has a charming, traditional village, a great selection of hotels, natural hot springs for onsen and a vast ski resort featuring its famed juhyo (snow monsters), which can also be seen at Shiga Kogen (*see* p. 233).

The atmospheric alleyways of Nozawa Onsen *Opposite top* With a little imagination, twilight is laced with steamy dragon's breath *Opposite bottom* Jizō statues, the protectors of travellers and children, can be found on the side of the road

CHINA

China has big mountains – some of the highest peaks on Earth, including Everest and K2, are located on its western borders. As they're far from urban areas, they don't interest ski developers but China's large population does.

In the past decade, skiing has exploded in China. The 2022 Winter Olympic Games in Beijing and the growing middle class embracing leisure have served as springboards for all things snow sports.

After being awarded the Games in 2015, Liu Peng, President of the Chinese Olympic Committee, projected China would have 300 million winter sports enthusiasts by the time the Olympics slid around. Three weeks pre-Games, the goal was reached and the 'snow plan' for 2016–25 continued, including training tomorrow's skiers – and 5000 schools integrated winter sports into their curriculum.

However, there are some obstacles. Skiing is somewhat perceived as entertainment rather than a sport, and the trend is to buy a two-hour pass – so there's a low return rate. It's also still expensive, even for the middle class. Snowfall is scarce in many parts of China, meaning limited snowmaking, and Banff-type cold blights the country's northern resorts, where it easily dips to -25°C (-13°F).

Ski areas now number 700, but many are tiny beginner ski areas with one or two magic carpets; around three-quarters offer less than 100m (328ft) of vertical, leaving only about a handful that can be considered as true ski resorts.

There are lots of positive signs though – most skiers are millennials and young urbanites keen to reconnect with nature and inspired by social media. More ski-centric Club Meds are opening (there's no surer indication of predicted tourism success), and they've partnered with the École du Ski Français.

But the biggest boost to China's nascent ski industry isn't strategy or development – it's a person. American-Chinese multi-medal Olympic freeskier, Stanford student and model Eileen Gu is on a superstar level, a literal poster girl for winter sports.

Whichever way the Chinese ski industry goes, it will be a fascinating ride.

Coolest winter selfie

China has 36 snowdomes, including the three largest in the world. Or heard to Chongli, an hour from Beijing, for an 'Olympic-rings' background. If heading north, don't miss the Harbin Ice and Snow Festival in Jan and Feb with its incredible hand-carved pop-up ice city (tip, take a bird's eye view from the Snowflake Ferris Wheel).

Get appy

The ultra-trendy app Xiaohonghsu (Little Red Book, or just Redbook) has reams of ski-related queries. For social media, there's Weibo (kind of like Twitter), direct messaging app WeChat and Douyin (like Tik Tok).

Don't break the bank

Skiing in China isn't overly expensive, but it's unlikely you would visit for budget skiing alone. A hotel may seem expensive (a top one can be around US$200 per room per night) but check the inclusions which can be lift tickets, hot spring tickets and meals. And seeking out a local noodle bar will result not just in saved yuan, but will also give you a cultural experience.

When it snows

Much of China is a desert. The 2022 Olympic Games relied almost entirely on artificial snow, which is harder, slicker and denser than its natural counterpart - not so great for jumping sports, but a dream for alpine racers.

Domes of frigid, sinking air from Siberia typically block Pacific moisture from reaching north-east China during the winter. As a result, only 2 per cent of Beijing's annual average precipitation (1cm/0.4in) falls between Dec and Feb, but frigid temperatures are ripe for snowmaking.

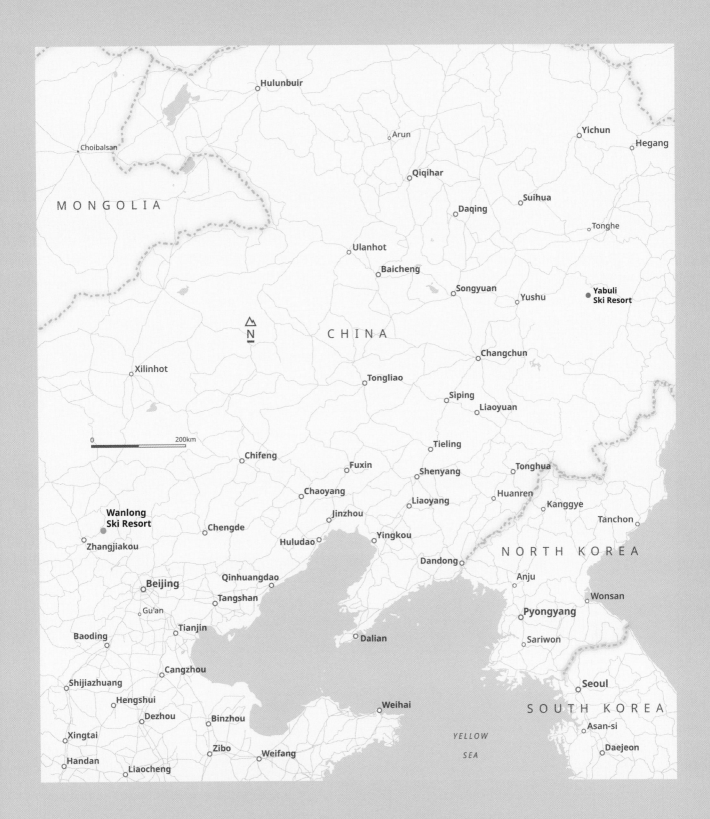

A Winter Olympic host, China slid into the global snow scene and Wanlong is the hub of the country's fast-growing ski industry.

Wanlong Ski Resort

THE LOWDOWN

Wanlong Ski Resort is around 250km (155mi) and about a 4hr drive north-east of Beijing in Heibei. You may know the name as the host of the parallel slalom snowboard events of the 2022 Winter Olympics. With an elevation of 1560m (5118ft) to 2110m (6923ft), it's one of the highest ski areas in China.

Wanlong and neighbouring resorts have been actively promoted as a new tourism sector. There's a distinct Chinese flavour too, you can lean into novelties like 'butt-pillow' options when renting equipment, with offers of a large stuffed panda or turtle strapped to one's derriere.

Wanlong has five chairs and one cablecar lift: three chairlifts reach mid-mountain, two more and a gondola converge atop the mountain. You'll find unexpectedly short lift lines and wide-open, uncrowded terrain here.

At the bottom of the mountain is a base lodge with shops and rentals (all Salomon) on the bottom floor, and a 400-person second floor, including outdoor decking, as well as two hotels nearby.

There's enough to keep you busy here for a weekend.

 Mountain stats
- Elevation top: 1560m (5118ft)
- Elevation bottom: 2110m (6922 ft)
- Vertical drop: 550m (1804ft)
- Skiable terrain: 22km (13.6mi)
- Longest run: 2.5km
- Beginner terrain: 18 per cent
- Intermediate terrain: 55 per cent
- Advanced terrain: 27 per cent
- Lifts: 6

 Run
Jinlong Trail is a great mid-mountain, 1.8km (1.1-mi) intermediate trail. The 2km (1.2-mi) Yinlong Trail is a challenging black trail on the west side.

 Experience
The Wanlong Wood House (made with wood imported from Finland) at the top has heated toilets and slippers included in a lunch buffet (at the base, your experience will include navigating a squat toilet in ski boots and clothes).

 Local's tip
At the ski rental shop, feel free to bust out a stern 'wo zai paidui' - which means 'I'm in line', or the slopes will close before you even get on them. You'll also need your ID or passport to rent equipment.

Opposite Cold temperatures means later morning starts won't affect the snow quality

THE MOUNTAIN DEBRIEF

Advanced skiers will find the more demanding slopes on the mountain's west face.

Chair 1 is a double chair to mid-mountain accessing one main trail and a terrain park side trail. If you want to explore further, the top of this lift connects with a new quad chair to the top of the mountain at 2210m (7250ft).

Chairs 3 and 4 serve expansion areas as the ski area grows to the west, taking in a new valley and ridge area. A new detachable six-passenger, high-speed lift now carries riders from the bottom of the western slopes all the way to the top of Chair 2. The gondola connects the base lodge with the top of the mountain and also operates in summer. The resorts also rotate through the trails for mid-day grooming, so keep an eye out for noon corduroy.

A RIDING ITINERARY

Start with one of the chairlifts on the east side and warm up with some blues, power charging on the upper slopes, which you'll have mostly to yourself, as most people seem to stay below mid-mountain. Don't miss the fun woods trail weaving through the forest, although it's unlikely you'll find stashes.

It's easy to move across to the gondola (all lifts except one originate at the base) at the western side of the base and from the top, enjoy some ridgeline skiing with top views before dropping down into one of the eight black options there. This is the newer side of the mountain and has some satisfyingly steep pitches from ridge to valley.

ADVENTURE

There is snowmobiling, but it's worth taking a few days to spend in Beijing exploring the grandeur of the Forbidden City or taking a side trip to the Great Wall.

Opposite A Wanlong weekend

OFF-MOUNTAIN MUST-DO

• At the **Shuanglong Hotel**, there are hot springs, and the kids will go crazy in an indoor basement pool with a splash park.

EAT UP & DRINK DOWN

• Choices for food are limited to the hotels and ski-area base lodges, but the choices themselves are varied and good. On offer are grilled lamb skewers, handmade dumplings, made-to-order noodle dishes, fried rice, fresh tandoori-baked naan and pizza. At around US$8/€7, it's a fraction of the cost at European or North American ski resorts.

APRÈS SKI

• Après hasn't really caught on here but if you're desperate, there is a karaoke room in the **Shuanglong Hotel**.

STAY

• The 100-room, three-star **Shuanglong Hotel**, renovated in 2016, or the newer **Yuelong Business Hotel** are both ski-in, ski-out and have the usual amenities you expect in slope-side hotels.

ALTERNATIVE - YABULI SKI RESORT

In Yabuli, there are 50.9km (31.6 mi) of winding slopes in an ancient pine tree forest, split between three domains of mainly non-challenging terrain. A 14hr drive north of Beijing, it's colder than Wanlong. The big drawcard here is Club Med, with all the bells and whistles like snow trekking, yoga lessons, an indoor swimming pool and one of the most reliable places in China to find French cheese.

Ideal conditions for beginners and intermediates *Opposite* Snow sports have taken off in China

Ski the World

Slide way (way) off the beaten track and explore the corners of the globe. A trip to these destinations are soul-stirring snow adventures, when it's just as much about the journey as the destination.

For snow explorers

These off-the-beaten-track destinations are for snow explorers – those among us who love a challenge, serious powder or ski touring. These are odysseys to places that you may not have even heard of, much less contemplated skiing at before.

Whether you want skiing crossed with cultural immersion in Romania's Poiana Braşov (*see* p. 258), to go where the pros go in Las Leñas, Argentina (*see* p. 264), or to ski (and then island hop) in Greece's Parnassus (*see* p. 259), it's all here. If you're in South Korea, go like the locals to Yongpyong Ski Resort (*see* p. 263) for slalom, or try skiing in in Azerbaijan (*see* p. 262) with its brand-new industry much championed by the locals.

Boasting rights are big in these destinations too: skiing in the Himalayas (*see* p. 261), Morocco's High Atlas Mountains (*see* p. 260) or the Andes (*see* p. 265).

And then there's Alaska ... a place like no other where heli-skiing and ski touring involve the highest mountains on Earth outside of the Himalayas and Andes.

Many of the destinations in this chapter are for experienced skiers and boarders only. They require careful research and planning, allowing extra travel time and utlising the services of guides for backcountry touring and avalanche knowledge.

Powder pilgrims, come and explore.

Previous spread Alaska offers extreme adventure and heli-skiing for hard-core riders *Right* Pristine skiing in the Carpathian Mountains, Poiana Braşov, Romania

Ski the World

Romania's best resort isn't just a ski holiday – it's saturated with culture.

Poiana Brașov

ROMANIA

Day passes for €32/US$34, ski rentals for the price of a coffee in Zermatt, a charming setting and Dracula's castle. These are the big things to know about Romania's swankiest and best-designed resort – but not all, not by a long shot.

The Brits have long been on to the bargain bounty of Romania. Cheap flights and tickets put Romania on their ski map - it was voted the most affordable European ski resort by London's *Telegraph* last decade. Luckily, it never became a Magaluf On Ice (read: booze-fest destination), and 10 years later, after tens of millions spent in infrastructure investment, it's retained a rich cultural heart - and it's amazing value. It's also one of the most pristine and well-preserved mountain areas in Eastern Europe (complete with wolves). That's enough to howl about.

The aforementioned day pass accesses 24.5km (15.2mi) of ski terrain, with a flavour that is deliciously different to other ski resorts, boasting a spellbinding setting in the pine forests of the Carpathian Mountains. Intent on creating the Romanian 'Alps', the early founders sent architects and engineers to study famous alpine resorts and apply the same design and quality principles in building Poiana Brașov. The result? A slick ski area.

Located deep in Transylvania, Dracula's Castle (or rather Bran Castle, which inspired Bram Stoker's fictional tale) is only 20km (12.4mi) away. The medieval city of Brașov is 10min down the road, and make sure you spend a little time exploring Bucharest, the capital.

Perfectly planned pistes and Transylvanian legends are an intriguing combination in Romania *Opposite* Greece is famous for summer fun, but also has a winter snow scene largely unknown to foreigners

Philotimo – Greek hospitality given with generosity and kindness – makes skiing here a joy.

Parnassus

GREECE

The Greeks have it all. As if their summer islands, historic cities and lip-licking cuisine aren't enough, they also have ski areas. Eighty per cent of Greece is mountainous and the highest peak is 2917m (9570ft). If you're hoping for a trip packed with more high points than Zeus's quiver of thunderbolts, say yassou (hello) to Greece.

Parnassus is the biggest downhill ski resort in the country and the most popular, only a 3hr drive from Athens. The resort itself consists of two connected areas with 23 ski runs totalling 34km (21mi) and 17 ski lifts and chairlifts, as well as a gondola. Since 2014,

a multi-stage overhaul has resulted in new lifts with names like Aphrodite-Bacchus (a Goddess of Love and God of Wine combo surely spells good times).

The Kelaria side of the resort is fairly open and flat, with mostly intermediate and beginner runs. Once you get to the top, woah - there's an eagle-eye view over the surrounding mountains with water visible on both sides: the Gulf of Corinth and the Euboean Gulf.

Skiing down the other side of the mountain - Fterolaka - you'll be flanked by pine trees, the terrain steepens, and fresh tracks can be found in the woods after snowfall. The Kelaria side is windier and gets more crowded (with newer facilities and the restaurant). Just avoid the weekends when the Athenian elite descend and lift lines can be longer than one of Medusa's snakes. But the best thing about skiing in Greece? The Greeks themselves. Specifically, their philotimo culture of welcoming foreigners.

Claim your boasting rights to the highest ski resort in Africa.

Oukaïmeden

MOROCCO

Exotic Morocco - home to sweeping deserts and historic cities such as ancient Fes, where life continues as it has for hundreds of years, and Marrakesh the famous red city with its chaotic medina (marketplace) - is not often associated with skiing. But only 78km (49mi) south of Marrakesh is the highest ski resort in Africa: Oukaïmeden in the High Atlas Mountains.

Standing at over 3000m (9500ft), there are 10km (6.2mi) of slopes, with seven lifts here, including six drag-lifts and a slow single chairlift to the more advanced slope. Jebel Attar is the highest peak and has five runs, the longest of which is a 3km (2mi) descent; the challenge isn't the gradient but lack of piste maintenance.

Ski touring beckons. Jebel Toukbal is North Africa's highest summit at 4167m (13,671ft) and gives access to the surrounding 4000m (13,123ft) mountains where you'll find open snow fields and some tight couloirs for your efforts. Or consider the beautiful ski traverse and ascent of Tizi'n Tadat at 3600m (11,811ft) with stunning panoramic views; a highlight is staying in Berber huts on the descent to the villages of M'zik and Imlil.

However, the slopes are not what you come for - it's the ambience of Morocco itself, street-food breaks at the base of some mountains, the fact that you're skiing in Africa and an excuse to stay at Sir Richard Branson's Kasbah Tamadot nearby to Jebel Attar.

Immense peaks, excellent hospitality and the challenge of limited facilities offer a Himalayan adventure like no other.

Gulmarg

INDIA

In 2005, it was announced that a new gondola was opening up in a ski area called Gulmarg in Kashmir in the Himalayas, and I decided to ride it.

The gondola was installed but hadn't opened yet, so I spent a week hiking and riding while it was teasingly tested by French POMA staff overhead. I stayed above a tea house, making friends with their chickens and convincing my perplexed (but welcoming) hosts that I was doing pretty well without a husband. And, yes, my dad had given me permission to leave.

That was in 2005, and Gulmarg was poised to take off. It still hasn't truly, despite featuring in a Warren Miller film with Lysney Dyer (and some other ski-umentaries). There are obstacles - traveller warnings, limited wi-fi, no alcohol or bars and power outages. But the sense of adventure - as large as the muscular mountain, Apharwat, which tapers to a 4200m (13,780ft) peak - atones for it all. Whether or not you're a skier, this sight fills the heart with equal parts awe and fear. All around, immense peaks pierce the sky and impale clouds.

From one of the world's highest gondolas (3747m/12,293ft), ridges run off in all directions like veins, the folds of the flanks hiding off-piste runs that mostly end in deep bowls of snow several metres deep. Gulmarg boasts of receiving the highest amount of snowfall in the Himalaya at the same altitude. And, by a divine conspiracy, a cold wind pattern ensures the snow is perfectly crisp for skiing and snowboarding.

The mountain is avalanche-prone so make sure you hire an experienced guide and be prepared to spend a few days acclimatising to the altitude too. Whatever happens, it'll be a snow trip like no other.

Skiing in the Himalayas is an adventure to remember, sure to involve some unexpected plot twists *Opposite* Morocco's High Atlas mountains offer a unique skiing and cultural experience

The Azerbaijanis have taken to winter sports with gusto as their brand-new, top-end ski industry grows.

Shahdag

AZERBAIJAN

Azerbaijan serves as a gateway between Europe and the Middle East, forming a geographical mezze plate with neighbours Georgia, Armenia and Iran, and with the Great Caucasus Mountains to the north. Ten years ago there was no industry here, just the opportunity to start from scratch and use best practices to get skiing off the ground in Azerbaijan.

Now it has an has an element crucial to its skiing development - a prime minister who's not only a great skier but believes there's a place for skiing in Azerbaijan. That's according to Gabriel Guevara, the Ski School Director of Shahdag Resort, and his private instructor.

Locals have embraced the new, exciting winter activity, and the large expat community has, not surprisingly, also gotten on board. Developments continue to expand the resort's capacity and they've started as they mean to continue - top end - with two gondolas, six quad chairlifts, and five magic carpets (some resorts don't even have one) on 1.08sqkm (267 acres) with 23km (14.3mi) of skiable terrain and 231 snow guns (snow cannons).

Off-slope there are snow-grooming tours, an alpine coaster, ziplining, snowtubing, ice-skating and snowmobile tours, plus a slopeside four-star hotel. With some top Andorran talent here - no doubt partly also behind the renaissance of Grandvalira (*see* p. 167) - Azerbaijan is starting off on the right ski boot.

Shahdag has expanded to offer top-end skiing infrastructure *Opposite* Join the weekenders from Seoul skiing at Yongpyong

Since the 2018 Pyeongchang Winter Olympics, South Korea is well and truly on the map of Asia's leading ski destinations.

Yongpyong

SOUTH KOREA

There are 12 ski areas within striking distance of the capital city Seoul, but the largest by far is Yongpyong Ski Resort with 28 slopes, 13.6km (8.5mi) of riding and 14 lifts.

With a compact size, Yongpyong gets crowded on the weekends - skiing is the Korean sport of the moment and the population of Seoul is 26 million. But you need to manage your expectations before visiting South Korea's ski resorts. It's not like Japan and only gets 2.5m (8.2ft) of snowfall.

The crowning glory is that six runs squeeze into the requirements of an FIS Giant Slalom course and Slalom course (Rainbow 1 and Rainbow 3), hence it has been both an Olympic and World Cup host. South Korea had to specifically build the Jeongseon Alpine Centre for the Downhill and Super G events.

Korean pop culture (beyond K-pop music and K-dramas) is running hot here, there's even a word for its popularity: hallyu, originating from the Chinese characters for 'Korean wave'. Seoul is just 200km away, the prime place to take a hangeul (Korean calligraphy) class, explore the 600-year-old historic neighborhood of Bukchon Hanok village, sleep in one of the dozens of hanoks (traditional wooden houses that have been restored) and live large with a KBBQ (Korean barbecue), but save room for the galbi jjim (short ribs).

Put this destination down as a combined skiing and cultural experience.

The stuff of legends – a big-mountain skiing nirvana where couloirs and cliffs riddle insanely steep slopes.

Las Leñas

ARGENTINA

Las Leñas is a magnet for pro skiers and film crews each season. It's accessed by the legendary Marte lift (described as heli-skiing by chairlift) and the lines - from the steep bowl directly underneath to Eduardo's 48-degree couloir - are practically limitless. Sold?

There's a catch though. Just like heliskiing, there are down days, and given this is the eastern side of the Andes, where winds snag around the peaks and whistle through the spires, conditions can lead to frequent closure. But that gives powder pilgrims a chance to partake of the buzzing nightlife, which starts late, finishes later and guarantees you won't be first at the lift.

A Marte lift closure won't bother families and intermediates. They come (from Buenos Aires) for intermediate groomers, lessons from instructors who teach in Aspen (*see* p. 13) doing endless winters, and the only night skiing in South America. On Minerva, slopes are named after Greek and Roman gods; maybe they're friendly with Parnassus (*see* p. 259).

Getting here can be a clunky affair too. It's 419km (360mi) from Mendoza and 1200km (746mi) from the capital (a sleeper bus makes the 12hr journey on winter weekends) and airfares can be expensive. Once here, you're greeted with altitude; Las Leñas is high with a base of 2240m (7349ft) and peak at 3430m (11253ft).

If you are travelling with non-skiers, consider Bariloche (also called Brazil-oche as it's a Brazilian favourite), the striking ski area of Cerro Catedral just 20min from Bariloche itself. The town, perched on pristine Lake Nahuel Huapi, is also a gateway to Patagonia, and a Swiss-like feel extends to an exponential array of chocolate shops.

Craggy peaks and powder make Las Leñas a legendary destination. *Opposite* Portillo is snowbound perfection.

This South American superstar is nothing short of epic, with local hospitality and uncrowded slopes.

Portillo

CHILE

My first trip to Chile was full of unexpected surprises. A prodigious Andean storm had encompassed Portillo, two hours from the capital, and an avalanche had cut off road access (and would take three days to clear). The resort was still accessible by helicopter though - and empty of other guests. So ensued three days of possibly the best riding of my life, and for all the times I've been told 'you should have been here yesterday', I think, 'I'll always have Portillo'.

Imagine a cruise ship marooned on a mountain, and there you have the big, yellow hotel with a slopeside

pool, four meals a day (including high tea), and reliable snow. With numbers capped at 450, there's an exclusive club feel here - you'll be saying hola (hello) to everyone by week's end.

The resort of 12.4sqkm (3042 acres) is serviced by 14 lifts, including several of the infamous Va et Vient (as used on the Roca Jack); a high-speed poma able to transport five skiers at a time, sling-shotting them up a steep, short slope. The treeless terrain provides the opportunity to explore the wide-open bowls, rocky chutes, and incredible off-piste; World Cup ski racing teams from the USA, Canada, Austria, Norway and others train here during their summer season.

A week here involves plenty of late-morning starts, long lunches at Tio Bobs, early hot-tub sessions, a siesta, dinners that start at 9pm and memories of mingling with like-minded skiers, pisco sour in hand. The bonus is a stopover in Santiago. Located in an Andes-Pacific Ocean sandwich, it's a surprise chiaroscuro (contrasting) package of cool European class and hot Latin blood.

A road through the heart of the Kootenay Rocky Mountains that is ingrained in powder folklore and trademarked by the local tourism authority.

The Powder Highway

BRITISH COLUMBIA, CANADA

This 1013km (630-mi) circular loop crosses the doorsteps of eight legendary ski resorts, as well as a smorgasbord of backcountry lodges and heli- and cat-ski operators. Altogether, there's an estimated 60 different powder providers along the route, punctuated by natural hot springs, storybook villages and pristine lakes. The landscape will take your breath away as you drive through, let alone ski.

But ski you must. Start your journey anywhere on the loop - a good choice is Fernie Resort with its 142 runs, 10.11sqkm (2500 acres) and 8.5m (28ft) of average annual snowfall, all just an hour's drive from the Canadian Rockies International Airport. Or maybe

click in at Revelstoke (*see* p. 55) where the craft beer scene, foodie offerings and nightlife are almost as renowned as the skiing. Otherwise, head for crowd-free lines in the pillowy playgrounds of Whitewater Ski Resort's 'Trash Glades' (ask a local how to find them).

Steep trees, stash-laden terrain and plentiful 'cold smoke' powder characterise this epic pilgrimage. But experiencing the funky ski towns of Kootenay is just as big a drawcard. Don't skip over historic Nelson, dubbed 'Queen City of the Kootenays' and listed as one of North America's Best Ski Towns by National Geographic.

Resorts on the Powder Highway:

1. Fairmont Hot Springs Resort
2. RED Mountain Resort (*see* p. 49)
3. Whitewater Ski Resort
4. Fernie Alpine Resort
5. Panorama Mountain Resort
6. Kicking Horse Mountain Resort (*see* p. 57)
7. Revelstoke Mountain Resort (*see* p. 55)
8. Kimberley Alpine Resort

Between the massive amounts of snow, the audacious terrain, and the breathtaking views, there's nowhere like AK.

Alaska

USA

So we'll just casually heli-drop Alaska in here. You know, only one of the most outrageous places to ride *in the world.* If you're going resort skiing, there are two ski areas near downtown Anchorage. But 45min away is the funky mountain town Girwood and Alaska's premier ski resort area, Alyeska.

Rated by *Skiing Magazine* as one of the world's Top 25 ski areas, Alyeska resort is an Olympian spawning ground, ejecting skiers like Tommy Moe and Rosey Fletcher. Alyeska isn't the biggest or baddest, but what it lacks in showboating it makes up for in skier cred.

The stats speak for themselves – 762m (2500ft) of vertical, over 5.66sqkm (1400 acres) of skiable terrain, a season that can stretch beyond 150 days and 16.5m (54ft) *on average* of silky pow. Throw in the Girwood après ski scene with dinner spots like Double Musky and Sitzmark Bar and Grill, and out pops an irresistible ski destination.

But that's just the tip of the iceberg in a state whose mere name conjures ski flick images of massive glaciers cascading off huge peaks, sharp spines dropping to oblivion and hard-core riders. When you've finished riding a chairlift and shredding Alyeska's famous steeps, Chugach Powder Guides has a helipad right at the resort; spend a few days here and you too will start thinking about hitching to the big-name and bigger-mountain Chugach Range.

From world-class heli-skiing out of places like Haines and Cordova to ski touring in the Thompson and Turnagain Passes, if you need to take your adventures to the next sky-high level, Alaska is the holy grail of powder prilgrms.

Towering mountains, back-country terrain and heli-skiing in Alaska *Opposite* There's a heaving smorgasboard of stellar ski areas on the Powder Highway

INDEX

PHOTOGRAPHY CREDITS

Cover (Burnt Mountain, Aspen Snowmass, USA) Tomas Zuccareno, Back cover (Val d'Isere, France) Andy Parant, Preliminaries iii Jungfraubahnen, iv Andy 'Rails' Railton, v Andrew Jay, viii Boris Molinier, ix David Andre, xi Rainer Eder, xii Treble Cone Ski Area, xv Caroline van 't Hoff - Dutchies Do Ski, xvi Frank Shine, xvi Kiera Skinner, xvii Chis Hocking, xvii, Alta Badia - Alex Moling; North America, xx Jordan Curet, 4 Jeff Engerbretson for Big Sky Resort, 6 Colton Stiffler for Big Sky Resort, 7 top Tom Cohen for Big Sky Resort, 7 bottom Max Lowe for Big Sky Resort, 8-11 Visit Jackson Hole, 12 Scott Markewitz, 15 Jeremy Swanson, 16 Dan Bayer, 17 Scott Markewitz, 18 Noah Wetzel, 20-21 Steamboat, 22 & 25 top Telluride Tourism Board, 25 bottom Kiera Skinner, 26 Ben Eng, 28 Justin Olsen, 30 PC Vanderlinden, 31 top Scott Markewitz, 31 bottom John Entwistle, 32-37 Peter Morning, 38 Joe Kusumoto/U.S. Paralympics Alpine Skiing, 42-7 Mike Crane, 48&52 Ashley Voykin, 50-1 StackedFilms, 53 Rory Court, 55-6 Hywel Williams, 57 left Michelle Laureen, 57 right Supplied by ROAM, 58 Paul Zizka, Banff Lake Louise Tourism, 60&63 Banff Lake Louise Tourism, 61 Reuben Krabb, Banff Lake Louise Tourism, 62 Noel Hendrickson Banff Lake Louise Tourism, 64-9 Big White Ski Resort, 70 Supplied by Chris Davenport; Europe 75 Saint-Gervais-Mont-Blanc, 76 Loic Bouchet, 78 Chris Konig, 79 top Loic Bouche 79 bottom & 81 Oreli.b Photography 80 Oliver Godbold, 82&87 Andy Parant, 84-7 tignes.net, 88 Guillaume Borga, 90-3 Boris Molinier, 94 Mathis Decroux, 96&97 top Courchevel Tourisme, 97 bottom Mathis Decroux, 98-103 OT Chamonix-Mont-Blanc, 105 Moritz Ablinger, 106-8 Patrick Baetz, 109 Felicity Byrnes, 110 Moritz Ablinger, 112 Mirja Geh, 113-4 Daniel Roos, 115 top Daniel Roos, 115 bottom Mirja Geh, 116 Dominic Daher, 119 Freddy Planinschek, 120-2 Harald Wisthaler, 123 Manuel Righi, 124 Daniele Molineris, 125 top Foto Bisti, 125 bottom Daniele Molineris,

126 &, 131 Alex Moling, 128-130 Freddy Planinschek, 133 Engelberg-Titlis Tourism, 134, 137 & 139 Pascal Gertschen, 136 Wenger Leander, 138 top Rainer Eder, 138 bottom Andrew Geraci, 140 Engelberg Titlis Tourismus, 142 Roger Gruetter, 143 top Oskar Enander, 143 bottom Christian Perret, 144 Alaïa Bay, 146 Luciano Miglionico, 147 Crans Montana, 149-153 Jungfraubahnen, 155 & 158-9, Visit Levi, 156 Teemu Moisio, 160 Levi Ski Resort, 161 Visit Levi, 163-5 Shutterstock, 166 & 169 Marketing Grandvalira, 168 Alexis Boichard, 170-1 Supplied by Chemmy Alcott; Australasia 172 Andrew Railton, 176-181 Thredbo Resort, 182-7 Courtesy of Perisher Ski Resort, 188-191 Andrew Railton, 192 Matt Hull, 194 Goodtimes Falls Creek, 195 top & middle Falls Creek, 195 bottom Goodtimes Falls Creek, 196 Chris Hocking / OWIA, 200 Cardrona Alpine Resort, 203 top Cardrona Alpine Resort, 203 bottom & 204 Treble Cone Ski Area, 205 Cardrona Alpine Resort, 206 & 209 Miles Holden, 210-11 QueenstownNZ.co.nz, 212-6 Mount Hutt, 218 Pally Learmond; Asia 220 Furano Tourism Association, 224-6 Niseko United Marketing Team, 227 left Skye Niseko, 227 right Kumo Restuarant, 228 Furano Tourism Association, 231 top Caroline van 't Hoff - Dutchies Do Ski, 231 bottom Shutterstock, 232 top Caroline van 't Hoff - Dutchies Do Ski, 232 bottom Furano Tourism Association, 233 Caroline van 't Hoff - Dutchies Do Ski, 234-9 Rusutsu Resort, 240-3 & 245 Courtesy of Skimax, 244 Nagano Tourism Organization, 248-53 Imaginechina Limited/Alamy Stock Photo; Ski The World 254 CSNafzger/Shutterstock, 258 Courtesy of Poiana Brasov, 259 Discovergreece.com, 260 The Photolibrary Wales/Alamy, 261 ImagesofIndia/Shutterstock, 262 Lizard/Shutterstock, 263 KoreaKHW/Shutterstock, 264 Whit Richardson/Alamy Stock Photo, 265 Frank Shine, 266 Nick Nault, 267, CSNafzger/Shutterstock, 272 Engelberg-Titlis Tourism, 274 Flip Byrnes.

Opposite Olof Larsson surfing the ridge above a cloud sea in Engelberg, Switzerland

ABOUT THE AUTHOR

It would be hard to find someone with more snow experience than journalist and snow marketing specialist Flip Byrnes, who's skied on every continent from Courchevel to Kashmir, Russia to Romania, Quebec to Queenstown and most places in between. A lifelong snow industry career has amassed mountains of knowledge of every facet of the industry, as an instructor, a ski journalist, a resort PR and Greenland expeditioner whose lived in the French Alps, Colorado USA and Snowy Mountains Australia. She's equally happy snowboarding, skiing, split boarding or kite skiing. Sled hauling she can take or leave.

With an Antarctic explorer and photographer in great-grandfather Frank Hurley, it may be reasonable to think that Flip has snow-love in her genes. But despite clicking on skis at age two, it wasn't until pulling T-bar during university breaks that Flip fully succumbed to the white addiction. So much so that following her degrees in journalism and a post-graduate degree in tourism management, (including a thesis on infrastructure for snowboarding within ski areas) she headed to St Moritz for her first ski season, before returning to Australia to be a snow report at Perisher.

That lead to eight back-to-back winter seasons, between Perisher Australia, and Aspen Colorado where she gained her snowboarding instructor ratings. Since then her career has included being a ski columnist for the *Sydney Morning Herald*, writing on snow for publications ranging from *The Telegraph* and *Vogue* in the UK to *Skiing USA* and *Outside* magazine, working on two winter Olympics (for the organising committee and the Australian Olympic Committee), contributing to various guidebooks and currently writing communications strategies and media plans for international ski resorts.

At one point Flip morphed from snow bunny to pole cat and is drawn to the polar and remote areas. She has kite skied halfway across Greenland as part of an international kite ski team (as the recipient of The North Face Young Adventurer of the Year grant) and is the first Australian woman to have climbed and snowboarded down Elbrus in Russia, the highest in Europe at 5642m. She's climbed three of the seven summits, saying 'the rest are too scary', except maybe Aconcagua or Vinson, where she would love to finish off some of her great grandfather's Antarctica adventurers.

Flip met her husband, a German UIAGM mountain guide, at Everest Basse Camp and they are raising two mini mountain mad girls, dividing their time between Australian and Europe.

Flip at base-camp Garabashi-Bochki (Barrels) on Mount Elbrus, Russia

Flip believes snow sports are for everyone, not just those who look cool when cruising through the ski resort carpark. She hopes her stories will enourage others to have adventures both big and small and, most importantly, to never stop exploring.

ACKNOWLEDGEMENTS

Three were three major players involved in this project while I was writing around the clock. Gold medals to Till for cuddling our kids and keeping the ship sailing patiently when I was working around the clock. To Monique Choy, my clever cyber space editor who was a warm and calm tonic of efficiency. And Alice Barker who with Monique gently cut my wordiness to word count; an incredible team who allowed me to forge ahead and write, taking care of the rest.

To the wider Hardie Grant team: publisher Melissa Kayser, designers Andy Warren and Susanne Geppert, typesetter Megan Ellis and cartographers Jason Sankovic and Emily Maffei – thank you all for your expertise. Thank you to other 'Ultimate' series authors: Benny Groundwater, Lee Atkinson, Penny Watson, Catherine Best, Andrew Bain and Laura Waters, as well as author Lee Mylne, for tips on pulling together 50,000 words.

I appreciate the snow chats of the ever-knowledgeable snow mate Sarah Plaskitt, founder of Scoutski (a boutique ski operator), Paddy Maher who always has the stoke, Rob Stewart for welcoming this antipodean into the UK ski world, and danke Kaisergarten's classy Felix, Dom and team for a warm and welcoming place to write.

I am deeply grateful to the super stars who generously shared both time and knowledge. In Australia, Mount Buller's Rhylla Morgan (the best PR in the snow game), Dani Wright, Deb Howie, Narelle Evans, Krista Sturday; and in New Zealand Mount Hutt's Richie Owen, James Urquhart, Jen Houltham, Rachael Milner, Sally Norman, Ross Whitelaw, Scotty Dennis and Geoff Wayatt.

In *bella Italia*, grazie to Sabrina Frizzi, Nicole Dorigo, Dr Diego Clara and Vanessa Fisher; in Switzerland Sabrina Marcolin, Nadia Sommer, Tasha, Sanne and Samira from Ski Lodge Engleberg, Dario Gross , Alan Ramsay and Pierre-Henri Mainetti; in Austria, Astrid Gruchmann-Licht, Kathrina Denk, Heli Gausli, Wilma Himmelfreundpointner and Katharina Laimer; in France, merci to Laury Eloy, Chloé Harlé, Theo Lejeun, Orianne Tian, Coralie L'Enfant, Eloane Roche, the Team Club Med; in Finland, Maarit Koelle, Essi Toikkanen, Lydia Lassila; and in Andorra, Albert Canes and Ellen Powell.

North America, incoming! Thanks to Mary Zinck, Jessie Boyd, Salina McNamara, Nickie Mabey of Mabey Ski, Fliss Harley, Dane Gergovich, Erik Kerr, Chantelle Deacon, Kevin Manuel, Laura Meggs, Nikki Wiart, Bob Parsons, Steve Pampel, Sarah Pearson and Avery Price in Canada. In the USA, Maureen Poschman, Carol Breen, to Maren Franciosi, Stacie Mesuda, Bob Ambrose, Eric Seymour, Nate Berenson, Tony Harrington, Lauren Burke, Neev Zaiet, Benny Wisner, Tom Watkins, Melanie Mills and Maddy Condon.

Japan was a slippery noodle. A huge *arigato* to Peter Douglas at Nozawa Tourism, Ross Swiney of Whiteroom Tours, James Winfield of Hokkaido Collective, John Dyer, Eri Kikuo, Chieko Kashino, Amberlie Boyd and Snow Travel Expo's Phil Osborn, Erica and Cassie at Skimax for pics, and Travelplan's Sylvia Schmiedl for Asian contacts.

Lastly to the Aspen crew, especially Lucy Lea Tucker, for being awesome.

This book is dedicated to my mountain babies and polaris Lotte and Leni. Being your mamma is the most magical and best adventure of all my loves.

And to my Mum and Dad who've always championed and encouraged my writing and adventures, my biggest cheerleaders and personal and professional role models, I love you both to bits.

Published in 2023 by Hardie Grant Explore, an imprint of
Hardie Grant Publishing

Hardie Grant Explore
(Melbourne)
Wurundjeri Country
Building 1, 658 Church Street
Richmond, Victoria 3121

Hardie Grant Explore
(Sydney)
Gadigal Country
Level 7, 45 Jones Street
Ultimo, NSW 2007

www.hardiegrant.com/au/explore

All rights reserved. No part of this publication may be reproduced,
stored in a retrieval system or transmitted in any form by any means,
electronic, mechanical, photocopying, recording or otherwise, without
the prior written permission of the publishers and copyright holders.

The moral rights of the author have been asserted.

Copyright text © Flip Byrnes 2023
Copyright concept, maps and design © Hardie Grant Publishing 2023

The maps in this publication incorporate data from the following
organisations

www.openstreetmap.org/copyright - OpenStreetMap is open data,
licensed under the Open Data Commons Open Database License
(ODbL) by the OpenStreetMap Foundation (OSMF). https://
opendatacommons.org/licenses/odbl/1-0/

Any rights in individual contents of the database are licensed under
the Database Contents License: https://opendatacommons.org/licenses/
dbcl/1-0/.

Made with Natural Earth. Free vector and raster map data
@ naturalearthdata.com.

© Commonwealth of Australia (Geoscience Australia), 2004, Creative
Commons Attribution 4.0 International (CC BY 4.0)

Contains data sourced from the LINZ Data Service licensed for reuse
under CC BY 4.0

Cartographic Boundary Files - Shapefile Source: US Census Bureau,
Geography Division

A catalogue record for this
book is available from the
National Library of Australia

Hardie Grant acknowledges the Traditional Owners of the Country on
which we work, the Wurundjeri People of the Kulin Nation and the
Gadigal People of the Eora Nation, and recognises their continuing
connection to the land, waters and culture. We pay our respects to
their Elders past and present.

For all relevant publications, Hardie Grant Explore commissions
a First Nations consultant to review relevant content and provide
feedback to ensure suitable language and information is included in
the final book. Hardie Grant Explore also includes traditional place
names and acknowledges Traditional Owners, where possible, in both
the text and mapping for their publications.

Traditional place names are included in *palawa kani*, the language
of Tasmanian Aboriginal People, with thanks to the Tasmanian
Aboriginal Centre.

Ultimate Skiing & Snowboarding
ISBN 9781741178777

10 9 8 7 6 5 4 3 2 1

Publisher
Melissa Kayser

Project editor
Alice Barker

Editor
Monique Choy

Proofreader
Collin Vogt

Cartographer
Jason Sankovic, Emily Maffei

Design
Andy Warren

Layout
Susanne Geppert

Typesetting
Megan Ellis

Index
Max McMaster

Colour reproduction by Megan Ellis and Splitting Image Colour Studio

Printed and bound in China by LEO Paper Products LTD.

The paper this book is printed on is certified against
the Forest Stewardship Council® Standards and
other sources. FSC® promotes environmentally
responsible, socially beneficial and economically
viable management of the world's forests.

Disclaimer: While every care is taken to ensure the accuracy of
the data within this product, the owners of the data do not make
any representations or warranties about its accuracy, reliability,
completeness or suitability for any particular purpose and, to
the extent permitted by law, the owners of the data disclaim all
responsibility and all liability (including without limitation, liability
in negligence) for all expenses, losses, damages (including indirect or
consequential damages) and costs which might be incurred as a result of
the data being inaccurate or incomplete in any way and for any reason.

Publisher's Disclaimers: The publisher cannot accept responsibility
for any errors or omissions. The representation on the maps of any
road or track is not necessarily evidence of public right of way.
The publisher cannot be held responsible for any injury, loss or
damage incurred during travel. It is vital to research any proposed
trip thoroughly and seek the advice of relevant state and travel
organisations before you leave.

Publisher's Note: Every effort has been made to ensure that the
information in this book is accurate at the time of going to press.
The publisher welcomes information and suggestions for correction
or improvement.